Wholeness in Learning

"*Wholeness in Learning* gives us a form of learning that is whole, in the sense of being undivided and complete. It involves not only growth through experience, but also increasing self-awareness, and the ability to let go, to open up to what is new and other. This holistic form of learning allows us to connect directly with ourselves, others, and the mystery of life. It integrates learning as the acquisition of knowledge and skills with learning as opening up and letting go. This allows us to gain knowledge and experience in a way that is ever more competent, while at the same time bringing us closer to who we are deep-down."

Antonie Zweers is an independent scholar with a PhD in the Philosophy of Education from University College London (IOE). His research aims to uncover the deepest potential in human flourishing: to be truly open to life, to become ethical and good, to find meaning and fulfilment in our day-to-day existence. This individual learning is then connected with the collective learning of groups, communities, and even society as a whole developing new ways of living, so that eventually the course of history itself may become a process of collective growth.

He lives with his partner in the New Forest, Southern England.

Wholeness in Learning

*Heidegger, Authenticity &
How We Become Who We
Are*

Antonie Zweers

CorMundi

Published by CorMundi Press 2011
Copyright © Antonie Zweers
Website: www.educationandlove.com
All rights reserved. This book or any portion thereof
may not be reproduced or used in any manner whatsoever
without the express written permission of the publisher
except for the use of brief quotations in a book review.
ISBN-13: 978-0-9928313-4-9
ISBN-10: 0-9928313-4-2

Contents

Introduction
1. The two faces of learning — 1

Authenticity
2. Authentic Dasein — 21
3. "Turning away from the world" and "turning back" — 37

Conventional learning — 51

Authentic understanding
4. Gaining an authentic understanding of oneself — 73
5. The nature of authentic self-understanding — 79
6. Dasein understanding itself as finite process — 85
7. Understanding learning to be authentic — 94
8. Authentic attunement — 103
9. Authentic attunement — 103
10. Moods of authenticity — 111
11. Attunement learning to be authentic — 120

Authentic being-with
12. Heidegger's account of authentic being-with — 131
13. The call of conscience — 148
14. The richness of authentic being-with — 158

Authentic Learning
15. Learning to be authentic and conventional learning — 179
16. The tapestry of authentic learning — 208

Bibliography — 223

Introduction

The two faces of learning

Wholeness in learning

Wholeness is the quality or condition of being whole, of being undivided, of being undamaged and having all its parts in due connexion. Thus wholeness refers to that which constitutes a complex unity, in a way that has nothing wanting, suggesting completeness and perfection (OED 2009). When there is wholeness in learning, the learning itself is whole.

The aim of this investigation is to show how learning can be something that is complete in a way that involves the whole person. Such learning is sound and undamaged. It is genuine in the sense of being authentic. And as a result of this learning, the person becomes whole in themselves. With Heidegger's discussion of the question of what it is to be human in *Being and Time* (1962) in mind, this whole form of learning will be called *authentic learning*.

In setting out this holistic notion of learning, I will take learning to be something we all do all the time. Whenever we meet a situation where we cannot rely fully on our automatic responses (and this is, I would argue, most situations), we need to adjust, adapt, let-go, or open-up in some way or other. That is, in so far as our habitual ways of responding to what happens are not attuned one-hundred per cent to the situation we are in, there needs to be learning. Whether this involves getting used to a new colleague at work or figuring out how to operate a new kind of software, whether this involves learning to be less impatient or getting one's head around a theoretical proposition, there is some form of learning. And the deeper experiences of life too require constant learning, grasping things anew as well as letting go of old ways of being, for example, when we first fall in love, when we become a parent, or when the time comes for us to let go of earthly existence. Learning is almost always part of life, in its most mundane moments as well as in moments of existential change.

In taking learning as formative much of the person we are (really just excluding those ways of being that are innate), I am following current thinking in the fields of developmental psychology, adult learning, neurology, and education. To cite one example, Peter Jarvis, writing within the field of adult education, defines human learning as "the combination of processes whereby the whole person - body (genetic, physical and biological) and mind (knowledge, skills, attitudes, values, emotions, beliefs and senses) experiences a social situation, the perceived content of which is then transformed cognitively, emotively or practically (or through any combination) and integrated into the person's individual biography resulting in a changed (or more experienced) person" (Jarvis 2006, 13). As we will see in Chapter 3, this notion of learning as lying at the basis of most of who we are makes it one of the central processes in our lives. The idea is, therefore, mistaken that learning is done mostly by the young or in formal educational settings.

In a very real sense the whole of life is learning. And this is not something to lament, because as soon as we notice that life is new (as opposed to a mere repetition of the past) there is the need to learn. It is not just that the ever-changing nature of existence obliges us to continually adapt, the very possibility of experiencing life as creative and rejuvenating depends on our ability to open up and to learn. The fact is, however, that we do not always adapt to the challenges life puts to us or have the openness to change that allows us to experience life as new. On the one hand, we sometimes get stuck in ways of being that fail to do justice to the changing world, with the result that we no longer respond adequately to what is happening. On the other hand, we sometimes become so set in our ways that life loses its sparkle and freshness, because we have lost our openness to what is new and different.

So, the first thing I want to show in what follows is that when learning is whole, in the sense of complete and healthy, there need to be two sides to it. On the one hand, learning needs to involve the modification of existing ways of understanding, feeling, acting, thinking and relating. This aspect of learning is about continuity, about what is learned always building on something that is either innate or learned previously. On the other hand, learning needs to involve openness to what is new, to that which we do not already understand, feel, do, and think. This aspect of learning is about discontinuity, about that which is learned being different from what was already innate or learned previously. Wholeness in learning will, therefore, need to combine moments of grasping and growth with moments of letting-go and opening-up.

But as we will see, these two sides of learning rest on a deep tension in the way we tend to look at ourselves and at life as a whole. This tension between continuity and discontinuity comes to a head in our notion of learning. On the one hand, learning needs to allow us to build on previous experience, to become ever-better adapted, more skilful and knowledgeable. While, on the other hand, there needs to be discontinuity in learning, so that there can be openness to what is new and other; and I will argue in Chapter 2 that this can really only come about when we let go of some or all of the experience we have accumulated over the course of our lives. But as we will see in Chapter 3, our conventional notions of learning are mostly associated with continuity, growth, and increased experience. Because of this, these notions of learning tend not to be able to account for moments when we let go of what we have previously learned, open up to life, and connect with that which is completely other than we ourselves.

Because our conventional accounts of learning tend to lack a well-formulated notion of letting go and opening up, they cannot really account for some of the most valuable experiences in life. Because, if learning is all about the accumulation of experience, how can we ever come into contact with the ground of experience itself, which, presumably, is somehow prior to any particular experience? If learning is all about assimilating what we encounter in life into our existing understanding, how can we ever open up to other people, or to life itself in its depth, given that these may not be able to be understood in terms of our particular way of understanding things? Likewise, this inner contradiction in our notion of learning expresses itself in the question whether we can ever experience the newness of life, or whether we remain forever caught in a web of sameness and repetition. To anticipate some of the Heideggerian terminology I will be using: how can we ever come to get the being of those entities right that are new, other, or basic to any form of understanding, if we always already relate to them with an existing idea of what they are?

Related to this question of openness to the being of entities is the aspect of learning as that which helps us be who we really are. This is the side of learning that concerns not so much the entities we find in the world but ourselves. To anticipate again some Heideggerian terminology we will be looking at later, if we are in essence open to the being of entities (to what is new, other, or basic to experience itself), then being who we really are involves being truly open. In that sense, a form of learning that involves opening up is a form of learning that helps us be who we are. And this means that when there is wholeness in learning, this will involve a sense of healing, of making whole again that which has been fragmented. So, a truly whole form of learning would not only allow us to build up experience in relation to things and people in a way that remains open to the being of what is new and other. A whole form of learning would also integrate the parts of ourselves that life may have separated: it would get our own being right. Again, our conventional ways of thinking about learning do not really allow for this possibility, because there is never a moment in conventional learning that is as truly open as our most basic way of being in the world.

In our common ways of talking about learning, we do take learning to involve both continuity and openness to what is new and other. And there is also a sense, I believe, in which many of us take learning to ultimately be something that ought to bring us closer to who we really are, that ought to connect us with ourselves and give us a deeper understanding of our own being. But as we look more deeply at conventional notions of learning, we find that the emphasis tends to be on continuity and growth as opposed to openness and letting go. We also find that in virtually all conventional notions of learning a division is maintained between inner and outer, self and other, in the sense of the learning having an intentional object, thus lacking in a true sense of wholeness. As we will see, these tensions within our ideas about learning can only be resolved if we go deep into the fundamental structures of experience. As already indicated, I will use Heidegger's ideas, notably his notion of authenticity, to help bring together learning as continuity and growth with that of opening up and letting go. This notion of authenticity will also give us a first indication of what it would be like if learning helped us become who we really are, in that it does justice to the fundamental openness that exists in us. And all this will be tied together at the end of the investigation, where we will see that there is a form of learning that is whole, in the sense of complete and undamaged, when the two movements of what I will call *conventional learning* and *learning to be authentic* come together in a single process of *authentic learning*.

Conventional learning

In the remaining sections of this introductory chapter, I will discuss the key notions of learning I will be using in the book: *conventional learning*, *learning to be authentic*, and *authentic learning*. This will hopefully prevent later confusion of these terms, as well as set out in more detail the challenge of restoring a sense of wholeness to our notion of learning. I will begin by introducing, in this section, the notion of *conventional learning*. This is the kind of learning we are all familiar with. It is the kind of learning as adaptation that we tend to have a common-sense understanding of and which underlies most, if not all, accounts of learning used in psychology and education.

A child needs to learn to speak, as it moves from being fully dependent on its caregivers to someone who is increasingly a member of a family and community in their own right. When, later, the child goes to school, there are changes to the environment the child needs to adapt to. And when they get their first job, yet another adaptation is called for. And this sort of life changes continues throughout life on a scale that is sometimes large and sometimes small. So, even someone who grows up and stays in a single, stable community will need to adapt continually, because their world changes, for example, when in old age they become dependent on the care of others, where before they have been proudly independent.

But the communities we live in are themselves never completely stable, as technology, the climate, and the social, political and economic context change. This puts an extra burden on our ability to learn, because it is not enough to simply adapt to existing roles and positions in the communities in which we live. Collectively, we need to discover new ways of doing things, for example, when a new generation needs to make sense of the prospect of human-made climate change in a way that, by all accounts, no earlier generation of young people ever had to. And this need for collective adaptation means that our notion of learning needs to go beyond that of enculturation into an existing social order and include the ability to find truly novel solutions.

Regardless whether the adaptation is to an existing role or position or to a reality that is truly new, part of the adaptation consists in a modification of our existing ways of relating to entities, events, ourselves, and other living beings. And this notion of learning is well-established (in Chapter 3 we will see that almost all learning is thought of as the modification of an existing way of being). We saw at the start of this chapter, learning really involves all aspects of life, from feeling, to acting, or thinking. And whichever aspect of the person is involved, the underlying assumption is that there is an existing way of relating to oneself, others, things, and the world, and that this existing way of relating it modified, as a result of a process of learning. This is the conventional notion of learning as modification and growth.

In the background of this idea of learning is that we are born with certain innate responses to things that happen to us, and that learning happens in the first place when these innate responses get modified. The result of this is that we then not only have innate but also learned responses to things that happen. Subsequent learning can then also happen with regard to the learned responses themselves: now the learned response itself is modified as a result of further experience, for example, when someone who has learned to eat with knife and fork learns to eat with chopsticks. In either case, the learning in question involved the modification of an existing way of relating to things, whether this existing way is innate or itself learned. As we will see in Chapter 3, the notion of learning as building on an existing understanding of the entity one is relating to has a long and respectable pedigree, which in Europe goes back to at least the late middle ages (Miner 2004), and which can be seen in contemporary accounts of learning from constructivism to behaviourism, to Hebbian learning.

But, as I explained in the previous section, when learning is thought of as involving a modification of existing ways of relating, this raises the question as to whether it is possible to be truly open towards that in relation to which we are learning. To put it differently, if we always start off with an existing understanding of the entity we are learning about, can we ever learn something that is completely outside the range of what we already know? Do we not limit any further learning about the entity, when we start off with an existing way of understanding the entity? Can we really learn something that is completely different, if we always base the process of learning in what we already know?

This question of whether we can ever be really open, if we always begin with our current understanding, is especially pertinent when it comes to relationships which cannot be grasped with any existing understanding, any innate way of responding, any sense impression. For example, the origin of the experiences we ourselves have cannot, by all accounts, be caught in any sense impression, innate understanding, or understanding of being we may have. Likewise, when we meet another living being, we are in relationship with something that goes beyond our sense impressions, our innate responses, and our understanding of what it is to be a person, because the other person will at least to some extent have their unique way of experiencing life. Finally, the paradigmatic example of what cannot be grasped in terms of that which we already have an understanding of is that of the divine, of that which lies beyond anything we can understand in terms of what is already at least to some extent known.

Drawing on Heidegger's early philosophy, I will, in the central chapters of the book, argue that this shortcoming of conventional learning is especially there in relation to what he calls the being of entities. According to Heidegger, every existing way of relating involves an understanding of the being of the entity we are relating to. For example, when we are relating to someone on the phone, we take this person as a human being, where a human being has a different *being* from, say, a speech robot. So, when, in the middle of the call, we realize that we are talking to a speech computer, we need to adapt to the *being* of the voice we are relating to at that moment. Then, once we have adapted to the *being* of the voice (it turns out to be a computer) we have to work out a way of relating to it that is in line with their *being* (for example, we need to speak clearly and there's no point making a joke about the weather to the computer).

In this way, every modification begins with an understanding of the being of the entity one is relating to. The adaptation may leave the being of the entity in place, as when we adapt to a foreigner on the phone, speaking more slowly, but sticking to our understanding that we are dealing with a human being. Or the adaptation may involve a change in the kind of being we take ourselves to be relating to, as when in a museum we realize that what we took to be a coatrack turns out to be a work of art. In either case, the learning involves an understanding of the *being* of the entity. And regardless whether the adaptation also involves a change in what we take to be its being, the learning remains grounded in an understanding of the being of the entity.

Note that, where the notion of an understanding of the being of the entity is taken from Heidegger, others have put the most basic foundation of our ways of relating in things like our biological givens or sense impressions. But setting our beginning in an understanding of being is not necessarily in contradiction with the involvement of biological givens and sense impression, because we can see an understanding of being implied in many biological givens, for example, where even new-borns appear to distinguish between people and inanimate objects, and where almost all people learn to distinguish between something that is materially real and something that is an idea, a mental representation. So, if we now take our understanding of the being of entities as a way of indicating our most basic way of understanding them, the question arises whether it is possible to be open to the being of the entities we are learning about. This, as we will see in the chapters that follow, one of the challenges facing conventional learning: if all conventional learning builds on previous learning, going back to an essential understanding of the *being* of the entities involved, how is it ever possible to learn about the *being* of entities?

So, if all our learning is a modification of an existing way of relating to things, how can we ever learn about that which is totally different from anything we already know? This limitation to the notion of conventional learning can be seen when someone comes in a situation that is totally strange to them, for example, because it happens in a strange cultural context, where they have no way of making sense of what is going on. This limitation can also be seen in relation to that which is by its very nature different from anything we know. Together these limitations to the concept of conventional learning do not only limit the kind of learning that can be accounted for, they also limit what kind of person can grow out of this kind of learning: if openness to what is new and other, to the being of entities, is part of our true nature, conventional learning cannot lead to us becoming who we are.

We will look at all these issues in more depth in Chapter 3, where we will also see how things like forgetting that are accounted for in conventional learning still fail to allow for the kind of openness we are after. But before that, we will return to the idea that part of learning involves an openness to beings which goes beyond the mere modification of existing ways of relating to the entity involved which conventional learning tries to explain.

Learning to be authentic

Even when it comes to practical, day-to-day learning, there is a sense in which we need to have a degree of openness to what we are learning about, if we want to truly learn. Thus, learning to speak a new language, we need to be able to hear the sounds of that language for what they are and not hear merely the sounds in our own language that resemble them. When the languages involved are close enough, we may still be able to say that all that is needed is a modification of an existing way of hearing the sound, for example, by saying that their 'd' sounds a bit like our 't'. But there comes a point where we need to let go of our habitual way of, in this example, hearing the sound, so that we can hear it as it is.

This need to be able to let go of our habitual ways of understanding something, so that we can begin to understand it anew, is especially important where there is no guidance given as to how to understand it. To return to the previous example, so long as there is someone who tells us what to listen out for (as in, "their 'd' sounds a bit like our 't'"), we can make our way to the right understanding by modifying our habitual understanding. But what if there is no one to act as a bridge between our current understanding and the one we need to be aiming for? Then the only way of guiding the modification of our current understanding comes from what we ourselves understand to be the correct understanding. But how are we to know how we ought to hear a sound in a foreign language, if we do not hear what it ought to sound like in the first place? (I return to the challenge of remaining open to sounds in foreign languages in Chapter 3). There may, of course, be feedback mechanisms, such as when repeated difficulties in communication make us try different sounds, to see what works, but not all learning situations have that sort of feedback, with the result that we may go through life not even aware of the fact that we have become stuck in a less-than-adequate way of responding to certain things.

The need to be open to what we are learning about is no less there in relation to other people, say, when we meet someone from a different culture and need to learn to understand the meaning of their gestures and facial expressions, not only in terms of their culture, but also in terms of what these mean for the individual personally. And when it comes to our own experiences in life, the need is also there to sometimes begin anew, to connect with what we are feeling, thinking, and doing in a way that is not already shaped by previous experience. We need to be able to be open to what it is to be us, not only when we are going through something that we have not experienced before, but also when we want to examine our own lives in a deep way. After all, learning about ourselves necessarily involves coming upon new ways of experiencing who we are: we can only *become who we really are*, in so far as we open up to ourselves in a way that goes beyond what we already take ourselves to be.

Learning throughout life involves learning about ourselves, because life demands that we change in constructive ways, as the world around us changes. This is clear to most of us, in the sense that we would not consider a person's development healthy, if all throughout life they responded to things exactly as they did when they were a toddler. But even in adulthood a healthy psychology requires us to mature, to open up to life at different points in such a way that the very person we are changes, for example, when we attain a more senior position in the company we work for and different qualities need to come to the fore, for us to meet the demands of our new job. Likewise, growing old gracefully, accepting the limitations that come with age and being generous to the generations that follow us, all these require us to open up in new ways to life, ourselves, and others.

As indicated earlier in this chapter, some of the more valuable things in life also require us to open up in a way that is not restricted to ways of relating we had already acquired. To come into contact with the mystery of life is, almost per definition, something for which we need to be truly open in a way that is not held back by existing ways of relating to life. Feeling a sense of wonder at the very fact that there exists anything at all is not something we can do in terms of any particular way of experiencing we already have, because to sense the fulness of life requires us to do so in the very moment, in a way that is not mediated by previous ideas, goals, or desires. A sense of wonder at the existence of the universe is something we can only experience if we do so in terms of itself only, and not in terms of some other experience; and this means that we need to be open to existence in a deep way, if we are to come into contact with the mystery of life itself.

Likewise, when we want to really learn to relate to another living being, we need to be able to let go of some of our own notions of what it means to exist. This is because the other person (or animal) has their own way of experiencing life. Yes, all of us probably share certain experiences, for example to the extent that we have some of the same kinds of emotions or sense perceptions. But if there is something truly unique about the individual's experience of life, we can only connect with the other, in so far as we are open to experiencing something that completely other. To take a very common example, when a man and a woman connect, they can only come to understand each other, if each one is able to let go of some of their own, gendered ways of interpreting what is happening, in order to 'see' life from the perspective of the other.

To say that we need, to become who we really are, to be able to open ourselves up to new ways of experiencing life is not to claim that this can always be done in an absolute way – though it does not preclude that possibility either. In the context of this investigation, we are looking at processes of learning, and learning is a movement which may or may not reach its final, perfect, destination. Thus, we may never be able to understand completely what it is like to live life as someone of another sexual orientation. We may never be able to fully experience life in its bare form, as the simple feeling of existence in the here and now. We may never be able to completely let go of our attachment to life, so that we can face our own ending fully, when the time comes that our health and powers slip away. But to say that we may never reach the perfect state does not mean that we ought not go as far as we can. And note that the idea that it may be right to enter a path of learning even though we may never reach its ideal end is there in virtually all learning. When we learn about the meaning of a poem written centuries ago, we will probably never reach a perfect understanding of it; but this does not mean that we should not try to get as far as we can. Likewise, no science has ever grasped all there is to the material universe, but this does not mean that we give up on science altogether. Indeed, the question of what kind of knowledge can possibly be perfect appears to be a perennial one, answered differently at different points in time: for some it has been the existence of the thinking self, for others it has been self-evident mathematical truths, for others it has been the impermanence of all that exists. Important and enlightening as each of these may be in their own right, none of them has managed to become universally accepted.

So when we admit at the outset that, in leaning to open up to what is hitherto completely unknown to us, we as individuals may not be able to fully grasp that which we are opening up towards, this is merely the acknowledgement of something that appears to pertain to virtually all learning. But we are not here primarily concerned with the possibility or impossibility of perfect openness. Rather, we are looking at the kind of learning that is whole, in the sense of not lacking and in the sense of being true to who we are, and this learning, it seems, involves a moment of opening up. And just as it is widely accepted that no student of history will ever know all historical facts, we do not need to posit the possibility of total and complete openness, in order to see the importance of learning to open up to the entities with which we are in relationship. Learning is a verb, so the important word here is not the noun, openness, but the verb, opening up.

As will be explained in Chapter 2, I will use Heidegger's notion of authenticity as that way of being that is open to the being of entities. And I will call the process whereby we come to this authentic openness *learning to be authentic*. If then there is a moment of learning where this *learning to be authentic* combines with the kind of *conventional learning* described in the previous section, I will call this *authentic learning*, the learning that is whole in the sense of integrating grasping and growth with letting go and openness.

The quest for authentic learning

So far I have suggested that *conventional learning* tends to build on what we already know, for example, when we use our familiarity with software we have been working with to find our way around in a new software application. This learning is a form of adaptation, which begins with an existing way of relating to the entity we are learning about. Following Heidegger, I will look at this aspect of learning as one that involves an understanding of the being of the entity we are learning about. To stay with the example, we know what kind of thing software is (it is, for example, not a human being and won't run any faster when we get impatient with it), and when we learn about a new piece of software, we do so on the basis of the kind of being we know software to be. As already indicated, focusing on our understanding of the being of entities is not to deny or ignore our biological givens or the role of sense-impressions, but a way of generalizing a great number of cases by using the formal category of being.

It has also been suggested (and all of this will be worked out in more detail in the coming chapters) that there are limitations as to what kind of learning can come out of one that consists of adaptation on the basis of an existing understanding of the being of the entity we are learning about. In relation to the origin of our own experience, to other living beings, and to life itself as a whole, there is not really any existing understanding of being that can help us connect with what can only be understood through a kind of unmediated acquaintance. Any preconceived ideas about what it is for us to experience life, for example, will only get in the way of finding out what it means for us to experience life, if only because the ideas we have are themselves already the outcome of experience and not the fullness of experience itself. And this means that there is a natural limitation to what learning as an adaptation based in an existing way of understanding can achieve. To put it differently, no preconceived attitude, method, habit, or idea can take us to what is truly new, because that which is preconceived is, per definition, not new.

As indicated, it is not only in the kind of limit cases like coming to the foundation of all experience that openness to that which is new is required. Indeed, there seems to be a moment in all learning when we need to let go of some of our preconceived ways of feeling, acting, or thinking. We already saw that, in learning a new language, we need to be able to somehow let go of our native way of listening, so that we can really hear what the new language sounds like. Likewise, when starting work for a new company, we need to open up to a new organizational culture, where we can only really understand what it means, for example, to be a colleague or a subordinate, if we let go of at least some of the notions of company culture from our previous workplace.

So, it appears that most successful learning involves both an understanding of the being we are learning about and an openness to the entity, including its very being. If there is no openness, what we can learn will be restricted by what fits within our preconceived notions of the entity we are learning about. At the same time, for there to be actual, concrete learning, there will need to be an understanding of what the entity is we are learning about; if there is only openness, there is no ground in which any new ways of relating to the entity can take root. Because attitudes, skills, and knowledge invariably build on existing attitudes, skills, and knowledge, any learning that is to make a concrete change in how we feel, act, and think will need to have a basis in former learning or innate ways of responding to what happens to us, and openness by itself cannot give us this.

What this comes down to is that learning needs to be based in both existing understanding and in the kind of openness that has let go of that existing understanding. Such learning would combine the *conventional learning* and *learning to be authentic* we just looked at. The quest for this kind of *authentic learning* is there, in some ways, in a well-known "learning paradox" from Plato's Meno: how can we learn about something, unless we already have a way of understanding what we are learning about; while at the same time, learning is only truly learning, in so far as it concerns something we do not already have an understanding of. As we will see, Heidegger, though he does not explicitly address this particular form of the learning paradox as such, solves it with the help of what he calls the mode of authenticity. There is, according to Heidegger, a way of being in the world that allows for there to be an understanding of the being of entities which retains the kind of openness to these entities that allows us to relate to them in a way that is new. So, I will take Heidegger's notion of authenticity and apply it to the question of learning of how to reconcile *conventional learning* (as the learning that already in some ways knows what it is learning about) with *learning to be authentic* (as the learning that opens up to the very being of the entities involved). This will then result in a notion of *authentic learning*.

A focus on learning itself

Heidegger's notion of authenticity is, we will see in Chapter 2, one where there is both an openness to the being of entities and an understanding of the being of these entities. As such, the mode of authenticity can be taken to be one in which the two sides of learning I described above can co-exist. When a person is in a mode of authenticity, they should be able to learn in such a way that actual and concrete learning can happen that is based in an understanding of the being of the entities, even while there is a fundamental openness to the being of the entities. We will further see, also in Chapter 2, that there is among certain more recent philosophers writing in the field of education an understanding of the importance of this kind of learning. Useful though Heidegger's account of authenticity is, for our purposes it needs to be supplemented in important respects.

Heidegger did not write much about learning itself, and certainly not in the period before the publication of *Being and Time* (1927/1962), which is the period I will be mainly concerned with. In his later writings, there are some references to learning, but these do not explicitly discuss the learning paradox mentioned in the previous section. Thus he writes that "[t]o learn means to make everything we do answer to whatever essentials address themselves to us at a given time" (Heidegger 1976, 14). ("Lernen heisst: das Tun und Lassen zu dem in die Entspechung bringen, was sich jeweils an wesenhaftem uns zuspricht" (Heidegger 1954, 49).) This definition recognizes the importance of both an active ("to make everything we do answer...") and a receptive component, in that what we do needs to "answer to whatever essentials address themselves to us". There is, that is, implicit in this the need to open up to that which "addresses itself to us", in a way that in some ways puts the agency of learning in what we are learning about. But we do not find in Heidegger any further discussion about existing accounts of learning, and how these may need to be modified in order to allow for such opening up.

Heidegger's main interest seems to have been, following the tradition in which he wrote, in knowledge rather than in the process of knowledge acquisition, and in openness to what is other rather than in the process of *opening up* to what is other. This means that we have to reconstruct what learning would be like in the mode of authenticity; and in doing this we will find that, though there are substantial clues as to what such authentic learning would look like, many gaps in Heidegger's account need to be filled in. Though there is in Heidegger a continued understanding of the need for both an active and a receptive aspect in the way we relate to entities, he does not give us a notion of *authentic learning* as such.

To say the same thing differently, though Heidegger wrote a lot about authenticity, he did not write much about the process of *becoming* authentic. So even if we accept that, once a person is in a mode of authenticity, the learning they will engage in will be *authentic learning*, we are still left with the question of how one becomes authentic in the first place. We need an account of the process of becoming authentic, even if we accept that once a person is authentic there is both openness and an understanding of the being of entities that can form the basis for the concrete acquisition of attitudes, skills, and knowledge.

Here we then come upon a modified version of the learning paradox: in order for there to be *authentic learning* (one that combines openness with an understanding of the being of entities) the individual may well need to be in the mode of authenticity (what exactly that means will be explained in Chapter 2); but how is a person to come to the mode of authenticity, if not via a process of authentic learning? As we will see in the coming chapters, this paradox is well-understood by Heidegger to be genuinely paradoxical, and it culminates, in Chapter 6, in the question of how a call, a communication, can come through to us, if we have no register for it, no way of hearing that call. This is similar to the paradox of learning a new language, where we have to learn to hear sounds in new ways, in the face of our predisposition to hear these very sounds as being part the palette of sounds we are already familiar with from our native language.

But, as already incited, I will *not* work on the assumption that the individual needs to have arrived at the kind of authentic way of being that Heidegger describes, in order for there to be the kind of *authentic learning* that combines grasping with letting go. Still, *authentic learning* depends on the learner at a minimum going into the direction of authenticity. What is more, the mode of authenticity, as described by Heidegger, contains a strong sense of what it would be like to be who we really are. As we will see in the next chapter, we can characterize the very process of becoming authentic as that of *becoming who we are*. Because of this, there will, in what follows, initially be a focus on the question of *learning to be authentic*. In this way, the process of *learning to be authentic* functions as a paradigm case for *authentic learning*, in that the mode of being authentic is one that can only come about as a result of the kind of openness to what is new and other I have been referring to. At the same time, learning to be authentic takes us into the direction of who we really are. And this means that our quest for wholeness in learning has its natural starting point in the process of *learning to be authentic*. Once we have an understanding of the kind of learning process that leads to authenticity, we can then consider how such learning to be authentic can be integrated with accounts of conventional learning. This integrated form will then give us the kind of *authentic learning* that is able to grasp the being of entities from out of an authentic openness towards the being of those entities.

Overview of the book

The purpose of this book is to find a form of learning that is whole, in the sense of complete, sane, and healthy. Such a learning would involve the whole person, their body, emotions, actions, and ideas. It would also be understood that learning does not only happen in special circumstances or settings, but happens in most situations: yes, we may be able to rely heavily on previous learning in many situations, but there is almost always something that, if we have the required openness, means that we need to modify our response to the situation in subtle or not so subtle ways. Taken together, this means that a whole form of learning is something that operates most of the time, even if much of that time it happens automatically, as part of the very natural process of adapting ourselves to the specificity of the situation we are in.

Apart from being in operation most of our waking lives, such whole learning would, as we saw in the previous sections, involve both grasping and letting-go. It would focus on an object of learning as well as open up to the very being of the object. And, as will become clear fairly soon, of the two it is the element of opening up that is underrepresented in both academic and common-sense notions of learning. So, we will begin, in Chapter 2, by looking at Heidegger's notion of authenticity as one that puts openness at the very core of the human being. And we will see that, according to Heidegger's notion of the human being as openness, this very openness allows the human being to not only be *who it really is*, it also allows it to get the being right of the entities it is in relationship with. This, then, gives us a first starting point in our quest for wholeness in learning: for learning to be based in a correct understanding of that which we are learning about, this learning needs to be based in a fundamental openness.

In Chapter 3 we will take an in-depth look at our conventional notion of learning, as we find it in some of the main scholarly accounts of learning (psychology, information-processing, neurology, and education). Here we find that learning tends to be thought of as always having an intentional object, involving continuity and processes of association, amounting to a notion of learning that consists of modification and growth, in terms of ever-increasing integration and differentiation, resulting in an ever more stable, ridged even, way of relating to the intentional object. So, while these notions of learning go a long way in explaining what happens when we acquire attitudes, skills, and knowledge, they have no room for the kind of true openness that needs to be part of a whole form of learning. Yes, there is in these conventional accounts room for change and forgetting, but the processes described do not really have room for moments where letting-go is a conscious process that is grounded in an understanding of the need to open up.

Having, in Chapter 2, brought the notion of authentic openness into focus and, in Chapter 3, seen that our conventional accounts of learning cannot get us to that openness, we will in Chapters 4 through 6 work out a detailed account of how such authentic openness can come about. For this we will use Heidegger's ideas as these are found in his early philosophy – roughly around the time he wrote *Being and Time* in 1927. Within the totality of the human being (what Heidegger calls Dasein), he distinguishes the faculties of understanding, attunement, and being-with. And I will take one chapter for each of these three, in order to work out the process by which authentic openness is achieved (by which we become who we are). This will involve a detailed analysis of Heidegger's notion of authenticity, and at certain key points complements Heidegger's writings, because these do not contain many indications as to what the process of becoming authentic entails. This study of the process of *learning to be authentic* will be contrasted with the fundamental principles of conventional learning set out in Chapter 3, so that a picture emerges in what ways the process of conventional learning falls short of describing a process of learning that can be called whole, in the sense of complete, sane, and healthy.

In this discussion of the process of becoming authentic it will become clear that the main weakness in Heidegger's account relates to the notion of being-with. Being-with is Heidegger's notion of the relationship between human beings, where he, rightly, indicates that the way we human beings are related (and I would include other living beings, such as animals and plants, in that category) is different from the way in which we are related to objects in the world. We find in his notion of being-with important indications of how our relationships with ourselves and each other need to be based in a sense of oneness combined with respect for the unique individuality of each. But in many ways Heidegger fails to move beyond these promising beginnings, so that his account of authenticity shows important gaps, when it comes to the faculty of being-with. And because so much of our learning happens in relationship with other humans, I will spend considerable time augmenting Heidegger's account, introducing, for example, important interpersonal emotions, such as affection and love, in what would otherwise be a fairly barren account of this important dimension of life.

The book will end in Chapter 7 by bringing together *conventional learning* and *learning to be authentic* in a single process of *authentic learning*. As already indicated, authentic learning weaves together the openness of authenticity with the concrete moments of *conventional learning* as involving an intentional object that is grasped in a way that involves continuity, modification, and growth. Here we first look at the possibility of authentic learning for each of the three faculties (understanding, attunement, and being-with), but then we consider *authentic learning* in relation to the person as a whole. We find that *authentic learning* weaves together the strands of *conventional learning* and *learning to be authentic* in such a way that within each moment of *conventional learning*, there is a dimension of opening up, while at the same time, the authentic openness that emerges at the level of pre-reflective self-awareness is able to contain within it such a moment of *conventional learning*. We, further, see that by weaving together these two strands of learning, a form of temporality emerges that integrates the linear movement of *conventional learning* and the momentary nature of *learning to be authentic* in a way that is quite natural. In this way, *Wholeness in Learning* gives us a form of learning that is whole, in the sense of being undivided and complete. It involves not only growth through experience, but also increasing self-awareness, and the ability to let go, to open up to what is new and other. This holistic form of learning allows us to connect directly with ourselves, others, and the mystery of life. It integrates learning as the acquisition of knowledge and skills with learning as opening up and letting go. This allows us to gain knowledge and experience in a way that is ever more competent, while at the same time bringing us closer to who we are deep-down.

Authenticity

Authentic Dasein

In the previous chapter it was suggested that all of us need to be able to learn throughout life, because the world around us is changing all the time, and we ourselves are changing too. This kind of learning for life, I suggested, has two aspects. First, for learning to make an actual difference to how we feel, act, and think, it needs to build on existing ways of feeling, acting, and thinking – some of which may be innate and all of which involve some sense of the being of the entities we are learning about. And, second, learning needs to be able to open up to what is truly new and other. These two aspects are, on the face of it, mutually exclusive, and this leads to the kind of learning paradox mentioned in the previous chapter, where the continuity aspect of learning seems to preclude openness to novelty, while true openness seems to rule out grounding the new experience in a way that leads to real changes in our actual, concrete ways of responding to things, events, and people. I then suggested that Heidegger's notion of authenticity can show us a way out of this paradox. To get a firmer grasp of what Heidegger's notion of authenticity entails, we will begin this chapter by looking at what some philosophers writing in the field of education have written about authenticity.

The term "authentic" is the translation of the German "eigentlich", which is a concept with its roots in "what one really or actually is" and its branches in "what one is in potential". On the one hand "eigentlich" simply means "really" or "in actuality", as in, for example, "he is really very ignorant". On the other hand, "eigentlich" refers to a possibility rather than an actuality, the possibility of realising one's true potential of being "who one really is". So, when someone becomes authentic, there is a double movement of "becoming who one already is in reality" and of "becoming one's true self." One way of putting this is to say, as Heidegger does, citing Pindar, "Become what you are!" (Heidegger 1962, 186). This at first sight paradoxical statement is explained by Ian Thomson: "I can indeed become who I am if the one who I am now is not my own self (a self I have made my own), but merely a borrowed self, a self-understanding appropriated piecemeal from 'everyone and no one'" (Thomson 2004, 448). In this way, becoming authentic as becoming *who one is* is a movement from being an inauthentic to an authentic self.

Further examples from educational philosophy tell us that the notion of authenticity, of "becoming who one is", can be taken to be either *contrary to* or *in line with* conventional values. Ilan Gur-Ze'ev, for example, calls for a "counter education", setting authenticity up as contrary to the way education (and by implication society at large) is, which, he believes, alienates the individual from themselves. This critique of society and mainstream education is, of course, a familiar one that resonates with many of what are sometimes called critical pedagogies (See, for example, Freire 1970/1996), that see the task of education as one of liberating the individual from the socialisation that normally occurs in education, because, to cite Gur-Ze'ev, "Then, and only then ... will the overcoming of the given be possible and truth as uncovering realize itself" (Gur-Ze'ev 2002, 71). In this way, the notion of authenticity is presented as going against the grain of the mainstream of society.

Michael Bonnett (2002), on the other hand, while not denying the need for a certain amount of resistance, argues that the notion of "personal authenticity" is one that resonates with the central value in a liberal society of allowing individuals to be who they are and to engage in forms of learning that are personally meaningful. That is, "in characterizing some central components of what might be meant by 'human integrity', [personal authenticity] provides a view of personhood and therefore, in a liberal tradition, a view of what must be respected and developed" (Bonnett 2002, 230). This possibility of interpreting the process of "becoming who one is" as both *counter to* and *in line with* the basics values of western society reflects some of the deep inner tensions within our society. And the notion of authenticity can be taken as capable of helping us resolve that tension.

In this way, several philosophers of education have written about Heidegger's notion of authenticity as a valuable one for education. But with the exception of Bonnett's account of "poietic thinking" (2002), which we will look at in some detail later in the chapter, none of these accounts have set out to describe the process of becoming authentic itself in terms of learning. They have mostly been occupied with setting out a view on the nature of authenticity and making the case for authenticity in education, where authenticity may refer to either an educational aim or to a quality of the process of education, without addressing the question of learning directly. As my interest is first of all in the process of becoming authentic, I will not discuss in detail the arguments for making authenticity central to educational practice here, but merely reiterate some of what was said in those accounts, to fill it some more details as to the nature of Heideggerian authenticity. As indicated, I will remain within the field of educational philosophy in this chapter, because it is there that the question of learning has its natural home, while in the chapters that follow the focus will shift to other branches of philosophy, such as epistemology and ethics.

One early voice arguing that we ought to put authenticity at the heart of education is found in the writings of Donald Vandenberg, notably his *Being and Education: An Essay in Existential Phenomenology* (Vandenberg 1971). Vandenberg puts the question of the being of entities at the heart of his educational philosophy, and links it with self-awareness and authenticity. Here we see the notion of an understanding of the being of entities at work, where Vandenberg argues that learners ought to develop an understanding of being itself, as the most fundamental way in which we relate to entities. We could say that, according to Vandenberg, people with an understanding of *being as such* would be able to learn in a way that conforms to what the entities one learns about really are. Following Heidegger (see Chapter 4 in this book), Vandenberg gives in this priority to the individual's self-understanding which, he argues, forms the basis of its relationships with other entities, including those that lie fundamentally beyond what our habitual ways of feeling, acting, and thinking can grasp.

More recently, Gur-Ze'ev has taken up Vandenberg's call for an education that links self-awareness and self-realization with an understanding of the being of entities. As we saw earlier, Gur-Ze'ev calls for a "counter education", an education that is to counter the effects of "normalizing education", the socialization that brings about this inauthentic self-understanding, what

Heidegger calls the understanding oneself from out of "*das Man*"[1]. As we will see in more detail later, "*das Man*" is Heidegger's term for an understanding (both of things in the world and of oneself) that is neither one's own understanding (after all, it is one that one has been socialised into), nor an understanding that is true to the being of the entities it tries to understand (notably living beings). Thus, *Das Man* gets the being of entities wrong, in that through it one understands oneself as a (practical or theoretical) object rather than as that which one is in oneself. This "normalizing education", according to Gur-Ze'ev, constitutes a kind of violent imposition of a thing-like identity on the learner, in that it "produces the human subject as some-thing that prevents her from becoming some-one, a true subject" (Gur-Ze'ev 2002, 66). As with Vandenberg, we find that understanding oneself in a certain way and being in a certain way are inextricably linked, to the extent that we could say that one *is* one's self-understanding.

But Gur-Ze'ev does not only focus on how the individual understands his or her own being practically and intellectually. He also identifies the way that education tends to frame our relationship with the world at an emotional level and the way it motivates the learner to conform. With this he brings in an important affective element into the question of what it means to be authentic. Thus, he writes that, to be authentic, "the human subject must [...] resist the threats and temptations of security, pleasure, and success offered by [das Man], by society" (Gur-Ze'ev 2002, 71). This emotive or affective aspect, as we will see later in this chapter, resonates from Heidegger's notion of "attunement", the way we find ourselves located emotionally in the world, and which we will look at in detail in Chapter 5. That is, both the understanding of being and the openness that are part of authentic learning are not merely an intellectual or practical understanding, but contain an important affective component.

Bonnett identifies a further aspect of authenticity, when he writes that the "openness to things themselves" plays an essential part in the individual's being and becoming authentic. In relation to this fundamental openness Bonnett uses the phrase *thinking as poiesis* (bringing forth), which is, as indicated, not unlike the kind of learning we are after, in that it is a form of "thinking as engagement with things which is both personal in its commitment and transporting through its openness to things themselves"

[1]   I will be using the original "das Man" throughout the book, though most philosophers writing in English have used either "the they" or "the one".

(Bonnett 2002, 238). Importantly, this poietic thinking "requires constant and close attention to the signs which are its way, to a sense of that which is as yet withdrawn, not yet manifest. It requires a genuine listening to that which calls to be thought in the evolving situation" (Bonnett 2002, 239). With this emphasis on listening, a communicative dimension is introduced to authenticity (see also Chapter 6), where one's "understanding of being" is not a construction of the mind, but rather something that is informed by one's fundamental "openness to things themselves". Thus it is in this poietic (authentic) thinking, Bonnett argues, that "contingency and the many-sidedness of things is recognized and the non-human powers involved in the arising of things is sensed and responded to" (Bonnett 2002, 238).

In sum, for the philosophers of education cited, becoming authentic involves a true understanding of one's own being, a certain way of being located emotionally in the world, and a way of being open to things themselves, which has an important communicative dimension. What all this means in practice will be spelled out in detail in Chapters 4 to 6. For now, let me just point towards an emerging understanding of *learning to be authentic*, where there is a sense of self-renewal (in becoming who one really is), where one opens up to the being of entities, notably one's own being, with the result that one can get the being of these entities right. As such we can see the contours of a notion of learning that allows for both the continuity of building on existing understanding and the discontinuity of openness to what is new and other.

Dasein as concerned with the being of entities

Looking back later in life at the time when he wrote *Being and Time*, Heidegger wrote, "I have been concerned with renewing the question of ontology—the most central question of western philosophy—the question of being" (Heidegger 1980). Heidegger's philosophy is deeply imbued with the question of being, to the extent that his notion of the human individual, Dasein, also puts the question of being centre stage.

Dasein literally means existence, and it is Heidegger's term for the human individual. But Dasein is not only existence, it is also concerned with existence, with being. Because we ourselves are Dasein, and Dasein is concerned with being, the first step towards authentic existence is getting our own being right: only if we relate to ourselves in a way that is commensurate with our being, will we be able to relate to ourselves in the right way. And only from out of an authentic relationship with ourselves will we be able to relate in the right way to other entities, other living beings, the world as such.

And the issue of getting the being of entities right is not simply a practical one, but existential. Thus Heidegger writes that the "meaning of Dasein's being is not something free-floating which is other than and 'outside of' itself, but is the self-understanding Dasein itself." (Heidegger 1962, 372). That is, Dasein *is* its self-understanding, a notion which we saw in the previous section has been taken over by both Vandenberg and Gur-Ze'ev. To Dasein, its being matters, in that "Dasein is an entity for which, in its being, that being is an issue" (Heidegger 1962, 236).

So, Dasein is concerned with the being of entities, and as a result, one of the main challenges it faces is getting the being of entities right. Authentic Dasein gets the being of entities (including itself) right. So, the notion of authenticity as realizing our true potential (as becoming who we are) involves an authentic understanding of being. Such an authentic understanding of being begins with an authentic self-understanding, and once that is in place, Dasein is thought to be able to get the being of other entities right as well. As we saw earlier, this line of argument was adopted Donald Vandenberg, who in *Being and Education* writes that "Each province of meaning has its own mode of awakeness, i.e. its own temporal structure, cognitive style, and sense of reality, and each has to be 'entered' through a specific bracketing or 'leap' from another mode of awakeness and province of meaning" (Vandenberg 1971, 5-6).

Ian Thomson takes up the idea of authenticity as involving self-realization in his *Heidegger's Perfectionist Philosophy of Education in Being and Time* (Thomson 2004), where he turns to *Being and Time* (1962) to answer the question "*How do we become what we are?*". He writes that "The goal of this educational odyssey [of becoming what we are] remains simple but revolutionary: To bring us full circle back to ourselves, by first turning us away from the world in which we are most immediately immersed and then turning us back to this world in a more reflexive way" (Thomson 2004, 457).

To clarify the idea of becoming what one (already) is Thomson uses Thomas Hurka's account of perfectionist ethics, and he argues that in *Being and Time* Heidegger (a) had the idea that there is something distinctive and unique about human beings, that (b) our "greatest fulfilment or flourishing follows from the cultivation and development (hence the perfection) of these significantly distinctive skills or capacities", and that (c) there is a link between these two in that we are either, by nature, naturally disposed to reach this fulfilment or flourishing, or that we need to struggle for it, as it is against our nature (Thomson 2004, 440-442). Thus, according to Thomson, "Heidegger singles out Dasein as the unique possessor of an understanding of being", in that Dasein can disclose an entity as either a practical (ready-to-hand) one, a theoretical (present-at-hand) one, or an entity with the nature of Dasein itself (simply put, a being that is like us, human beings).

In perfectionist terms, (a) Dasein's *understanding of being* is distinctive and unique about it, (b) the flourishing that comes from the cultivation of this distinct and unique *understanding of being* is, according to Thomson conceived of "in terms of an embodied stand – 'authenticity' – that each of us is capable of taking on our own being". In other words, it is in the mode of authenticity that our understanding of being becomes "our own" and that we come to see ourselves and the entities we encounter in the world as they really are. And (c) the link between this *understanding of being* and the "embodied stand of authenticity" is "[a]uthenticity's double movement of death and rebirth [...] is a movement in which we turn away from the world, recover ourselves, and then turn back to the world, a world we now see anew, with eyes that have been opened" (Thomson 2004, 443).

So here we have Heidegger's fundamental beginning of the way we understand an entity, that of understanding its being. The understanding of the being of the entity would then provide the ground for continuity, in our search for an account of learning that is able to build on an existing understanding of the entity we are learning about. That is, we build our new understanding of the entity we learn about on an understanding of the being of that entity. This is not to say that innate predispositions and sense perception play no role, but that any learning that is more than the mere conditioning of the body's reflexes involves an understanding of the being of the entity we are learning about. And we also have in Thomson's account a first indication of what the process of becoming authentic could be like, that of a "double movement of death and rebirth", where the renewed understanding of being would be the foundation of the rebirth, and where the moment of opening up would be a kind of existential death.

Dasein as openness

Dasein is, according to Heidegger, not only that being for whom being is an issue; Dasein is also open to the world. Indeed, at the most basic level, Dasein is often referred to as an empty space, an openness where being and beings can be experienced. And as we will see shortly, becoming authentic involves a process of letting go, as a result of which Dasein becomes the openness which it is at heart, what in the reference to Thomson in the previous section was called "death."

Sometimes Heidegger uses for this openness the term "clearing", as in a clearing in the forest, an empty space among the otherwise dense growth of trees and shrubs, where light can enter. Another way of putting this is to say that Dasein is being-in-the-world. This means that Dasein *is* worldly existence, that it *is* its engagement with the entities it finds in the world, and that there is nothing substantial (like a soul) that exists as something internal, which then needs to reach out to (transcend to) the things that are external to it. Rather, Dasein is the very process of standing in relationship to the entities it encounters, of what Heidegger calls transcendence, where this transcendence in itself is nothing but openness to what is other. The process of *learning to be authentic* would, therefore, be one of opening up the individual (Dasein) to the world.

In the clearing of this openness the processes arise that give us the actual manifestation of the individual Dasein: understanding (*Verstehen*), attunement (*Befindlichkeit*) and being-with (*Mitsein*). These are the three ways in which Dasein finds itself in the world, and they will form the basis of Chapters 4 to 6. Ultimately, understanding, attunement and being-with constitute a unity; they are separated mainly as a way of gaining analytical clarity. Their ultimate unity notwithstanding, we find in Heidegger's writings discussions of authenticity for each of the three, so to get more clarity about Heidegger's notion of Dasein's openness, let us first look more closely at the tripartite structure of the way Dasein relates to the entities it finds in the world.

"Understanding" involves both our *practical know-how* of dealing with things and our *theoretical knowledge* of it. Heidegger's word understanding (Verstehen) is to be understood in the sense that whenever we engage with an entity, when we perceive it or act in relation to it, we have an understanding of what the entity is and we gain further understanding of the entity by relating to it practically and theoretically. This way of conceiving of action and perception is in many ways in line with the main accounts of learning we will look at in Chapter 3, at least in so far as these are not representationalist, because Heidegger's idea is not that there is in the individual somewhere a representation which is modified as a result of perception and which serves as a basis for action. Rather, understanding is an embodied way of being in the world that has both a practical and a theoretical dimension. We will look at understanding and the possibility of authentic understanding in depth in Chapter 4.

The aspect of "attunement" is the basic emotional way of being we have at any given point in time, where this emotional way of being discloses both the world and ourselves in a certain way – much like the mood that may disclose a person's world as a dreary place and himself as a failure, if they have just fired from their job or, conversely, the world as a beautiful place and him or herself as the beneficiary of good fortune, if the person they are in love with has just reciprocated their feelings. Attunement as mood is, for Heidegger, the basis for emotions that are directed towards a certain object (a person we are angry with or a child we feel tenderness towards), in that even emotions that are clearly directed towards an entity have the structure of disclosing both oneself and the entity in a certain way (the person as annoying and oneself as irritated) in a way that the two are not separate (one cannot emotionally experience a child as endearing without feeling something like tenderness). Importantly, mood is something that *arises* or *comes over one*, in that we do not experience a mood as *originating from* a certain particular place (in the way perceptions and actions do) or as *directed towards* a certain particular place (as perceptions and actions also do), but as colouring *the whole* of experience, even if, as we saw, it may also involve a directional element. We will look at attunement and authenticity in depth in Chapter 5.

Heidegger takes "being-with", our way of being related to other human beings, as constitutive of Dasein just as much as understanding and attunement. This is perhaps unusual in western thinking, with its emphasis on the individual as the ultimate unit of analysis, because the being-with dimension is part of Dasein itself. "Being-with belongs to [Dasein], which in every case maintains itself in some definite way of concernful Being-with-one-another" (Heidegger 1962, 204). Rather than saying that the individual is *primarily* an independent entity which only *secondarily* finds itself in relation to other individuals, Heidegger maintains that being-with-one-another belongs to the very essence of the individual. One could say that the individual is part of the social world they belong to in just as fundamental a way as it is understanding and attunement. As such, Heidegger, unusually perhaps, does not base communication in action-perception (as when messages are transferred from one to the other) but in a prior being-connected of human beings and other living creatures. We will look at authentic being-with in depth in Chapter 6.

As indicated, for all three Heidegger has an authentic mode, a way of understanding, being attuned, and being-with that is in keeping with who we really are. And for all three this authentic mode involves a certain openness: *authentic understanding* means that Dasein understands itself (is open to itself) in terms of itself rather than the things it finds in the world; *authentic attunement* means that Dasein has an affective stance in life which does not identify itself with things in the world and yet maintains a nearness (openness) to these things; *authentic being-with* means having direct, wordless, unmediated communication with others, which is likewise based in openness. To say the same thing, anticipating some of the Heideggerian terminology we will encounter later in the book, authenticity is "constituted by anxiety as attunement, by understanding as a projection of oneself upon one's ownmost being-guilty, and by discourse [communication] as reticence" (Heidegger 1962, 343).

The openness we find in authenticity has an effect on Dasein, because when there is this openness, things are *disclosed*, things enter into experience. That is, the most basic way of characterizing how we understand, grasp, or encounter things and living beings is that these are *disclosed* in this openness. And what is disclosed most fundamentally is the *being* of entities. Here we find the understanding of being (that which can ground learning in an existing way of understanding the entity one is learning about) come together with the openness that, I argued, is necessary for a true account of learning: as Dasein opens up, the being of entities is disclosed.

As we saw earlier, the being of entities is disclosed in different ways: as practical (what Heidegger calls the ready-to-hand), as theoretical (what Heidegger calls the present-at-hand), or as belonging to the human domain (what Heidegger calls *being in the world* or *entities with the nature of Dasein* or *existence*). If something is disclosed as ready-to-hand, it is disclosed as a practical entity, something we interact with, handle, manipulate, the way we do objects we find in our practical dealing with things: objects of use and pieces of equipment are by their very nature ready-to-hand entities. If something is disclosed as present-at-hand, it is disclosed as a theoretical entity, something that we take to have an essence and properties (qualities and relations), and we relate to it in the way we relate to theoretical ideas and representations.

Inauthentic Dasein tends to disclose *itself* as either ready-to-hand or present-at-hand too, and this is where, according to Heidegger, things start to go wrong, because Dasein itself is neither something ready-to-hand or present-at-hand, but something with the being of Dasein itself, of being-in-the-world, of existence. The main change from inauthentic to authentic existence, therefore, consists in Dasein learning to take itself as an entity with the nature of Dasein, as openness. This is what earlier we saw Vandenberg refer to as "getting the being of entities right." And only when Dasein discloses itself as an entity with the nature of being-in-the-world will it disclose the being of the other entities it encounters in the world in the right way (sometimes as practical or theoretical entities but, more importantly, also other entities with the nature of Dasein, as would be the case with other humans, and, in contrast to Heidegger, I would add animals and plants).

So when we say that learning needs to involve an understanding of the being we are learning about (for only then can this learning result in concrete, actual change in the way we feel, act, and think) while at the same time there is an opening up to the entity we are learning about, we begin see that the openness in Heidegger's account of openness is intricately linked to his notion of an understanding of being. It is this combination of *opening up* and coming to an authentic *understanding of being* that, I hope to show, can provide the starting point for learning.

In opening up, Dasein can disclose the being of entities

As indicated in the previous section, Dasein's opening up is not inert but can, in its own way, help it engage with the entities it encounters in the world, in that it can help disclose the being of these entities. This mix of opening up and grasping the being of entities can then act as the basis for a form of learning that combines the continuity of existing understanding with the discontinuity of openness. In this way, the paradox of learning being at the same time new and a continuation of previous learning (and innate responses) can possibly be solved. How exactly this works will occupy the remainder of the book, but for now, let me begin by clarifying one of the most pressing questions: how can an understanding of being come out of the process of opening up?

One answer to how an understanding of being can come out of a process of opening up is that the openness itself is receptive to the being of entities. Early Heidegger appears to take this route, when he refers to Dasein's openness as "a structure which makes possible for it being-fulfilled by certain goods of the life-world" (Heidegger 2004, 250). Thus Dasein's openness is not thought to be inert but consists in the "essential *openness to values* and *primary love of meaning* of the personally existing being" (Heidegger 2004, 250). I will, however, not go as far as to say that the openness itself gives us the being of entities, first, because merely stating this to be the case does not answer the sceptic and, second, because my interest in is the process of opening rather than some state of openness.

This focus on the process of opening up rather than a state of openness comes, first of all, because in my experience there can for most people be regular moments of opening up, where it is much rarer that one experiences an actual state that is completely devoid of any presupposition about the entities one is in relationship with. And when there is such a moment of complete openness, it tends to be fleeting, tends to not be concerned with the actual entities one finds in the world or with oneself as an individual Dasein, and tends to leave behind no concrete understanding of being that subsequent learning can build on. In other words, from the little experience of complete openness I have had, this openness appears to do exactly what one would expect complete to do, which is to have very little direct effect on subsequent learning. What it does seem to do is set in motion an internal reorganization of the way one is, one that is felt at the bodily level as a reordering of the energy one feels oneself to consist of. The result of this reorganization at the level of energy is, however, not something that I can pin-point as having any particular effect on my way of being, other than that it seems to leave behind an increased openness and an ability to see things more clearly as they are.

So, from the little experience I have of it, moments of complete openness do not produce the beginnings of further learning in relation to any particular entity, even if they result in an increased ability to open up. Without wanting to dismiss states of complete openness (others may, for example, have experienced more lasting ones and, as a result, experienced other effects), I will, therefore, focus mostly on the process of opening up. Moreover, because the meaning of complete openness lies, per definition, in the experience of it and not in its conceptual explication, the process of opening up will always have priority: if we discover how the process of opening up takes place, this may help us eventually come to a state of complete openness. There is, in this, the same priority that the process of learning has over its outcomes: when we try to learn something, the most important thing is that we get there, not that we talk about what it would be like if we got there.

Another reason for the priority of the process of opening up over the state of complete openness is that, at least in my experience, the actual being of entities is disclosed in the process of opening up itself rather than in the moment of complete openness. This may, at first, sound strange, for how can the process of opening up achieve more (disclosing the actual being of entities) than the perfect state of openness itself? But it makes sense, if we take into account that what complete openness discloses may lie beyond the being of entities. After all, let us not too readily assume that the being of the entities we find in the world is the most fundamental truth about existence that can be disclosed. Yes, Heidegger appears to have referred back to the medieval notion of that which is absolute (God) as being. But we do not need to follow him in this. What is more, even if complete openness discloses the being of the absolute, this does not mean that the absolute has the same being as the entities we find in the world – and this possibility of the absolute having its own distinct mode of being was well-understood in the tradition in which Heidegger found the notion of the absolute as being.

So, it may be the case that the process of opening up to the being of those entities we find in the world (things, ourselves, other living beings) has its perfection in complete openness. It may, however, also be the case that, if and when complete openness happens, we come into contact with a form of being that does not tell us how to relate to those beings we find in the world around us, even if that contact changes us inwardly. And, yes, that contact with another form of being that comes with complete openness may well be more important than anything we can learn about the entities we find in the world. But it is not the aim of this book to talk about that other way of being or its effect on those who come into contact with it. My goals are more modest (and still possibly beyond my reach), namely, that of bringing into focus a process of learning that involves opening up, and showing how this can help disclose the being of the entities we are in relationship with on a day-to-day basis. If, in following through the need to open up, some of us occasionally find ourselves in a state of complete openness, I will take this as a step-change in our way of being, of which the process of opening up as described here may show traces, but to which it is not connected in any necessary way.

The question driving this investigation concerns the process of learning, as we engage in it on a day-to-day basis. This process of learning, it has been argued, has two aspects which can easily appear to be in contradiction with each other: learning builds on an understanding we already have of (the being of) the entity we are learning about, while at the same time learning demands that we open up to (the being of) the entity we are learning about, so that we can come to a new understanding of it. So far I have argued that, though there may be cases of learning where all we see is a gradual modification of our existing understanding of the entity, in most cases learning has a discontinuous element, where new learning cannot be said to be based solely in previous learning. We saw that this is especially the case, when the learning happens in relation to that which is by itself in some ways beyond what we can know, such as the origins of our own experiences, other living beings, and life itself. But the need to let go of existing ways of understanding the entity we are learning about is also there in more practical situations; and, indeed, moments of creative insight are often reported as having just such a moment of discontinuity. Thus "the appearance of [a sudden insight] contains a character of discontinuity : it surges forth with a leap, unexpectedly, out of our control" (Petitmengin 1999, 2): the importance of opening up is also there in our attempts to find new solutions to new problems.

It has been suggested that we can resolve this apparent contradiction between the need for learning to be based in an existing understanding and the need for learning to let go of just such an existing understanding with the help of Heidegger's notion of authenticity. Because authentic Dasein combines genuine (authentic) openness with a genuine understanding of the being of entities, it appears to be in the right position to learn. But, as was explained in Chapter 1, more important even than an understanding of the authentic mode of being-in-the-world is an understanding of the process that will get us there. And this brings us back to the question of the process of becoming authentic, as both the paradigm case for authentic learning and that which may lead us to such authentic learning. We will end this part of the chapter by looking briefly at the way in which some philosophers writing in education have characterized the process of becoming authentic. In the second part of this chapter, we will then return Heidegger's own characterization of the process.

Becoming authentic as "turning away from the world" and "turning back"

Earlier we saw that Thomson wrote about authenticity as a movement in which we "turn away from the world, recover ourselves, and then turn back to the world" (Thomson 2004, 443). Bonnett refers to this same movement of "turning away from the world" and "turning back", when he frames this movement in terms of both an active and a passive element to authentic learning. Authentic learning (and I would add, *learning to be authentic*) is active in the sense that "[p]ersonal authenticity is an achievement", in that "[w]e have to extricate ourselves from the frame of mind that constitutes [*das Man*] and which proximally and for the most part conditions our perceptions" (Bonnett 2002, 232). The "rebirth" for Bonnett, citing Charles Taylor, happens against a "horizon of significance ... a valuation system of a historically grown community – the authoritative principles, rules, values, and norms that are expressive of the socially prevalent conception of the good life" (Bonnett 2002, 233). Thus, the "understanding of being" that Thomson identifies is, according to Bonnett, brought to "perfection" only in "openness to things themselves."

Ilan Gur-Ze'ev refers to this openness as "lettings-things-be", which is a term used by the later Heideggerian, *Gelassenheit*, referring to the ability to let things present themselves to consciousness "as they are", which harks back to Meister Eckhart. Gur-Ze'ev contrasts this "lettings-things-be" with the "normal violence directed at imposing realities and meanings" (Gur-Ze'ev 2002, 71). The "turning away from the world" is thus a turning away from the world as handed down to us through *das Man*, through "normalizing education", a world whose "realities and meanings" are imposed, projected onto the world, taken over in an inauthentic way by the individual from society. Gur-Ze'ev contrasts this inauthentic way of knowing the world with "transcendence ... in which Being, which is normally veiled and exiled, reveals itself" (Gur-Ze'ev 2002, 71).

After this "turning away from the world", the moment of "rebirth" or "turning back" occurs when one returns from this openness to the resources of one's cultural tradition, to appropriate them in a way that is authentic. As

Michael Bonnet writes, there is an important passive element to authentic learning with the existence of a "superordinate cultural normative framework [which] directs the focus of discussion away from the notion of the authentic individual as somehow operating in splendid isolation from the real world and places it instead on the quality of his or her relationship with the world" (Bonnett 2002, 233). In other words, the individual can only be authentic within human society, which necessarily involves things like language, culturally sanctioned knowledge, socially constructed ways of doing things, and so on. This "return" to *das Man* is inescapable, but if it is done in an authentic way, it is done in a way that is open to the being of entities, both of oneself and of entities other than oneself.

As we will see at different points in the book, the language surrounding authenticity is often dramatic, with words like death, guilt, and anxiety. This is partly so, because the process of becoming authentic involves the whole person, the totality of one's life, all the way down to one's deepest feelings, one's most fundamentally held beliefs, and one's most basic ways of being in the world. To put it differently, giving up what is given to us through *das Man* involves giving up much if not most of the person we are. It is for this reason that authenticity involves a moment that is often characterised as a kind of "dying", though I prefer the milder term of letting go. It is also for this same reason that the moment of "rebirth" necessitates a return to these culturally given ways of seeing and doing things, as these are simply the "currency" in which human life is transacted.

In Chapter 7 we will look at what this "return" or "rebirth" may look like in some detail, because it constitutes the moment at which, from out of openness to the being of entities, we return to the acquisition of attitudes, skills, and knowledge that is so much part of education as a socially useful practice. That is, whereas much of what has been written about authenticity in education is about opening up, the true test for an account of *learning to be authentic* will be whether it is able to bring the practice of attitude, skill, and knowledge acquisition into this openness. Education as enculturation, enabling the individual to play a productive role in society, will need to have a place in the openness that comes with one's "turning away from the world." It is only when this return to society, with all its practical demands, is done in a way that is in harmony with Dasein's essential openness that we can expect the demand for authentic education in the Heideggerian sense to be taken seriously in the mainstream.

To sum up, Heidegger's notion of authenticity has been discussed by a number of recent philosophers of education as a double movement of both *becoming who one really* is and reaching one's full potential as a human being. In so far as the process of becoming authentic has been described by these philosophers of education, it has been characterized as a kind of "death and rebirth", a "turning away from the world" and a "turning back" in such a way that one gains an authentic (*genuine* as well as *one's own*) understanding of one's own existence as well as that of the entities one encounters in the world. In order to deepen our understanding of this process of "turning away" and a "turning back", I will now return to Heidegger's own description of this process. This will then give us a foundation from which to construct a detailed account of *learning to be authentic* in Chapters 4 to 6, where *learning to be authentic* is both a paradigm case and a precondition for *authentic learning*.

"Turning away from the world" and "turning back"

Disclosure as Dasein's most fundamental way of being in truth

As was explained in the introduction, if we want something like opening up to the being of entities to play a role in the way we learn, we need an account of how we can learn this kind of opening up, an account of the process of *learning to be authentic*. Heidegger himself did not give a detailed account of this process, but where he does refer to it, he writes about a process that can be characterized as *awakening, giving oneself up*, or *finding one's true self*. We will take a closer look at these three ways of characterising authenticity in this part of the chapter, and do so against the backdrop of the distinction Heidegger makes between disclosure (we briefly looked at disclosure in the first half of this chapter) and discovery. This is the existentialist distinction between *disclosing* the being of entities (What things can possibly exist?) and *discovering* actual entities (Which things do actually exist of all the things that could possibly exist?). Importantly, of the two, disclosure is for Heidegger a more fundamental form of truth than the kind of truth we may discover.

Heidegger characterizes disclosure as Dasein's primordial truth. Thus he writes that resoluteness, as a "distinctive mode of Dasein's disclosedness", is existentially "the primordial truth", and that "[s]uch truth is primarily not a quality of 'judgement' nor of any definite way of behaving, but something essentially constitutive for being-in-the-world as such [Dasein]" (Heidegger 1962, 343). As David Cooper puts it, Heidegger's notion of truth contrasts with the notion of truth as the agreement (we could also say "correspondence") between a proposition or a representation and objects or facts in the world. Thus, Cooper writes that, while the "conception [of truth as correspondence] is not simply mistaken, Heidegger levels two criticisms against those who subscribe to it. First, they treat 'agreement' as a matter of similarity between two entities, a representation and an object or fact represented", which he rejects as unintelligible. "Instead, he argues, we should think of a true assertion as disclosing or uncovering an object". Second, "it is not ... assertions or judgements which are the primary vehicles of truth. For it is we – Dasein – who disclose and uncover" (Cooper 2002, 54). It is Dasein itself that is in truth or untruth, just as it is the individual him or herself (and not their ideas or representations) that can open up to the being of entities.

Disclosure is a concept Heidegger uses for the way in which the being of entities is accessed by Dasein. Disclosure is, therefore, essentially about Dasein's understanding of the being of entities. The German word for "to disclose" is *erschliessen*, which consists of two parts: the prefix "*er*[2]", which functions in much the same way as "dis" does in disclose, and "*schliessen*" which means to close. In German the word *erschliessen* means "to open up", where what can be opened up is, for example, a country for trade, an oil well or a mine for extraction, a book for meaning, the heart for experience, a hotel for guests. *Erschliessen* can also mean that something reveals itself to someone, the meaning of a book can be revealed to the reader, nature can reveal itself to the poet, someone can reveal themselves to a friend. In so far as the process of becoming authentic brings us into contact with what is true and good at a fundamental level, it discloses, first and foremost, the being of the entities involved.

---

2   Note that the German prefix "ent" usually means the same as "er", which is a further indication of the closeness of the terms *entschliessen* (to decide) and *erschliessen* (to disclose)

What happens in the event of true disclosure is that Dasein itself is disclosed to itself (we will see later that this happens through a form of a pre-reflective self-awareness) at the same time that the being of the entities it is in contact with is being disclosed. "Whenever a 'there' [the most basic truth about Dasein is, according to Heidegger, that it is the openness of 'a there'] is disclosed, its whole being-in-the-world—that is to say, the world, being-in, and the self which, and an 'I am', this entity is – is disclosed with equal primordiality" (Heidegger 1962, 344). This is in line with the idea presented earlier, that the being of entities is disclosed at the level of what is called the apriori, at the point where both the "active" *intentio* and the "passive" *intentum* of the relationship emerge. Authentic disclosure thus brings together "what we take something as" with "how something presents itself to us." We could say that what is disclosed in authenticity is the deep structure, the apriori, of *the way something presents itself* or of *what it is taken as*. And because there is in this disclosure as yet no distinction between the *intentio* and the *intentum*, it is one of unity.

The truth of disclosure is more basic than propositional truth, the truth of a judgement, or the truth of an action, of a way of behaving. Hence it would be misleading to say that authentic existence consists of holding certain propositional truths or behaving in a certain way; this is not about the attitudes, skills, or knowledge we may acquire. Because disclosure is the way in which Dasein first discloses anything (itself and the world) one could say that before (prior to) disclosure there is nothing for Dasein but openness to entities. In contrast, for Dasein to *discover* something, there needs to already be both a world in which things can be discovered, and "things", in the broadest sense of the word, to be discovered in that world: if Dasein has no *world* of any sort and no sense of what kind of *entities* exist in that world, it is impossible for Dasein to discover anything. In this way discovery presupposes disclosure: disclosure happens at the apriori level, where there is a sense of unity, because there is not yet a distinction between self and other, between *intentio* and *intentum*. Because opening up to the being of entities happens at the level of the apriori, the process of becoming authentic will involve the disclosure of the possibility of authentic existence to Dasein.

Awakening as discovery and disclosure

The first characterisation of the process of becoming authentic we will look at is that of Dasein disclosing both itself and the world, in a process that I would characterize as an awakening. An example of this can be found in the following quote from *Being and Time*, though Heidegger himself does not here use the word awakening: "If Dasein discovers the world in its own way and brings it close, if it discloses to itself its own authentic being, then this discovery of the 'world' and this disclosure of Dasein are always accomplished as a clearing-away of concealments and obscurities, as a breaking up of the disguises with which Dasein bars its own way" (Heidegger 1962, 167).

Those familiar with the religious discourse used in many mystical traditions will recognize the reference to the falling away of the veil of illusion in which most of us are thought to be caught most of the time. As with religious awakenings, the disclosure that comes with authenticity refers to a renewed understanding of both the self and the world. Note that this is linked to Heidegger's notion of the aim of philosophy as opening up the individual to the deep truth of life itself: "Plato says in one of his major dialogues that the difference between the philosophising human being and the one who is not philosophising is the difference between being awake … and sleeping…" (Heidegger 1995, 23). In this way, "Heidegger understands philosophy as an awakening of life itself" (de Beistegui 2005). The kind of awakening Heidegger is interested in is, in his words, ontological (pertaining to the *being* of entities) rather than ontic (pertaining to actual entities). In other words, disclosure is primarily ontological and discovery is ontic, and we will take them as being two distinct ways in which Dasein has access to being and beings, even though disclosure, as more fundamental than discovery, is sometimes also used as encompassing both.

When thinking about authenticity in terms of awakening, there is the risk of conceptualising the state from which one awakens and the state in which one wakes up in terms of our ordinary (practical or theoretical) conceptions of things. An example of this would be if a daughter discovered that her father, who she had hitherto held up as her hero, was, in fact, deeply corrupt in his dealings with a business partners. For the daughter this could amount to a discovery which brings about a kind of awakening. Her father is suddenly seen in a different light and with this may well come a change in how she sees her own world: no longer is the beautiful house she grows up in the fruit of honest labour and business nous, as it now represents the ill-deserved gains of dishonesty and manipulation. Though this kind of discovery represents an awakening of sorts, it is not the kind of awakening Heidegger refers to when he talks about authenticity. The ontic discovery shows the daughter what kind of person, of all the possible kinds of persons, her father actually is. But this is different from ontological disclosure which would be the disclosure of what it is to be human, what the possibilities of being human are, in the first place.

In our common-sense conception of learning we often find the *ontical* approach to awakening, where the learner becomes aware of actually existing things, which is different from the *ontological* emphasis in authenticity on disclosing the *being* of entities. Thus, in many critical forms of learning the idea is that the learner awakens from the slumber of traditional ways of seeing things. Often the word narrative, or grand narrative, is used for the ways of looking at the world and themselves that the learner grows up in. The awakening these critical forms of learning imply is that of the learner seeing what is false about these narratives. For example, the idea that people in western democracies are free could be critically analysed, shown to be a narrative which hides many aspects of our lives that are not free, as a result of, for example, media manipulation or the lack of any real political choice. It is then thought that a person who is able to critically engage with such narratives is better able to be an autonomous person, because they can form their own opinions and are not as much subject to being told what to think as people who have not learned to think critically in such a way.

Though there is, I believe, a lot of merit in many of such critical forms of learning, they do not think of awakening in the same way as Heidegger does. For Heidegger awakening, in the context of a discussion of authenticity, does not wake up to the fact that X is not Y but Z (e.g. "the education system is not there to help the individual flourish but to serve as a tool of an oppressive social order"), not even to the fact that there are such things as Xs, Ys, and Zs (e.g. "in this world there are oppressors and the oppressed and usually the oppressor, if successful, hides behind a mask of benevolence"). What Heidegger's authentic awakening discloses is that as human beings we are, more often than not, lived by the public discourse of *das Man* (his term for an understanding of things and ourselves that we have been socialized into and is, as already mentioned, developed further in the first part of Chapter 6) but that there is a way of relating that is deeper than (prior to) *das Man*. In contrast, the examples of critical education given above aim for the learner to awaken to the true nature of *das Man*.

That is, the process of becoming authentic is not so much a critical analysis of *das Man*, but an awakening to the fact that as human beings we tend to get lost in a socialized understanding of ourselves and the world. At the same time, becoming authentic opens us up to the possibility of an authentic way of being in the world: as part of awakening to the fact of socialization, there is the awakening to the possibility of a deeper connection with ourselves and the world, the possibility of letting go of *das Man* itself and opening up to the being of entities. So, at the same time that we awaken to the fact that we tend to take the entities, including ourselves, as practical or theoretical entities, the possibility of true openness is disclosed to us. This awakening to one's "lostness" in *das Man* constitutes an awakening to the being of the world and others; it puts the whole of human existence in a different light by realizing the possibility of authentic existence.

Giving one-self up as discovery and disclosure

A second way in which authenticity can be characterised is that of "giving oneself up". Thus "[a]nticipation [the realisation of the finitude of one's existence, which we will look at in Chapter 4] discloses to [Dasein] that its uttermost possibility lies in giving itself up, and thus shatter all one's tenaciousness to whatever existence one has reached" (Heidegger 1962, 309). Here the act of giving oneself up (of letting go of all the ways one has adopted from *das Man*) can be seen as an act of resolve in the face of the disclosure of the truth of one's most authentic way of being as openness; it is similar to the notion of "turning away from the world" and existential dying we looked at earlier in this chapter.

As in the case of awakening, the danger with the notion of "giving oneself up" is that of conceiving of the self in terms of our ordinary everyday understanding as either a practical or a theoretical entity rather than in terms of an entity with the nature of Dasein. Thus, sometimes such "giving oneself up" is thought of in terms of the individual giving up a belief they have about themselves, in order to discover a truer self – for example, when a young man, who believes that his most cherished asset is his reputation as a womaniser discovers that he can give up that part of his self in order to become who he really is, for example, the faithful lover who is set to become a dedicated husband and father. In such cases, the self is not truly given up, rather, one way of being oneself is exchanged for another. The point is not that we should never move to a notion of ourselves that is more in keeping with who we really are, but that, in order to open up to the being of entities, including ourselves, all forms of self may need to be let go of. Rather than saying that there is a true self hidden underneath the person that is there now, or that the person needs to be shaped in the right way, this notion of "giving oneself up" implies that *any* form of self needs to be relinquished.

But even where there is the understanding on the part of the individual that all forms of self, however noble, get in the way of authentic relationship, there is the risk that this "giving oneself up" is taken in a way that assumes either a practical or a theoretical stance and, as a result, does not happen at the level of the apriori. The danger of understanding such "giving oneself up" in practical terms is that the self is taken as ready-to-hand (we saw earlier in this chapter that a ready-to-hand entity is a practical entity like an object one could give up by leaving it behind). The self is then seen as a nuisance, the cause of suffering, or the impediment to one's full realisation as a human being. And such a discovery of the self as an impediment is likely to result in one *acting* towards the self, trying to change things practically. For example, one may deny any "nourishment" to the self and renounce all worldly goods; or one may set out to punish oneself for any manifestation of selfishness in order to teach oneself not to allow the self to take over; or one may subject oneself to a regime or the will of another person, as monks do in monasteries when they pledge absolute obedience to the abbot, as a way of practicing surrender to god. In this way one would practice life without the self, but this practicing would presuppose a practical attitude (Heidegger's ready-to-hand) and would as such not be at the level of the apriori, and therefore not part of *learning to be authentic*.

Another way of taking the self that is not at the level of the apriori is to do as something present-at-hand (we saw earlier in this chapter that a present-at-hand entity is a theoretical entity like a concept one could give up by replacing it with another one, and we will look at this in more depth in Chapter 4). When taking the self as a theoretical entity, the individual has a representation of the self as an entity with qualities and relations that explains what the self is and what it does. Staying with the notion of "giving up", the self may be thought of as a mere theoretical posit, one that is not based on any empirical evidence, but a kind of optical illusion. As a result of such an inauthentic, theoretical, notion of the self there may then be either an account of how "giving oneself up" is possible and even inevitable, or of how giving up is impossible, and the self just something one needs to learn to live with or requiring an act of grace to be given up. All of this may then suggest things one could do (which would take the self as ready-to-hand understood from within the present-at-hand scheme), or it could suggest that all one needed to do was adopt a true representation of the person as one without a self. Again, such a theoretical (present-at-hand) approach to the perceived need to give up the self would not happen at the level of the apriori, because the theoretical attitude is itself based in a certain apriori stance about the being of oneself, others, and the world.

A further way of explaining why any notion of the self as practical or theoretical runs into difficulty is that it is not clear what or who it is that would give up the self in the first place, when the self is taken as either ready-to-hand or present-at-hand. For there to be something ready-to-hand or present-at-hand there needs to be something that takes the entity as ready-to-hand or present-at-hand. But in the case of *giving up the self* what is it that could give up the self other than the self? It is, therefore, not a matter of discovering that the self must be given up, but of disclosing the self in a way that is prior to any practical or theoretical take on it. The result of such a disclosure at the level of the apriori is then not a judgement or a way of behaving but, rather, a way of being. Heidegger then claims that in the very instance of disclosing the nature of the self "all one's tenaciousness to whatever existence one has reached" is shattered (Heidegger 1962, 309). Thus the "letting go" of the self is neither the result of an action one takes nor of a theoretical judgement one makes about how things are, but something that happens in the moment of disclosure itself.

Finding one's true self as discovery and disclosure

A third way of characterizing the process of becoming authentic is that of finding one's true self. Heidegger writes that "because only the self of the [self belonging to *das Man*] gets appealed to [by the call of conscience] and brought to hear, *das Man* collapses. ... [and] the self, which the appeal has robbed of its lodgement and hiding-place, gets brought to itself" (Heidegger 1962, 317). Here the idea is that of the inauthentic self (which is constructed out of or by *das Man*) collapses and the true, authentic self comes to the fore. Characterizing the process in this way is clearly linked with "giving oneself up" as the inauthentic self "collapses" and with awakening, as one awakens to what one is authentically (one *becomes who one is*) in finding one's true self.

This "finding" is an instance of disclosure, of revealing to oneself what the possibilities are that the self has, rather than finding any particular actualisation of these possibilities. In Heideggerian terms we would then say that the self of *das Man* is being let go of, and a true sense of who one is is disclosed in that very act of letting go. Note that the true self is often conceived of as present-at-hand, in that it is thought to have certain characteristics which are true to it. For example, a person may have conformed to certain expectations from others and, as a result, behave and think like the person they feel they are expected to be. In this case the true self would behave and think differently from how they now behave and think. This person would then, in discovering their true self, find out that "deep down" they are inclined to behave and think differently from how they normally do, like the young man mentioned in the previous section, who finds out that he is not really made to be a womanizer but a loyal husband. But, as we also saw in the previous section, because such a discovery is not at the level of the apriori, it does not constitute the kind of disclosure that leads to authenticity. Again, in line with what we saw in the previous section, the true self is often seen as a ready-to-hand entity, when the person uses it as if it was a physical object in the environment. Thus the person may "assert themselves", take a stand on who they are, say "this is the kind of person I am", or "fight for their right" to be themselves, again, in a way that would need to be characterizes as ontic rather than ontological, and, as a result, not really part of the process of becoming authentic.

It is important within the context of a phenomenological investigation to acknowledge that such a theoretical or practical discovery of a true self is often based in experience, with its own validity. It is, therefore, not to dismiss reports of cases where individuals find their true self, for example, because they discover that a certain role does not suit them and they assert themselves as a different person. The question that needs to be raised in the context of authenticity, though, is whether what is now being experienced as the true self is not simply a different version of the inauthentic self, as when a person who was told to behave and think in a certain way is now told to behave and think differently: from a Heideggerian perspective both are inauthentic, it is just that one is, for example, older than the other, and may, therefore, feel like the more authentic one.

Indeed, it is not at all clear what such an ontic "true self" would consist of. We may tend to behave and think in ways that are heavily influenced and shaped by our environment, but it does not follow from this that there is something that behaves and thinks, like a prior self, which is not affected by our environment. To put it differently, when we believe there to be an ontic true self, we seem to imply that there is a way of being formed by *das Man* which is authentic, whereas Heidegger's point is that all ways of being in *das Man* are inauthentic and that the only true self is that of openness. What is more, because every human being grows up in some sort of an environment where some sort of demands will be made of it, where certain things will be expected of it, where there is, at a minimum, a preference on the part of other people as to what constitutes desirable behaviour and correct thought, it becomes difficult to see what would be a coherent account of a self that is truer than the one that one has grown up to have (other than, perhaps, the openness that constitutes authentic being).

For Heidegger the authentic way in which Dasein may find its true self is when it understands itself not in terms of something practical or theoretical, but as something with possibility (and openness) as its essence. It is, therefore, not any particular actual way of being that is true to Dasein's self but existence as possibility, as not any particular characteristics in the way that practical or theoretical entities have characteristics. This is again the essential openness at the core of Dasein we encountered before, where it is from out of the moment of opening up (which has possibility as its essential nature) that the *actual* ways of a particular Dasein emerge. None of these actual ways are authentic in themselves, because they are all the result of having grown up into *das Man*. Finding one's true self, therefore, does not consist in finding any particular way of being oneself, but in opening up, a possibility that exists when the actual ways of being a particular person are being let go of.

In sum, the notions of awakening, giving oneself up and finding oneself can easily be taken to refer to discoveries one makes about oneself at the level of the ready-to-hand or present-at-hand, and when this happens they are taken in a way that misses the point Heidegger wants to make. In looking for authentic existence, one is, according to Heidegger, not looking to awaken to "facts" about life or oneself one did not know before, but to what it means to be a human being, to what is possible for a human being in the first place. One is not looking to get rid of or explain away the self, but rather to disclose to oneself that the kind of entity one is has "giving itself up" as one of its essential possibilities, because only this giving up will allow one to open up. One is not primarily looking for one's "own" way of *seeing* or *doing* things (though these do have their place), but for one's own way of *being*, where being cannot be reduced to what one does and believes but comes *prior* to that. To repeat part of an earlier quote, the disclosive truth of authentic existence is "something essentially constitutive for being-in-the-world as such" (Heidegger 1962, 343). For Heidegger, authentic existence does not lie at the level of how one sees or does things, but at the level of existing as openness and possibility.

First characterization of the process of becoming authentic

In this chapter we have looked at a first characterization of authentic existence and of the process that, according to Heidegger, leads to authentic existence. We saw that Heidegger's Dasein is, in essence, openness and possibility, that within this openness the processes of understanding, attunement and being-with emerge, and that authentic existence contains a moment where these processes are let go of, as part of a process of opening up.

We saw that in relation to the question of truth, Heidegger speaks of disclosure as being more fundamental than truth as the correspondence between a proposition or a representation and reality: the truth of disclosure is more basic than propositional truth, the truth of a judgement, or the truth of an action, of a way of behaving. As authentic, Dasein is "in truth" in that Dasein itself is disclosed to itself at the same time that the being of the entities it is in contact with is being disclosed.

We saw further that a number of recent philosophers of education have conceived of the process of becoming authentic in terms that are essentially perfectionist (in the technical sense of the term), conceiving of it as a double movement of both *becoming who one really is* and *reaching one's full potential as a human being*, as a result of a "death and rebirth", a "turning away from the world" and a "turning back", in such a way that one gains an authentic sense of one's own existence as well as that of the entities one encounters in the world.

In all this, the first moment of the process of becoming authentic, the part that involves a "turning away from the world", is characterized by Heidegger as "bringing oneself back from lostness in *das Man*". This involves two, related aspects: extracting oneself from the ways of understanding things into which one has been socialised, and understanding oneself *in terms of oneself* (as openness and possibility) and not in terms of practical or theoretical entities. The subsequent moment of "turning back" then involves a return to *das Man*, we could say to those attitudes, skills, and knowledge available to us in our culture.

Finally, we considered characterizations of the process of becoming authentic we can find in early Heidegger's writings. We looked at the ways in which the process has been described as one of "awakening", of "giving oneself up", and of "finding oneself", where we saw that all three refer to processes of disclosure of the kinds of things that can *possibly* exist rather than to the discovery of things we *actually* believe exist, and where the self is disclosed as something that is neither practical (ready-to-hand) nor theoretical (present-at-hand). The result involves changes at the level of the apriori, including a different understanding of what it is for Dasein itself to be.

Based on the above, we can say that the process of becoming authentic involves a process of letting go that occurs at the level of the apriori, at the level where we take a stance on the *being* of the entity in question (practical, theoretical or as belonging to *life and living beings*). In all this a connection with the entity remains, even as the basic faculties of relating to the entity (understanding, attunement and being-with) are subsiding. This process is a "turning away from the world", a turning away from understanding things (material entities as well as living beings) in terms of categories handed to us through enculturation (*das Man*). It also involves a turning away from engagement with practical and theoretical entities, even as a connection with the entity remains. That is, in spite of this "turning away" the connection with the entity one is learning about remains, made possible by Dasein's essential openness. As we will see in detail in Chapters 4 through 6, this process of opening up includes radical self-renewal and a change in the structure of experience, in such a way that it is not based in the relation to an object of learning or even in the existing state of the learner, and where the result of the process is that of Dasein opening up to *the being* of entities in themselves.

This process of opening up is essentially one of letting go, which is then followed by a "turning back" to the world in a new way, where what is new has been disclosed at the level of the being of entities (the apriori). Attitudes, practical engagement, and ideas may then become part of the relationship once again, in a way that is in keeping with the being of entities that has been disclosed in the process of opening up.

And here it is instructive to have another look at the way in which Heidegger qualifies this moment of letting go, of "giving oneself up". Heidegger writes that in giving itself up lies Dasein's "uttermost possibility" (Heidegger 1962, 309). That is, this moment of "giving itself up", this letting go is not simply one of the many possibilities of Dasein, but rather its "uttermost" possibility, you could even say its most "perfect" possibility, using terminology from the tradition of perfectionism we looked at earlier in this chapter. And the special importance of Dasein letting go, of "giving itself up", lies in that it enables Dasein to become authentic, and thus become who it really is. But, as I wrote earlier in this chapter, this does not commit us to positing complete openness, giving ourselves up completely. We do not have to posit an "uttermost" mode of being perfectly authentic, in order to say that the process of opening up needs to be part of learning.

So we will stay with the processes of opening up rather than put forward some notion of perfect openness. And, as indicated in Chapter 1, as soon as we look more closely at the process of letting go that are part of authentic being-in-the-world, we discover that any such a process poses considerable challenges with regard to the way we tend to think about learning. The most pressing challenge being that the kind of letting go that is required for authentic being is not something that current notions of learning can account for. Regardless whether we turn to neurological accounts, information processing accounts, behaviourism or constructivism, we find the same thing: the currently dominant notions of learning preclude the possibility of a letting go that leads to authentic openness to the being of the entities we are learning about. These limitations of the currently dominant accounts of learning will be the focus of the next chapter, so that in subsequent chapters we can return to Heidegger's notion of authenticity, to construct an account of learning to be authentic and authentic learning.

Conventional learning

Can learning make us authentic?

The aim of this chapter is to show how certain metaphysical assumptions about learning made in the theories of learning that inform both common-sense thinking and education rule out the possibility of the kind *authentic learning* we discussed in the previous two chapters. These metaphysical assumptions are found in a number of mechanisms according to which learning is believed to always involve an object of learning as well as a process of growth, where this process is rooted in the existing way of being of the learner, and characterized by increased integration and differentiation, ultimately leading to increased stability, even rigidity. These assumptions, it will be argued, rule out a learning that involves the kind of opening up to the being of entities that constitutes *authentic learning*. And because *learning to be authentic* is itself an instance of authentic learning, our common-sense notions of learning also rule out an account of *learning to be authentic*.

As we saw in the previous chapter, authentic learning involves opening up to the *being* of the entities involved – including oneself – where existing notions of the of the entities are being relinquished. During this "giving up" there is a sense of discontinuity, because when one is "dying an existential death" anything that follows is in some ways a new beginning, giving rise to a sense of self-renewal. To return to some of the terminology used in the previous chapter, there is in the authentic way of learning a dual process. First, there is a process of "turning away from the world", turning away from understanding things as a result of enculturation (*das Man*). This is a process of letting go and opening up at the level of the apriori. And because we want to begin to think about this process of letting go and opening up in terms of learning, this is the first sense of *learning to be authentic* in the light of Heidegger's notion of authenticity.

But this "turning away" is followed by a "turning back" to the world in a new way, where what is new has been disclosed at the level of the being of entities. Attitudes, practical engagement, and ideas will need to become part of the relationship once again. But they need to do so in a way that is in keeping with the propensity for opening up that is part of authentic learning. This turning back is also a process of learning. And as we will see in this chapter, this return to grasping and construction is the one process of learning that is widely acknowledged in both common-sense discourse and education; I will call it *learning as modification and growth*. For there to be authentic learning, this process of attitude, skill, and knowledge acquisition will need to happen in a way that does not invalidate the authentic ability to open up, or obstruct any subsequent letting go and opening up.

As indicated, such a dual understanding of *learning to be authentic* where that attitudes, skills, and knowledge may be acquired in a way that is in keeping with the openness of authenticity is not compatible with most contemporary notions of learning. Having said that, current notions of learning are much more inclusive than those in many past cultures, when learning tended to be more closely associated with things like imitation, repetition, and memorization. As we will see in the next section, there has, at least in the field of in education, been a steady widening of what forms of human development and change are thought to fall under the broad category of learning. Still, as we look more deeply at the underlying assumptions we find in contemporary accounts of learning, we discover that at a fundamental level, such processes of learning are incompatible with the process of becoming authentic, because of their emphasis on grasping and construction, and their inability to account for the kind of opening up that is part of authentic learning.

In order to make up for the lack of a concept of *learning to be authentic*, I will begin by setting out some of the main characteristics of the *learning as modification and growth* that is currently dominant in education. This will then make clear why, in the way we currently tend to think about learning, we cannot expect the process of *learning to be authentic* to have a prominent place in education or our own life-long learning: our very notions of *learning as modification and growth* make it all but impossible for an individual to come to such openness using conventional notions of learning. At the same time, looking at the way in which *learning as modification and growth* limits what can be learned will anticipate some of the demands we will make later in the book on the way attitudes, skills, and knowledge should be learned. In this way, this chapter will clear the ground on which, in the chapters that follow, I will construct a positive notion of the process of *learning to be authentic*.

Learning as formative of much of existence

One characteristic of the state of authenticity is that it concerns the whole person. If Dasein is essentially the kind of openness that can only be disclosed if there is a kind of existential death, this openness will necessarily concern the whole person and not just a part. And if, as a result of awakening to their true nature, the authentic person becomes who they truly are, this too will necessarily involve the whole person. One way of putting such a letting go of all one's established ways of being is that one needs to forget everything one has become as a result of growing up, of being enculturated (into *das Man*). And, as we will see in this section, we could just as well say that, in order to let go of all our ways of being enculturated, we need to let go of everything we have learned.

One aspect of current understanding of learning as it is found in the influential accounts of learning we will be looking at in this chapter is that it is the whole person who learns. Thus, Peter Jarvis, writing within the field of adult education, defines human learning as "the combination of processes whereby the whole person - body (genetic, physical and biological) and mind (knowledge, skills, attitudes, values, emotions, beliefs and senses) experiences a social situation, the perceived content of which is then transformed cognitively, emotively or practically (or through any combination) and integrated into the person's individual biography resulting in a changed (or more experienced) person" (Jarvis, 2006, p. 13).

Though there have traditionally been many theorists who believed that learning concerns primarily the acquisition of knowledge and skills, such as D. W. Hamlyn who writes that learning is the "acquisition of a form of knowledge or ability [skill] through the use of experience" (Hamlyn, 2005), there is a trend in education towards a more holistic view of learning. Paul Hager, for example, writes about an "emerging understanding of learning" where learning "includes not just propositional understanding, but cognitive, conative [to do with the will] and affective capacities as well as other abilities and learned capacities such as bodily know-how, skills of all kinds, and so on" (Hager, 2005b, p. 662).

The importance of the idea that learning involves the whole person is twofold. On the one hand, it is, as Jarvis puts it "the whole person [who] experiences a ... situation", which means that in principle the whole person is involved in any learning event: even the simplest feat of memorization involves physical, social and emotional aspects as well as cognitive ones, even if, say, the emotional aspect is so marginal as to make no noticeable impact on the outcome. On the other hand, the involvement of the whole person means that it is not just "propositional understanding" but things to do with the will, emotions, practical skills, and so on, that are affected by learning: what motivates us, how we feel about things, how we move and act, are all shaped as a result of learning.

What is more, many contemporary theorists of learning would contend that "learning and development are inseparable" (Ireson, 2008, p. 14). This means that from the day we are born, even during gestation, we are learning, and that "learning processes share all of the complexity, organization, structure, and internal dynamics once exclusively attributed to development" (Kuhn, 1995, cited in Ireson 2008, p. 14). Recent discoveries that "maturational changes can be triggered by learning mechanisms" (Manukata & Pfaffly, 2004, p. 145, emphasis added) only help to reinforce the notion that the learning and development are inseparable. This emphasis on learning is not to deny that some things may be innate, such as the tendency in babies to visually track moving objects, or to be more interested in human faces than inanimate objects. What it means is that the development of the innate beginnings of the person is more and more thought of as a process of learning, and that therefore the person as such, apart from their innate reflexes (for example, blinking at flashes of light), is itself largely the result of learning. There is not much in who we are as individual human beings that is not affected by learning: we are the result of an on-going process of learning, a process that began as soon as we started to exist, involves all the different aspects of our being, and is continually integrating all the different aspects of the process into the person we are.

If, now, we return to the question of what kind of (learning) process will bring us authentic openness to the being of entities, we can say that any such openness is likely to be one that has let go of that which has been learned: if who we are as individuals is largely the outcome of learning, returning to the openness we are deep down will involve a radical kind of unlearning. At the same time, we may want to question the very notion of learning that divides the acquisition of attitudes, skills, and knowledge from the process of letting go of existing structures: why would we restrict the idea of learning to the construction of ways of being and exclude from our notion of learning the possibility of a radical opening up? Is this not similar to saying, for example, that breathing is only about inhaling air and that the process of exhaling air is of a different nature? Should our idea of what learning is not include the moment of letting go, even the moment of letting go the very structures of intentionality and the self? After all, only if we encounter a notion of learning that encompasses both the moment of construction and that of letting go and opening up will we have found a notion of learning that can lead to authentic relationships with living beings.

The contemporary understanding that learning involves not only knowledge, but also the will, emotions, practical skills, and so on, means that there is not much in who we have become in growing up that is not the result of learning. It is the whole person who is formed through learning, where all the different aspects of the person are involved in virtually all learning. Even the primarily biological processes of maturation and development are affected by processes of learning. And this means that a state of authenticity that concerns the whole person cannot ignore the facts of human learning. We need to ask what the process is that leads to such radical openness, as well as what processes of attitude, skill, and knowledge acquisition need to be like, if these are to happen in such a way that they are based in openness to the true being of the entities we encounter. And to come to such a positive formulation, we first need to understand why it is that our conception of *learning as modification and growth* cannot account for a process of *learning to be authentic*.

Learning has an intentional object

In a survey of theories of learning Ireson writes that "there is no single unifying framework" for learning (2008, 28). This sentiment is echoed in the philosophical literature about learning. Thus, in *The Philosophy of Human Learning* Christopher Winch discusses philosophical questions concerning learning, but expressly disavows any attempt at what he calls "grand theory building" (1998, ix); he does not attempt to arrive at one, overall concept of learning, even if it "might be inferred [from the book] that Winch views 'learning' as a family resemblance concept" (Hager 2005, 660). Hager, on his part, denies even such a family resemblance, arguing that learning is merely a label: "it seems plausible to view learning as a conceptual and linguistic construction, one that is widely used in many societies and cultures, but with very different meanings, which are at least partly contradictory and contested. Put differently, there is no external, reified entity that is 'learning'" (Hager 2008, 682).

In trying to understand learning in the context of the possibility of *learning to be authentic*, we do not need to adjudicate between Hager and Winch. We can take from the above that there is no unified theory of learning, even as much of what we call learning shares certain characteristics. Without wanting to set out a comprehensive definition (catching its essence in terms of what necessarily belongs to it, and identifying those characteristics whose presence are sufficient to call something learning), we can say that most, if not all, currently dominant notions of learning share a number of assumptions about the process of learning: *learning is generally conceptualized as a process of growth that has an intentional object, involves a continuity between the existing and a possible future state of the learner, leading to increased integration, differentiation and stability*. And in the remainder of this chapter I will try to show that the presence of these characteristics excludes the possibility of a process of learning that results in the kind of radical openness that belongs to the state of authenticity. I will begin with the assumption that learning has an intentional object.

Hager reports how Hirst and Peters proposed that one of "the two necessary conditions for learning" is "that it has an object" (Hager 2005, 651) (we will encounter Hirst and Peter's second necessary condition shortly). This is such an "obvious" aspect of conventional accounts of learning that many theorists do not make it explicit: whenever we learn something we are engaging with something (a thing, a state of affairs, a person, an idea) and as a result of the learning we acquire a feeling about, knowledge of, an attitude towards, or a way of acting on *something*. In this section, will contrast this notion of learning as necessarily object-related with the possibility that learning occurs in such a way that it is not in relation to any specific intentional object.

Marton and Booth, taking a phenomenological approach to learning, presuppose the intentional structure of consciousness in their discussion of learning. They write that "[t]he verb 'to learn' has to have an object" (Marton and Booth 1997, 84). This can be understood as having two moments or aspects, both of which stem from the assumption, taken from Brentano that all "psychic" (what we could nowadays call *psychological*) events have an intentional structure in that they are about something, something apart from themselves. We encountered this notion in Chapter 2, when we considered how both the *intentio* and the *intentum* emerge at the level of the apriori; and, indeed, Heidegger's use of these terms, writing within the phenomenological tradition, is rooted in Brentano's original insight. The idea that all psychic events have an intentional object is sometimes called the transcendental structure of psychic life, where the terms transcendental means *referring to something other than the organism itself*. Thus, Marton and Booth cite Brentano: "No hearing without something being heard, no believing without something believed, no hoping without something hoped, no striving without something striven for, no joy without something we are joyous about, etc." (Marton and Booth 1997, 84). Within this notion of intentionality Marton and Booth distinguish two different ways in which learning has an object: first, the way the object of learning is taken at the beginning of the learning process and, second, the way the object is taken as a result of the learning process..

First, there is what the learner is trying to do when they are learning (Marton and Booth's study focuses on situations where learners are intentionally setting out to learn something), stemming from the fact "that people have distinctly different ways of understanding [...] what learning is" (Marton and Booth 1997, 47). But it is not only within the phenomenological tradition that we find such an intentional object, reflecting the learner's initial grasp of it. Thus, in behaviourist terms the object would be the stimuli, both unconditioned and conditioned, as they are initially responded to. In neuro-scientific accounts of learning the learning object would be seen in terms of what neural networks are activated initially in relation to something, before the actual experience modifies the tendency of the organism to respond. We can see how this resonates with Piaget's notion of assimilation, where the object towards which the learner acts is taken in a certain way, as a certain kind of object. We can also see how this is similar to Vygotsky's current stage of development, where the learner has a current way of taking an object.

Second, there is the notion that learning has a second (in time) "direct object [in the sense of] the content that is being learned" (Marton and

Booth 1997, 84). In behaviourist terms this is the tendency of the organism to associate stimuli with other stimuli or with responses *after* this pattern of association has been modified as a result of experience. In neuro-scientific terms this is the way neural networks are being activated in relation to something, *after* their activation patterns have been modified by experience. We find resonances of this in Piaget's accommodation and Vygotsky's higher level of development, as it has been reached with the help of a more competent other. This direct object of learning also links in with the second "necessary conditions for learning" as proposed by Hirst and Peters, namely, "that some standard of achievement has been met" (Hager 2005, 651), where Hirst and Peters introduce the normative element that is often implicit in the other accounts of learning mentioned here.

Thus there are two moments to a learning object, first, the way it is taken at the beginning of the process and, second, the way it is taken at the end of the process. Or, to put it in a way that reflects the ongoing character of the learning process: the way the object is taken at $t1$ and at $t2$, where $t1$ is the earlier point in time and $t2$ the later one. These two aspects of the object of learning give us the *dialectic* between the existing and possible structures of the intentional relationship. They give us the temporal dimension of learning as a process from one state of being to another. They also tell us that the phenomenal object of learning needs to be thought of as being in a state of flux, because the way the object is experienced is continuously changing for the duration of the learning process. Ultimately the notion of learning having an intentional object is the consequence of seeing the psychic as necessarily intentional, and it is this notion that is challenged in Heidegger's notion of authenticity.

The state of authenticity includes a moment of openness to the being of the entity one is in relationship with, where there is no longer a distinction between the *intentio* and the *intentum* at the level of the apriori. There is in this state the sense of unity, and in the ideal case of complete openness, there may well be a sense of unity with the totality of life. Importantly, the suggestion that there may be a process of opening up that does not happen in relation to an intentional object does not dispute that thinking, perceiving and acting are intentional in nature: the acquisition of attitudes, skills, and knowledge are still thought to take place in relation to intentional objects. What it suggests is that there may be a process that occurs, as it were, at right-angles from the intentional relationship. Such a process would not occur in relation to the objects of intentional experience but at the level of the apriori, and concern the being of the entities involved, including that of the self which is experiencing the learning. And this means that the presupposition in most, if not all, contemporary accounts of learning, that learning happens in relation to an intentional object, calls into question the possibility of accounting for the process of becoming authentic by the established accounts of learning, such as behaviourism, constructivism, or contemporary neurological and phenomenological ones. *Learning to be authentic* cannot be accounted for in terms of *learning as modification and growth*, because the process of opening up to the being of entities happens at a level that is deeper than the intentional relationship between subject and object.

Learning involves continuity

In this section we will take the point that learning is usually thought of as involving an intentional object further, by showing how our mainstream theories of learning tend to conceive of learning as involving continuity between existing and possible structures: according to the theoretical accounts of learning we are considering, all learning is inescapably linked to previous learning, making it unlikely for an individual to learn something that does not build on existing structures, thus excluding the possibility of the kind of opening up (as a result of an initial dying towards one's existing ways of being in the world) associated with the notion of authenticity.

Paul Van Geert discusses the continuity between existing and possible structures in the learner at some length. He explains how, when computer models of neurological networks are given tasks to be learned "[t]he learning system obtains information [about what needs to be learned] in terms of its own current learning state by making errors. The errors lead to updating the connection weights, which eventually reduce the distance between the current state of the system (its actual state) and the properties exemplified by [what needs to be learned] (the potential state)" (Van Geert 1998, 5). That is, not only do the networks begin the learning process with their actual state, they also "understand" the information that is given to them "in terms of their current learning state".

This is perhaps more easily understood in terms of yet another theoretical approach to learning, information-processing theory, which understands learning in terms of the application of rules to information that comes into the system – where the system is usually understood in analogy with a computer. This approach "makes a distinction between rules or strategies on the one hand and the information resulting from applying those strategies on the other. The resulting information is then integrated in a way that either consolidates or modifies the available rules and strategy sets" (Van Geert 1998, 5). Again, what we see is that the system itself collects (selects) the information it uses (by applying rules to input), and that, as a result of the information which it has collected and the way it has processed this information, the very strategies of both collecting and processing information are modified.

With regard to Piaget's and Vygotsky's theories, Van Geert notes that "there exists a fundamental dialectic between a primarily subject- and a primarily object-driven force, which constitutes the motor behind the developmental process. This dialectic involves a tension between a consolidated, current level [...] and a potential, future level of development." What is perhaps most important in this for our discussion here is that the "potential, future level of development" is "still confined by the current state of the subject" (Van Geert 1998, 5). That is, not only is *the response* to the entity in the environment based in the current state of the individual, the way the entity in the environment is understood *in the first place* is also based in the current state of the individual.

So we can see that the inevitably conservative force we find in our learning about the things. This is important when, for example, we want to understand certain skills and knowledge build on existing skills and knowledge. But at the same time, we can see how understanding and responding to a current situation being inextricably linked to the individual's current take on the situation can put limitations on what kind of learning is possible. To return to earlier examples, approaching the origin of experience, others, or life as a whole may only get in the way of truly connecting with them. And this can have real practical implications; one only needs to think of all the long-standing conflicts between individuals or groups of people, where new events are understood in terms of a current understanding, which is based in the experience of past events. It is likely that, in such cases, prejudices get "confirmed" again and again, because what is happening now is invariably interpreted in terms of past events. This then makes it difficult to understand what is really happening, and it may well keep the relationship locked in a pattern, both sides unable to break out of it, because each interprets that actions of the other in terms of previous experience.

Note that the point about an authentic relationship is not that all previous experience is set aside for good, but that there is a moment of opening up, of "turning away", of letting go of one's previous way of relating, which will then allow the relationship to be reconfigured at the level of the apriori. This will, as it were, allow for the relationship to renew itself, even though in the "turning back" previous experiences will once again enter into the relationship, albeit in a way that has been modified by the moment of openness, so that the meaning of this previous experience may well have changed dramatically. For example, as a result of a moment of openness, a relationship of endless tit-for-tat may turn into one of reconciliation, because both parties have come to see each other differently, and as a result interpret past events, present actions, and future possibilities differently.

We can illustrate this giving up of continuity with existing states, by thinking about a teacher who is, after an arduous day at school, considering how to respond to a troublesome class. If this teacher lets go of their current ways of relating to the class, they let go of their current feelings, attitudes, and ideas about the class. But in doing this they can still be in contact with the class. This possibility of a connection without any concrete way of feeling, acting or thinking is, as we have seen, one of the crucial points about authenticity, and in Chapters 4 to 6 we will see more clearly how this is to be thought possible. For now, let us say that there is a form of connectedness that is so deep, that it is not based in any current way of feeling, acting or thinking on the part of the teacher. This makes it possible for the ways in which the teacher has hitherto structured their relationship with the class to fall away to a greater or lesser extent. And this may then result in a new-found contact with the situation and the troublesome class. This new way of relating to the situation concerning the class is not a mere modification of the existing ways of relating of the teacher, but emerges as a result of at least part of the previous state dissolving. One could object to this that the openness resulting from the dissolution becomes the new "current state" of the teacher and that, therefore, there is continuity after all. This is no doubt true in a formal sense, but it is also easily seen that, provided the dissolution is deep enough, there is no continuity between the previous state that was dissolved (at least in part) and the new way of relating that arose in the openness after the dissolution – and it is this kind of discontinuity that is the salient one with regard to learning to be authentic.

Coming from a notion of learning that is informed by the currently dominant accounts of learning, such a possibility of a response which is not a modification of one's current state is likely to sound unintelligible, because we very much see learning as involving the modification of an existing entity, so that, even if we were inclined to grant the possibility of "*a response* which is not based on one's current state", we would probably be reluctant to call such an event learning. But this seems arbitrary because, as we saw at the start of this chapter, learning has come to be seen as involved in virtually all the processes that make us who we are, including development and maturation. Why would we exclude from our notion of learning that which is potentially one of the most important formative moments in life, that of opening up to the openness which we are? Why, to return to an earlier analogy, would we restrict our idea of breathing to *inhalation*, consigning the all-important moment of *exhalation* to a different class of events?

The moment you allow for there to be contact with a situation even after the (partial) dissolution of existing structures it becomes possible to think of a form of learning that is not based in a continuity with existing structures in the learner (even though some of these structures may remain in place): the openness to being that characterizes the state of authenticity is not a modification of with the previous state of the learner in any but the most formal sense of the word. That is, having let go is not a modification of grasping, just as the dissolution of constructs is not a modification of existing constructs. In this way, learning to be authentic does not involve the kind of continuity that comes with the modification of existing intentional structures. Therefore, in so far as our notion of *learning as modification and growth* requires there to be continuity between existing and possible future states of the learner, it cannot account for a process that would lead to authenticity.

Learning involves association

A further limitation regarding the theories of learning used in contemporary education is that they tend to be based in processes that involve association, whereas the kind of opening up we are after cannot be associated with anything, because it is unlike any being, any entity, and if it can be characterized at all, this involves terms such as emptiness, nothingness, or the void. And this emptiness is such that no possible association can evoke it. Another way of putting this is, as we will see in the next chapter, to say that Dasein can understood only in terms of itself. This is not dissimilar to the notion that every human being in unique, but it takes this uniqueness to the level of being itself, in the sense that what is unique about us is not simply that we have a unique combination of characteristics (as in one person being female, tall and bright, and the other being female, tall and not so bright). Rather, every human being (and I would add every living being, including animals and plants) is not just a unique combination of characteristics but so much a one-of-a-kind creature that no comparison is possible at all, at the level of being where authenticity comes into being. That is, thought we may compare traits such as female and male, tall and short, bright and not so bright, such characteristics are superficial (and dependent on *das Man*) and do not concern the openness that makes up the essence of Dasein. This essential openness is, in Heidegger's account, absolutely unique for each individual Dasein, and can, as a result, not be compared or legitimately associated with anything else. As a result, no process of association can bring us into contact with that unique openness, either in ourselves or in others.

The principle of association is that one thing calls up the other thing. In everyday language we speak of associating one thing with another, as when we associate the smell of pipe tobacco with a particular person or when we associate a particular song with a week of clubbing on Ibiza. Thus, when we smell pipe tobacco, the memory of that person may be evoked, we may "see" the person, or "hear" their voice, feel emotions we have felt in the presence of that person, or think about something else related to the person, like their wife, who doesn't like him to smoke. This kind of associative memory can be said to be the co-occurrence of two experiences, one of which is actual (the smell of tobacco) and one of which is remembered (something that in the past co-occurred with smelling the tobacco). But there can also be an association between two experiences that are remembered, as when the smell of tobacco sets one off on a "stream of consciousness" series of associated memories. Likewise, when, back at work in the office, we hear the song we danced to every night for a week on Ibiza, we may "spontaneously" begin to move our body – before checking the urge to get up and dance. This is essentially the same mechanism as we find in the association between two stimuli, except that in this case the association is between a stimulus and a movement, a behaviour, an action, rather than a perceptual memory, such as that of a smell or a sound.

We find the principle of association in neuro-scientific accounts of learning. "Whenever one cell (A) repeatedly takes part in the firing of another (B), 'some growth process or metabolic change takes place in one or both cells' such that the efficiency of the first cell in firing the second is increased" (Fuster 2003, 42). This kind of learning is often called Hebbian learning, after the neuroscientist, Donald Hebb. "The basic tenet of Hebbian learning in neural networks is that 'units that fire together, wire together'" (Manukata and Pfaffly 2004, 141). Thus, once a set of neurons has "fired", been active, together, they are much more likely to "fire" together again in the future. This "firing together" can spread so that one group of neurons "fires" together with another group in the way that two experiences, each involving the "firing" of many neurons, are likely to occur together. This "firing together" may also involve a small, local, group of neurons setting off many large groups of neurons, as in a chain reaction, as when a small detail of something is experienced which evokes a world of association: we see a picture of a particular beach and the whole of a childhood holiday returns to us.

We further find the principle of association in behaviourist accounts of learning. In Behaviourist theories of learning the two main mechanisms, which in the natural world always work together, rely on association to work. On the one hand, there is the behaviour of the organism "as if it learns to associate" a stimulus (S) with a biologically significant event (S*). The paradigmatic case of this "S-S* learning" is that of Pavlov's dog, who behaved as if he associated the sound of the bell (the stimulus, S) with food (the biologically significant event, S*). On the other hand, there is the behaviour of the organism "as if it has associated" a behaviour or response (R) with a biologically significant event (S*). Here the case that exemplifies this R-S* learning is that of Skinner's box, where the rat behaved as if it associated pressing the lever (the response, R) with the food pellet (the biologically significant event, S*) (Bouton 2007, 28). In reality the two mechanisms are "almost inseparable", as every time a biologically significant stimulus (S*), like food, is associated with behaviour (R) it can also be associated with stimuli (S) that are present as well. And this goes the other way round as well, as the presence of a stimulus (S) can be associated with a biologically significant stimulus (S*), as well as with a response (R) (Bouton 2007, 29).

Piaget uses the term assimilation rather than association, but to essentially the same effect. "The dog that salivates at the sight of food will not salivate in this way at the sound of a bell unless he assimilates it ... to the schema of this action [of salivation]" (Piaget 2001, 107). Yet such a schema is itself a "structure or organization of actions as they are transferred or generalized by repetition in similar or analogous situations" (Cited in Murray Thomas 2005, 192). That is, the schema is what in the neurological account would be an associative structure. Even the case of accommodation requires there to be an associative scheme: "Since there is no assimilation without (prior or simultaneous) accommodation, there can be no accommodation without assimilation: this means that the environment does not simply induce the organism to register impressions or to make copies, but induces the organism to actively reshape itself" (Piaget 1967/1974, 165). For Piaget, something that fits into an existing scheme is assimilated, whereas something that does not fit is responded to by the scheme accommodating the new input, where in both cases the process is based in association.

As indicated at the start of this section, the difficulty for an account of learning to open up in such a way that there is openness to the being of the entity is that the openness that is essential to Dasein (and I would add other living beings) cannot be compared to or associated with anything else. This limitation is similar to (though distinct from) when in the previous section we looked at the limitations that come with associating learning with a sense of continuity. If a commitment to continuity cannot account for novelty, insistence on association rules out coming into contact with that which is completely unlike anything we know. And because the openness that is essential to each individual Dasein is completely unlike anything we can know (in this sense you could say that it is unknowable), we cannot get into contact with it through any process of association. Indeed, any comparison we could make with the openness of Dasein can only alienate us from its true nature, because its uniqueness does not allow for any kind of comparison or association whatsoever. And the same could be said of the ground of experience and the whole of life itself, in that these cannot be grasped through processes of association, because any process of association will, in the case of the former, be only one possible form of experience and, in the case of the latter, capture only part of the whole. In this way, association cannot account for the kind of openness that is part of authentic learning.

Learning is a process of growth, leading to increased integration, differentiation, and stability

So far we have seen that the way processes of learning are thought of in common sense and education excludes the possibility of resulting in authentic openness for different, albeit related reasons. First, learning is thought to always involve an intentional object, whereas the process of becoming authentic happens at the level of the apriori, where there is no separation between the subject and the intentional object, the intentio and intentum. Second, learning is thought to involve a degree of continuity between existing and possible future states of the learner, whereas learning to be authentic involves a degree of giving up of who one is, so that true novelty can occur. And, third, learning is generally thought to be based in a process of association, whereas the openness which authenticity brings us into contact with cannot be associated with anything, because it involves any entity that cannot be compared to any other entity.

If we now take all of these characteristics of the way learning is usually conceived, we see that the natural result of its object-relatedness, continuity, and association is a process of growth. Indeed, the traditional accounts of learning we are looking at can all be said to see learning as essentially a process of growth. Following Van Geert's reading of Piaget and Vygotsky, "the theories [of Piaget and Vygotsky] agree on the principle of developmental order: behaviours, actions, problems, tasks, and experiences (or whatever else constitutes the units of analysis) can be ordered along a developmental scale in terms of less or more developmentally advanced levels" (Van Geert 1998, 5). Indeed, Piaget writes, "All knowledge is continually in a course of development and of passing from a state of lesser knowledge to one which is more complete and effective" (Cited in Murray Thomas 2005, 192). Throughout development there is a process of growth, not only with respect to the knowledge we have about more and more things, but also with respect to our "conative and affective capacities as well as other abilities and learned capacities such as bodily know-how, skills of all kinds, and so on" (Hager 2005, 662). As a result, there is less and less in life that we have not acquired knowledge about, an attitude or feelings towards, a way of acting towards, a way of being towards.

Note that there is in the notion of learning as modification and growth also the acknowledgement that sometimes what has been learned is lost. We may forget or some of our abilities may diminish when they are not practiced. There are also processes of wear and tear, as when we lose certain capacities due to age or forms of deterioration, for example, as a result of disease. So it is not the case that contemporary accounts of learning are blind to the fact that we forget some of what we have learned. But this is not the same as the letting go and opening up that is part of authentic existence. When we let go of previously-acquired attitudes and ideas in relation to ourselves, another being, or life itself, this is not because we forget or because of age, but because there is an opening up to the being of these entities. In their focus on growth (on grasping and constructing) the major accounts of learning that inform our common-sense and educational notions of learning do not allow for such a process of opening up.

What is more, the process of growth described in the main theories of learning is one that leads towards increased integration and differentiation. Marton and Booth write that "development can be seen as continuous differentiation and integration of the experienced world", where differentiation is brought about by "separation" and integration is brought about by "simultaneity" (association) (Marton and Booth 1997, 138). Indeed, the possession of high levels of integrated and differentiated knowledge in a particular domain is often taken as being characteristic of expertise on the part of the individual. These two processes of integration and differentiation can further be seen at work in neurological, Hebbian, accounts of learning. On the one hand, there is increased "simultaneity" or association, where, as a result of certain input "Hebbian learning would increase the connections to [a certain] unit from relevant sending units, so the unit would become increasingly responsive to this correlation". On the other hand, there would be "separation", where "Hebbian learning would decrease the connections to this [same] unit from irrelevant sending units, so the unit would become less responsive to other correlations in the environment". Thus a certain unit (let's say a group of neurons) would become especially responsive to input from certain units and unresponsive to input from other units. What is more, "[t]hese other units could then tune their weights to respond to other correlations in the environment" (Manukata and Pfaffly 2004, 142-143). That is, as the first unit specializes in receiving input from certain units, the units that are ignored by this first unit may connect with other units. "In this way, Hebbian models can self-organize so that units specialize in representing distinct statistical regularities in the environment" (Manukata and Pfaffly 2004, 142-143), and the result is both greater integration and greater differentiation.

Note that these processes of growth, integration and differentiation can, according to some theorists, be explained purely in terms of self-organization, and can, as a result be said to be a function of the learning process itself. Thus Paul Van Geert writes that "development is possible ... [as] neural nets of the adaptive resonance type can construct higher levels of complexity without being issued with new resources or contents by an external source" (Van Geert 1998, 5). We thus have a notion of learning as necessarily involving "increasing complexity through self-organization" (Van Geert 1998, 5). But "[a]s connections change to strengthen certain neural responses to stimuli, this can reduce the possibility of other responses, which can impair learning" (Manukata and Pfaffly 2004, 144). Manukata and Pfaffly give the example of Japanese language speakers (we briefly looked at language learning in Chapter 1) who have learned, correctly, in their native language to hear the /l/ and the /r/ as the same sound, which they continue to do when learning English, where this is incorrect, a situation which is only remedied by them learning to hear the difference on the basis of exaggerated examples, which are made less exaggerated over time, to the point where they can hear the difference between the /l/ and the /r/ in natural speech. This example can be used to explain the existence critical periods in learning, but it is equally relevant in arguing that, as a result of integration and differentiation, there is a decreasing number of things and event for which the person does not already have a scheme. Because of the increased integration, this will then lead to a greater stability in what has been learned, while at the same time new things become harder to learn. That is, there are increasingly fewer things that an individual does not already have a schema for, while at the same time possible ways of being are being closed off, because these are being ignored, because the learner has become unresponsive to their input. This accords with the experience of many people who have seen older people become more set in their ways, when it may be said that "old habits die hard", or that it is no use trying "to teach an old dog new tricks".

The process of learning is generally though to involve growth, as well as increasing integration, differentiation, and stability. But as we take this idea of learning to its natural conclusion, where the growth, integration and differentiation seem to inevitably lead to a kind of rigidity, we also begin to see the limitations of this way of thinking about learning. Yes, there is plenty of evidence that, all else being equal, it is increasingly hard for people to acquire new attitudes, skills, and knowledge as time progresses.

But does this also have to be the case for the movement of opening up to the being of entities that happens at the level of the apriori? Yes, it is harder for us to learn new languages and skills, get used to new cultural norms and values, as we grow older. But are we less open to the being of entities, less able to let go of the structures of our understanding at the level of the apriori, where we suggested in the previous chapters any learning to become authentic will need to happen? If, indeed, there is the possibility of us opening up to the being of entities (other as well as ourselves and life as a whole) at the level of the apriori, this opening up would have to happen according to a different logic that the one described in the dominant accounts of learning, because these are committed to a learning that necessarily involves growth, increased integration, differentiation, and stability. Though these accounts of learning allow for things like forgetting and a wearing off of what has previously been learned, they do not allow for the kind of letting go that leads to openness at the level of the apriori.

Learning to breathe out as well as in

What we ourselves and the young people we educate can learn is to a large extend determined by the learning processes we are able to engage in. More than our goals and aims, more than the books we read or the content knowledge we teach, it is the learning processes we know to engage in that determine what is and what is not possible. As we have seen in this chapter, the processes that form the core of contemporary thinking about learning do not make room for the individual to come into contact with the openness that is part of the authentic way of being in the world. To put the same thing differently, if the origin of our own experience, other living beings, and life as a whole can only be understood in terms of themselves, we cannot learn anything about them through our conventional theories of learning, because these do not allow for a radical enough notion of opening up.

There are different directions in which we can go from here. As I mentioned earlier, one option is to say that an authentic openness to the being of entities cannot be attained via any form of learning, so that, in so far as we are interested in this openness, we need to think in terms of completely different processes, or of no processes at all – but as I explained earlier, this seems to be an arbitrary distinction to make. Another option is to say that our current conceptions of learning are deeply deficient, since they are unable to account for what are by all accounts real human possibilities letting go and opening up, so that our task is to completely overhaul current notions of learning. A third option is to say that while there is not necessarily anything wrong with our current conceptions of learning, they need to be supplemented with a process that, while it does not replace these current notions of learning, completes them, by adding a process that does enable us to make sense of the possibility of opening up to the being of entities.

In what follows I will begin by taking the third option, that of trying to supplement currently established notions of learning with an account of learning to open up to the being of entities. To go back to the earlier analogy with breathing: I will try to construct an account of breathing that includes a notion of exhalation, to supplement the conventional account of inhalation. Note that this leaves in place the core assumptions made in the accounts of learning as modification and growth discussed in this chapter. This raises the question whether the metaphysical assumptions that are made in contemporary notions of learning should also be questioned in the context of grasping and constructing knowledge and skills, with the possible outcome that the currently dominant notions of learning should be put on a different footing. Be this as it may, I will not try to propose an alternative here to the notion of *learning as modification and growth* as having an intentional object, involving continuity and association, while leading to growth, increased integration and differentiation, as well as stability and even rigidity. Rather, I will try to construct an account of learning to be authentic that is not in contradiction with these well-established theories. But though there will no attempt to put accounts of *learning as modification and growth* on a different footing, the identification of a process of *learning to be authentic* will not leave the practice of education untouched, not even the acquisition of attitudes, skills, and knowledge – this is something we will look at in more depth in Chapter 7.

In Chapters 4 to 6 we will look at the way in which we can come to an authentic openness to the being of entities. This will be a process of learning that goes into the opposite direction of the process of grasping and construction that leads to growth, integration and differentiation, and increased stability. We go from a state in which we have grasped to one in which we let go. And as we are letting go, opening up, we will encounter a set of apriori structures that are, as it were, the last ones in place before openness dissolves even those. These fundamental apriori mental structures will be the focus of the next part of the book, because they have a unique place in an account of learning that aims for it to happen in the light of authentic openness to being, in that they contain the possibility for both openness and construction. As openness these apriori structures allow for a true understanding of the being of entities, and as structures they allow for attitudes, actions, and ideas to be based on them. They are like the window that allows us to look both in and out.

In the next three chapters we will discovers such dual structures in the way in which we perceive and act, in the way in which we are emotionally attuned, and in the way we relate to other living beings. We find that Heidegger proposes the possibility of there being ways of feeling, acting, thinking, and communicating that are both concrete (in the sense that they can provide the basis for *learning as modification and growth*) and open to the being of entities in a way that allows an authentic relationship with living beings to enter into these concrete ways of being. As a result of becoming aware of these possibilities and inhabiting these authentic apriori structures in our daily lives, it will be possible for the acquisition of attitudes, skills, and knowledge to happen *in the light of* this an authentic understanding of being. The learning processes as they have been characterized in this chapter will not be substantially changed, but an authentic openness to the being of entities will guide them, and this, I hope to show, will make all the difference.

Authentic understanding

Gaining an authentic understanding of oneself

Understanding as projection

In Chapter 2 we had a first look at the three aspects of Dasein's "comportment", its ways of relating to entities (living as well as non-living beings). We saw that, according to Heidegger, there are in the clearing of Dasein's openness three processes which arise to give us the actual manifestation of the individual: the action-perception aspect of being-in-the-world, called understanding (*Verstehen*); the way in which being-in-the-world is coloured by emotion and mood, called attunement (*Befindlichkeit*); and the dimension of being-in-the-world that is connected to other living creatures and makes communication possible, called being-with (*Mitsein*). Though Dasein is essentially a unity (the openness itself is indivisible) we can distinguish these different processes for analytical purposes.

As we saw, understanding, for Heidegger, refers to both our practical engagement with things (the ready-to-hand) and our theoretical understanding of them (the present-at-hand). "If understanding is a basic determination of existence, it is as such the condition of possibility of all the Dasein's particular possible manners of comportment [ways of relating to things]… not only practical but also cognitive [theoretical]" (Heidegger 1982, 276). As a matter of fact, understanding itself does not only contain the possibility of understanding an entity as ready-to-hand, present-at-hand or existence, it is also something deeper than either practical or theoretical engagement, it is, as it were, the source of both.

Heidegger writes that "the understanding has in itself the existential structure we call projection" (Heidegger 1962, 184). Heidegger's word, projecting, is the translation of *entwerfen*, which literally means "throwing" something "off" or "away" from one, and it may also be used in the sense in which a geometer "projects" a curve "upon" a plane[3] (Heidegger 1962, 185, editor's footnote). Thus we understand something by projecting, by projecting it upon possibilities – like projecting what the possibilities of a certain situation are before understanding the entity one wants to understand in terms of those possibilities. Importantly, these possibilities are not usually explicit: "the character of understanding as projection is such that the understanding does not grasp thematically [i.e. explicitly] that upon which it projects – that is to say, possibilities" (Heidegger 1962, 185).

We could take as an example an individual's understanding of a hammer as something they may drive a nail into a wall with. In this case the hammer is encountered as a piece of equipment, as something one can use in an instrumental way, doing something with it in order to achieve a certain goal. The entity (the hammer) is thus projected onto its possibilities (being a piece of equipment) and only understood after these possibilities have been projected. Often humorous situations play on this kind of projection, as when a naive individual projects an entity (for example, a piece of modern art) onto the wrong possibilities (for example, onto equipment), with the result that they do something out of place (for example, hang their coat on the piece of modern art).

The word projecting is potentially confusing if it is taken in the sense analogous to "projecting an image on a screen" where the image determines what gets seen on the screen, just as when we say that "someone projects a feeling they have onto someone else", that is, when we use the word projecting in the same way as "sticking a label onto something", attaching a meaning to an entity that this entity does not have of itself. Rather, the entity that determines the meaning something can have is not an image, a label, a meaning that we project onto the thing but *that which the entity gets projected onto*. To return to the analogy of the screen, when the image

---

3   In ordinary German usage *Entwurf* is also used in the sense of "designing" or "sketching" some "project" which is to be carried through, but this is emphatically not the meaning Heidegger envisages.

is projected onto the screen, it is, in the way Heidegger understands projection, the screen that determines what image it is possible to appear on it (more on this possible confusion later). We can thus also say that we understand something "in the light of", "by projecting it onto something else", or "in terms of" something else.

Our theoretical understanding is based in our practical understanding

We saw in the section on Heidegger's perfectionist philosophy of education, that Dasein has, according to Heidegger, as its distinguishing characteristic that it has an understanding of being. Perhaps the first thing that springs to mind in hearing the phrase *understanding of being* is some kind of theoretical understanding, but a theoretical understanding is only one possibility. Heidegger posits that we can understand the being of an entity either theoretically, or practically or, indeed, in a way that is appropriate in relation to *life and living beings*. To understand these different possibilities, we will first look at the relationship between Dasein's theoretical and its practical understanding of being.

"[W]hen Heidegger singles out Dasein as the unique possessor of an understanding of being, he is referring primarily to the fact that Dasein is the only kind of entity which takes a stand on its being practically" (Thomson 2004, 443). We display an *understanding of being* in how we live our lives, in what we do, as much as in how we theorise. When we treat something as a certain kind of something (let's say, a pupil as a receptacle of knowledge) there is a certain kind of practical understanding of what kind of entity the pupil is, even if we do not hold the explicit (theoretical) belief that "the essential characteristic of a pupil is its nature as a receptacle to be filled with knowledge", but merely act in that way.

What is more, Heidegger thought of theory as derivative of practice. First, in the sense that we tend to only become theoretical about something, when our practical flow of engagement with the thing has been interrupted. Second, in the sense that our theoretical concepts are ultimately derived from our practical engagement with things. And third, in the sense that *being theoretical* is itself a practice. To return to the previous example, our way of dealing with the pupil involves a certain understanding of what kind of entity the pupil is, and it is only when our usual flow of interaction with the entity (the pupil) is interrupted (e.g. the pupil resists the knowledge being poured into him or her) that we may begin to try to understand *explicitly* and *theoretically* what kind of being the entity (the pupil) has, in which case we may bring into practice some of our theoretical skills (such as going to the library to read up on the topic and analysing the situation).

To give another example, the *theoretical* way of understanding things in terms of categories, classes, genus and species, is, according to Heidegger, derivative of such practical understanding of things. Thus we can classify a red fountainpen as a kind of pen, a pen as an implement for writing, an implement for writing as an instrument for communication, and so on. But we can also classify the same pen as a material entity, as a manmade material entity, as a machine-produced entity, and so on. The way in which these theoretical meanings of the object are derivative of the practical one is that the very question of what kind of theoretical entity something is *presupposes* a practical context. One only asks about the pen as an instrument for communication if one is interested in doing so, for example if one is researching the development of instruments for communication through history, which means that one is asking the question as a historian. Or, if one is asking about the pen as a machine-produced entity, one is perhaps doing so out of an interest in setting up a pen factory, which is again practical. Even the purely academic interest one may have in things presupposes an overarching practical context of the person who is asking the question.

Heidegger describes the origin of theoretical thinking in practical thinking in terms of an interruption in the flow of a smooth coping with things. If we are emerged in the flow of life, coping smoothly, we use things (like pens and doors and roads) without them becoming explicit (Heidegger would use the word "thematic"). Rather, Heidegger would say that these things are "transparent" when we are in the flow of things, in the sense of us not noticing them in any explicit way, as we are focussing on what we are doing, like writing, leaving a room, or driving on a road. It is only when things fail to go smoothly, when the pen runs out of ink, the door is stuck, or the road becomes pot-holed, that we begin to take explicit notice of them. This is, according to Heidegger, the origin of our theoretical, present-at-hand, understanding of things, an understanding which is, as such, based in our practical, ready-to-hand, understanding of things in the world.

Our practical understanding is structured by our self-understanding

Thus, we have practical understanding and theoretical understanding, where the latter is based in the first. For Heidegger, however, both are based in Dasein's self-understanding. As Ian Thomson writes, Dasein "lives in an intelligible world implicitly structured by the stand it takes on its own identity" (Thomson 2004, 443). What something means to us depends on how we see ourselves. For example, as a teacher, the exercise books and the red pen in my bag are understood in terms of marking student work (what Heidegger calls the "towards-this"), which I understand in terms of the monitoring and giving feedback that is part of the practice of being a teacher (what Heidegger calls the "in-order-to"), which, in turn, I understand in terms of my being a teacher (what Heidegger calls the "for-the-sake-of-which"). As Heidegger puts it (this time in the opposite order of our example), "The 'for-the-sake-of-which' signifies an 'in-order-to'; this in turn, a 'towards-this'" (Heidegger 1962, 120).

To put it differently, getting the meaning of these entities right (What kind of pens are these?) depends on getting their role in the activities right (What does it mean to mark student work?), which in turn depend on getting the whole of the role right (What does it mean to be a teacher?), which depends on getting oneself right (What does it mean to be me?). The questions put within brackets are phrased in an explicit (and theoretical) way but they are not questions one necessarily asks oneself explicitly, they serve merely as verbalisations of what is essentially tacit in the way we relate to the entities in question.

One could counter that with many practical activities we understand the activity in terms of the wider cultural practice rather than in terms of our self-understanding. Thus, we understand the activity of making a worksheet in terms of the cultural practice of being a teacher. But, Heidegger would argue, we understand this wider practice, in this case *being a teacher*, ultimately in terms of ourselves. And this is true regardless whether one is a teacher oneself; one could understand *being a teacher* just as well in terms of one's dislike of the teachers one had as a child, or in terms of one's relationship with one's spouse, who once wanted be a teacher. Though this may initially sound like too much of a self-oriented interpretation of what happens when we understand something in terms of the practices of our culture, it needs to be born in mind that the cultural context is, according to Heidegger, internalised as *das Man*, the cultural ways of understanding we tend to adopt uncritically because we socialized into them (there is a more in-depth discussion of *das Man* in the first part of Chapter 6). So, at least in so far as Dasein's practical understanding of entities is inauthentic (understood in terms of *das Man*), in so far as we do not take ourselves as openness, we are likely to understand the entities we find in the world in terms of our self-understanding.

As was said earlier, our understanding of ourselves is also something we project. Therefore, some of the confusion surrounding the meaning of projection is due to the fact that, to return to the analogy of the screen, one does not only understand entities by projecting them onto the screen, *the screen itself is also projected*, that which illuminates the entity one understands is also projected: one projects the entity one understands onto what is itself a projection. To return to the earlier example of understanding the red pen and the exercise books in terms of being a teacher, one does not only project the "pen and exercise books" onto the activity of "marking" and the activity of "marking" onto "being a teacher", one also projects "being a teacher" onto something. The question of understanding oneself then becomes a question of *what it is one projects oneself onto*: that is, *in the light of* what or *in terms of* what does one understand oneself? If we understand things in terms of the possibilities we project for those things, what are the possibilities that allow us to understand ourselves as a *human being*?

Heidegger, as we have seen, believes that the inauthentic individual understands themselves in terms of *das Man*, in terms of the ways of understanding and doing things they adopt unwittingly as they grow up in a particular society. Using the terminology of projection, we could say that the inauthentic individual project themselves onto a role, a kind of person, that exists in the discourse of the culture they live in, thus identifying themselves with being a teacher or some other persona from their culture. In effect, such an understanding oneself in terms of *das Man* means that the self-understanding is either as ready-to-hand or present-at-hand. When we understand ourselves in terms of, say, a role or a persona taken from *das Man*, we project ourselves onto *ready-to-hand* entities, thus understanding ourselves as an entity that can be used, for example to meet some expectation, to achieve a certain status, or to make a certain impression. And when we understand ourselves in terms of the theoretical categories that are given in *das Man*, we project ourselves onto *present-at-hand* entities, thus considering ourselves theoretically, for example as an immortal soul or an expression of the genetic code. As was said in Chapter 2s, this understanding of oneself as a practical or theoretical entity misses the essence of who one is, as one's being belongs to that of Dasein, as existence.

The nature of authentic self-understanding

Authentic self-understanding is understanding oneself in terms of oneself

We saw earlier that all understanding ultimately originates from or refers back to Dasein's self-understanding. It was also said that all understanding projects entities onto their possibilities, and that inauthentic Dasein projects its self-understanding onto *das Man*, onto the roles and categories given to it by its culture. The question then arises what it is that Dasein's *authentic* self-understanding is projected onto. Heidegger's answer is that Dasein's authentic self-understanding is projected onto nothing, because Dasein can be understood out of itself (contrary to the ready-to-hand and present-at-hand, which can only be understood by being projected onto something). And this goes right back to the point made in Chapter 3, that our current conceptions of learning cannot account for learning about something that can only be understood correctly, if it is understood in terms of itself and where the learning does not build on a preconceived understanding of the entity in question.

F. Volpi traces this notion of understanding something in terms of itself back to Aristotle[4]. He notes that Heidegger appropriates Aristotle's notion of *praxis* (as opposed to *poiesis*) to designate Dasein. *Praxis*, for Aristotle and Heidegger, cannot be understood in terms of anything but itself (and should, therefore, not be confused with the ready-to-hand, practical entity, which we saw tends to be understood in terms of Dasein's self-understanding). *Praxis* is something that is done for its own sake. "In the absence of

---

4   The same point is made in Dahlstrom, D. O. (2001). Heidegger's Concept of Truth. Cambridge, Cambridge University Press.

any region in which it can be constituted, *praxis* has to be self-constituting; and in this way it becomes the originary ontological determination, self-sufficient, its own objective. It becomes *ouheneka*, Worumwillen [for-the-sake-of-which]" (Volpi 1996, 50). Dasein exists "for its own sake" and not as an instrument for achieving a goal other than being itself. *Praxis* contains its own goal and is not instrumental: "the distinctive characteristic of *praxis* is the fact that it is not with reference to anything else (*henekatinos*) like *poiesis*, but that it contains in itself its own goal (*houheneka*)" (Volpi 1996, 56-57). What is more, this understanding of something *in terms of itself* only can be either *aware* of something or *ignorant* of it, rather than be right or wrong about it in the sense of having correct beliefs about it. Something that is understood out of itself cannot be misunderstood in the sense of being misinterpreted, it can only be missed altogether – and here we see that the notion of awakening we looked at in Chapter 2 fits in: when Dasein begins to understand its own true being, it awakens to its own true nature.

One could as an analogy to *praxis* think of a work of art, in the way that we sometimes think of art as existing for its own sake only – art for art's sake. If art is understood in this way it is, contrary to an instrument, a consumer good or an object of theoretical reflection, not made to serve any purpose other than itself. The notion of the individual existing for its own sake is sometimes expressed in terms of the individual "being an end in itself", or in terms of the individual having its origin in itself, in the sense of existing in terms of itself. This refers to the notion that the individual is neither an object to be used in instrumental ways nor one that needs theoretical justification. The individual human being exists for its own sake, and as such, can never be subsumed under something higher than itself (whether that be a practical purpose or a theoretical category). Because, according to Heidegger, all understanding projects entities onto an understanding of the being of the entity (in terms of the possibilities this kind of being has), Dasein is properly understood in terms of itself only, it cannot be projected onto anything but itself, if it is to be understood in an authentic way. In this way the moment of authentic self-understanding corresponds with what we saw in Chapter 2 as *finding one's true self*, and it happens as a result of *awakening*.

Authentic Dasein understands itself as process

Rather than understanding Dasein as a practical or theoretical entity, as something with an essence that persists through time, Heidegger conceives of Dasein as a process. As Reiner Schuermann puts it, "Heidegger's point of departure is the notion of subject as 'process' (*Vollzug*)" (Schuermann 2008, 57-58). And he adds that "[t]he meaning of the subject's being is time; the subject's Being cannot be referred back to anything other than Dasein, out of which it would then 'enter' into time" (Schuermann 2008, 57-58). There is not a substantive entity that is located within time (note that from a scientific standpoint the human body exists in time, but this investigation is about the structure of lived experience, which is accessible to each one of us directly and not tied to a scientific perspective), but rather, this entity itself is the process of time, it is *in essence* the process of time, temporality. "The 'essence' of this entity lies in its 'to be' [*Zu-sein*]" (Heidegger 1962).

In the next chapter, on authentic attunement, we will further develop the notion, already mooted, that Heidegger takes Dasein to be fundamentally openness, transcendence, in the form of being-in-the-world. In the present chapter we are seeing that, according to Heidegger, it is temporality, or process that constitutes the nature of this fundamental openness. Heidegger argues that authentic understanding means that Dasein understands itself in terms of temporality, where this temporality, unlike the things we find in the world and even the being of entities, is something that can be understood in terms of itself. We can, therefore, say that authentic Dasein understands itself in terms of temporality and that Dasein is, in essence, temporality.

To understand Heidegger's notion of temporality, we need to let go of both the common sense and the scientific notions of time. Both of these envisage time as a sequence of "nows", one that stretches from the indefinite past into the indefinite future. They envisage the individual as occurring "in" time, as coming into being at some point and going out of existence at a later one, not affecting the actual course of time itself. Again, this may be an adequate way of conceiving of the time of science, but it is, according to Heidegger, not the way in which we experience time in ourselves. Heidegger's phenomenological investigation tells him that we have to understand time differently, if we want to do so in a way that it corresponds with the way that things present themselves to our awarenss before they are coloured by common sense or scientific ways of thinking about the entity.

An authentic understanding of time has, according to Heidegger, several aspects. Daniel Dahlstrom mentions five aspects of "genuine timeliness [authentic temporality]" (Dahlstrom 2001, 337). The first of these is that genuine temporality comprises "ways in which to be-here is to be 'outside' or even 'beside oneself'" (Dahlstrom 2001, 337). This is very much in line with the notion of Dasein as openness and transcendence we looked at earlier and will discuss further in the next chapter. It is not that one exists and that, once that has been established, one may turn towards the past, present, or future. Rather one exists *as* turning toward the past, present, or future. In this, genuine temporality is not an entity but "it unfolds", it emerges. "Temporality 'is' not an entity at all. It is not, but it *temporalises* itself" (Heidegger 1962, 376-377).

Thus, temporality is the way in which Dasein is "outside" or even "beside itself", as a kind of reaching out toward things in a way that can be characterised as being turned towards the past, present or future. Dasein can, as such, be characterised simultaneously as openness and as process. As Michael Zimmerman puts it, "Human understanding, then, does not take place inside a mind locked in the skull. Instead, understanding occurs because human temporality is receptive to particular ways in which things can present or manifest themselves. ... [w]hat we ordinarily take to be the ultimate constituents of 'mind' – thoughts, beliefs, assertions, and so on – are for Heidegger phenomena that occur within the temporal clearing constitutive of human understanding" (Zimmerman 1993, 243).

We find more clues about process nature of Dasein, in Heidegger's discussions of the concepts of guilt and anxiety in *Being and Time*, where he talks about Dasein as "being-the-basis of a nullity" (Heidegger, 1962, p. 329). This concept of "being-the-basis of a nullity" defines the dual aspect of, on the one hand, Dasein being "thrown" into a world which is not of its own making, and, on the other hand, Dasein projecting the meaning of that world in understanding. We have here the picture of a free-floating process of finding oneself in a world (being thrown), while at the same time having no choice but to project one's understanding of that world, which represents Heidegger's notion of understanding.

To put it in more prosaic terms, how I normally understand things is based on my upbringing, my cultural background, my life experiences, but these are not essential to my being; even so, I need to take responsibility for the way I understand things. One could object here that one's cultural conditioning and the way one has been brought up are what is essential to one, and that to argue otherwise is to posit a substantive self, like a soul, at the core of Dasein. But we need to remember here that Heidegger does not posit some substantive essence at the core of Dasein, but rather a process of temporality: actual Dasein is nothing more than these processes, where the processes are open to the world and to Dasein itself.

When Dasein is authentic, is true to itself, it takes itself as temporality, as process. Going back to Chapter 3, we can see that our common-sense and educational accounts of learning do not really allow for a learning that happens in relation to something that is essentially processal. This is because process, when taken absolutely, does not allow for us to latch on to characteristics that we could learn about. There would not be an intentional object, because what is in constant flux cannot become an object we can then treat as independent of us. The temporal nature of Dasein means that it has no stable, substantive, essence in relation to which we can construct attitudes, actions, or ideas. And this means that the processal nature of Dasein, the way Heidegger proposes, excludes the possibility of our conventional accounts of learning getting a grip on it.

Dasein as finite totality and possibility

Another aspect of Dasein's authentic self-understanding is that it takes itself as finite. This is linked with Dasein understanding itself in terms of temporality. "Genuine timeliness [temporality]" (Dahlstrom 2001, 337), as Heidegger understands it, is finite. This is, of course, very different from the common-sense notion of time as an infinite succession of "nows". The grounds for such a statement again lie in phenomenological observation, in that Heidegger's claim is that, if we return to the way we experience time and take away all the "ideas", the presuppositions we have about time, we actually experience time as finite – at least in so far as we experience it from the first-person perspective. The evidence for such a claim (and its possible refutation) will lie in first-person phenomenological observation, and can never be scientific in any positivist sense. I will take the claim as initially plausible from a phenomenological perspective and hope that the following discussion will confirm this plausibility.

In the Chapter 2 we saw that the notion of authenticity can be understood in terms of a double movement of death and rebirth. We also saw that it could be understood in terms of Dasein giving up the existence it has arrived at. We looked at Heidegger writing that Dasein's "uttermost possibility lies in giving itself up, and thus shatter all one's tenaciousness to whatever existence one has reached" (Heidegger 1962, 309). These notions of existential death and "giving up oneself" can be linked with the experience of time as finite: in so far as Dasein actually understands itself as finite temporality, as a process that contains its own end as its ultimate horizon, it will understand itself as it really (authentically) is and thus become authentic in the perfectionist sense of both reaching its full potential and existing according to its real nature.

One way in which Heidegger puts the connection between understanding oneself as finite and being authentic is that only by understanding oneself as "being-towards-death" does one understand oneself in one's totality. This is because one's death is always already part of one's existence, in the sense that it is certain and as such a constant presence on the horizon of one's understanding of things (taking into account that one's understanding of anything is based on projections and projections are inherently futural). As Reiner Schuermann puts it, "In its process (Vollzug), the subject [Dasein], considered in itself, is … utterly finite. This … is the meaning of 'wholeness' or 'totality' (Ganzheit). Ganzheit is not the sum total of traits belonging to Dasein, but its finite autonomy; its utter facticity, with no recourse to an infinite subject" (Schuermann 2008, 57-58).

Dasein is, as we saw in the previous section, the basis of its own being, but it is the basis of its *whole* being only insofar as it is facing its *whole* being – and it does so only when it faces existential death, "the possibility of the impossibility of existence". As such death is not an event that lies in the future (though it is that as well, when taken from a third-person perspective, from a ready-to-hand or present-at-hand perspective) but something that is always part of the totality of Dasein's existence. "Death is not 'added on' to Dasein at its 'end'; but Dasein, as care, is the thrown (that is, null) basis for its death. The nullity by which Dasein's being is dominated through and through, is revealed to Dasein itself in authentic being-towards-death" (Heidegger 1962, 354). In other words, "Dasein exists as thrown Being towards its end" (Heidegger, 1962, p. 295).

What is more, because Dasein is process that is open to the world and to itself, and because it is possible for any particular form which this process may take to subside, we have to say that essentially, Dasein is possibility. After all, if any particular way of being emerges, then this is one of Dasein's "ways to be". But if Dasein is "in a certain way" it can be in other ways as well. The actual way in which Dasein is represents only one of many possible ways of being that could emerge. We can, therefore, say that authentic understanding involves Dasein understanding itself both as *possibility* and as *finite temporality*. Heidegger uses the word "transparency" to characterize this authentic self-understanding: "When one has an understanding of being-towards-death – towards death as one's ownmost possibility – one's potentiality-for-being becomes authentic and wholly transparent" (Heidegger, 1962, p. 354).

Dasein as possibility means that it is not possible for our conventional accounts of learning to progress in relation to it. This is similar to the point made in the previous section that Dasein as process precludes the possibility of making it into an intentional object without alienating it from its authentic nature. Similarly, if the deepest essence of Dasein is possibility, there cannot be the kind of continuity in relation to an intentional object that conventional accounts of learning require. This again comes down to the essentially open and undetermined nature of Dasein: where there is only possibility, there is nothing on which to base associative learning, nothing on which to base continuity. We, therefore, again see that when Dasein has an authentic relationship with itself, this cannot be the outcome of conventional forms of learning.

Dasein understanding itself as finite process

Authentic self-understanding as transparency

Now that we have a first grasp on what authentic self-understanding entails and why conventional accounts of learning will not get us there, we will return to the question of the process of learning to be authentic. As explained earlier, such a process of learning to be authentic will, first, be a paradigm case of authentic learning and, second, bring us to the mode of authenticity, which, it was suggested, is at the same time the state in which authentic learning can take place.

As we saw in the previous section, authentic self-understanding involves what Heidegger calls "transparency." In relation to this Benjamin Crowe writes that "[t]he image one gets [...] is that [Dasein] has become aware of itself somehow, has suddenly recognized that it has been living in a mode of [inauthenticity]. One has 'seen through' one's life as it has been lived" (Crowe 2006, 173). In a similar vein, Miguel de Beistegui writes about Heidegger's notion of Dasein that "what is most singular about the human Dasein is that it is open (on)to itself, open to its own openness, and so can, up to a point, become transparent to itself, and thus be in a position to grasp its ownmost possibilities. This is the *Durchsichtigmachen* of life itself, its self-clarification, or explication" (de Beistegui 2005).

This "seeing through" one's life is what Heidegger calls "transparency", which in German, *Durchsigtigkeit*, literally means "through" [durch] "sight" [Sicht]. Transparency is the way in which the whole of Dasein's existence becomes aware of itself as temporality, openness and possibility. "The sight which is related primarily and on the whole to existence [Dasein] we call 'transparency' [*Durchsichtigkeit*] (Heidegger 1962, 186-187). Importantly, "sight" is not to be understood in terms of sense-perception but rather in terms of knowing one's way around a situation, of being aware (in the most general sense of the term) of the situation and oneself in it. "In giving an existential signification to 'sight', we have merely drawn upon the peculiar feature of seeing, that it lets entities which are accessible to it be encountered unconcealedly in themselves" (Heidegger 1962, 187). Ultimately, Heidegger would claim, understanding is itself irreducible to something else (such as perception or knowledge), which is the reason why he uses "sight" not in a literal sense but as a word to indicate the way in which understanding can be *directed towards* entities, has *access* to entities, and *guides* its ways of engaging with these entities. In this book the terms "awareness" or "noticing" are sometimes used instead of sight, to indicate Dasein's access to beings and being itself in the most general terms.

Heidegger distinguishes "circumspection" [Umsicht], which allows for the access to, awareness of, ready-to-hand entities, "considerateness" [Ruecksicht], which allows for the access to, awareness of, other human beings, and "the sight which is directed upon being as such" [Sicht auf das Sein als solches], which allows for the access to, awareness of, the being of entities (Heidegger 1962, 186-187). Sight is used to denote what "guides" our interaction with an entity and what gives that interaction its particular "character" (Heidegger 1962, 98). It is like an awareness in which one looks around in order to find out how to comport oneself (how to relate) towards the entities one finds in the world (circumspection), towards the people one encounters (considerateness), towards the being of entities (the sight which is directed upon being as such) or towards oneself (transparency).

Transparency refers to the way in which we are *directed* towards ourselves, the way we gain *access* to ourselves and the way our engagement with ourselves is *guided*. An important aspect of this kind of transparency is that it is not a kind of reflective self-awareness[5], where the self becomes the object of reflection (practical or theoretical). If Dasein understands itself "this understanding, this becoming manifest of the self, is not a self-contemplation in the sense that the ego would become the object of some cognition or other" (Heidegger 1982, 277). What occurs is a kind of impersonal, unitary "*it* is disclosed that", which is a form of disclosure that discloses being-in-the-world as a whole, that is, both the individual and the world at the same time. Heidegger writes that "[t]he self is there for the Dasein itself without reflection and without inner perception, before all reflection. Reflection, in the sense of a turning back [reflecting *on*], is only a mode of self-apprehension, but not the mode of primary self-disclosure" (Heidegger 1982, 159).

Importantly, the pre-reflective nature of self-awareness goes for inauthentic Dasein as well as for authentic self-awareness. Thus Heidegger writes that "[t]he genuine, actual, though inauthentic understanding of the self takes place in such a way that this self, the self of our thoughtlessly random, common, everyday existence, 'reflects' itself to itself from out of that to which it has given itself over" (Heidegger 1982, 161). This is so, because Dasein "finds itself primarily and constantly in things because, tending them, distressed by them, it always in some way or other rests in things. Each one of us is what he pursues and cares for" (Heidegger 1982, 159). For example, one may understand oneself in terms of one's role in life, the things one possesses or would like to possess, the things one likes or dislikes, and so on. Heidegger's claim is that the authentic way of understanding oneself is more fundamental than the reflective ideas we may have about ourselves, because these reflective ideas are ultimately based in the pre-reflective ways of being in the world we have.

In this way, even our every-day (inauthentic) self-understanding is

---

5 See Chapter 5 for a discussion of pre-reflective self-awareness in relation to attunement.

primarily pre-reflective. For example, when we are asked what we are doing, we can usually tell directly (for example, "I am trying to fix the door") without having to step back from ourselves and reflecting on it. We could then say that, in so far as we are absorbed in the things we find in the world (fixing a door, explaining maths to a pupil, worrying about the mortgage), we pre-reflectively understand ourselves as absorbed in these activities. "It is as though the Dasein's [being] were projected by the things, by the Dasein's commerce with them, and not by the Dasein itself from its own most peculiar self, which nevertheless exists, just as it is, always as dealing with things" (Heidegger 1982, 289). That is, "[t]o understand ourselves from the things with which we are occupied means to project our [being] upon such features of the business of our everyday occupation as the feasible, urgent, indispensable, expedient" (Heidegger 1982, 289). We could say that according to the way in which we are engaged with things our understanding of ourselves will be shaped by those things. Dasein tends to understand itself "from out of that to which it has given itself over" (Heidegger 1982, 161).

All this means that the first step in the process of gaining an authentic understanding of oneself is to be pre-reflectively aware of the way in which we understand ourselves inauthentically. The first step is to notice how we tend to understand ourselves in terms of the activities and the things we are engaged with. We understand ourselves in terms of our engagement with those things, but what is lacking is that we are aware of the very process of understanding ourselves in terms of those things. So, the question becomes one of becoming aware of the process that yields our inauthentic self-understanding. To put it differently, our understanding becomes transparent in our "seizing upon the full disclosedness of being-in-the-world throughout all the constitutive items which are essential to it, and doing so with understanding" (Heidegger 1962, 186-187). As we "seize upon" (become aware of) "the full disclosedness of being-in-the-world" (the way we understand the things in the world as well as ourselves), we become aware of ourselves as we are (in a way that is pre-reflective). This is transparency: "Dasein is revealed to itself in its current factical ability-to-be, and in such a way that Dasein *is* this revealing and being-revealed" (Heidegger 1962, 355). In pre-reflective self-awareness the Dasein that is revealed equals the one revealing, because the self-revealing is not reflective but direct, from the inside out, as it were.

If we are then to characterize the process of going *from* understanding oneself in terms of one's engagement with these entities (where one understands oneself as a ready-to-hand or present-at-hand entity) *to* understanding oneself in terms of the very process of projection itself (where one understands oneself as the finite process of projection that is open to the world and itself), we can see that it is a process of, first, becoming pre-reflectively aware of the inauthentic way we have of understanding ourselves. We notice that we understand ourselves from out of the entities we find in the world and becoming authentic then involves a withdrawal from our absorption in the entities we find in the world. Such a withdrawal from our absorption in the world corresponds with the first part of the dual movement of "turning away from the world" and "turning back" I described in Chapter 2. In the next section we will look at the second part, the "turning back", but before that we will need to further specify the movement of withdrawal.

Letting go of one's inauthentic self-projection

To recap, authentic Dasein has a sense of itself as "thrown projection", a kind of free-floating process that has no substantial basis, that is finite, and that *understands* things, including itself, where understanding means that it can *direct* itself towards these things, have *access* to them and be *guided* in its engagement with them by this understanding. Authentic understanding, in contrast to inauthentic understanding, is the possibility that all this awakens to itself, becomes transparent to itself. The process of withdrawal from one's absorption in the things one encounters in the world is a process of not projecting the entities one understands onto the being of entities as projected but projecting them onto temporality itself. As we saw earlier, temporality projects itself and does not require anything to be projected onto. The withdrawal is, therefore, one of *not projecting* the being of entities or of oneself, but of allowing the entities to project onto temporality itself. To come to a full understanding, this process needs then to be further characterized as one of *ceasing to project* the being of entities, given that the, inauthentic, starting point of the process of becoming authentic begins with the projection of the being of entities in inauthentic understanding.

We can, therefore, say that the process of withdrawal needs to be understood, not in the sense of a "drawing in" or "drawing back", but of the cessation of the activity of projecting, which itself begins in the cessation of the *fixing* and *committing* to the projection of the being of entities. And we can see that this cessation of fixing and committing would make it difficult for conventional forms of learning to get a grip on it, because these conventional forms of learning necessarily start by fixing the being of the entity, to make it into an intentional object, in relation to which the processes of modification and growth can take place.

In contrast to the conventional form of learning as grasping the entity, becoming authentic is a process of letting go. What withdraws in this letting go is the commitment, the solidified state of being invested in, identified with, a projection. And this process of withdrawal itself is experienced as a letting go of what is being projected as soon as it is being projected. In this way, the mode of authentic understanding begins with one experiencing oneself as the on-going process of projection that is not brought to a halt by the fixing of a particular projection in one's commitment to it. In other words, being absorbed in the entities one finds in the world consists in fixing the being of those and committing to the way in which these are fixed. And refraining from this fixing and committing means that the projections, though they may still come[6], are allowed to go as well; this reveals understanding as a process.

Such a letting go of the being of entities that are being projected does, as was said, have to begin from a position where the being of an entity has been committed to and has become fixed. This means that the process of committing and fixing, of being committed and fixed, itself has to become transparent as such. This happens when the mode of being fixed is itself disclosed as essentially a process (an iterative process) of projection and when the being that is thus fixed is itself disclosed as possibility rather than something necessary. The understanding has to be one of oneself as projecting the understanding of being in question, so that what is initially experienced as fixed is now experienced as being the result of an iterative process of projection. And this particular projection of an understanding of being then becomes transparent as just one possible projection out of many, where the other (possible but not actual) projections are given as possibility. This discloses the projection of the being of the entity as just that, a possibility and a projection. "Seeing" this will result in the letting go of the fixed understanding of being that is being projected, so that the

6   Strictly speaking, Heidegger would say that the projections in the authentic mode come as possibility rather than actual projections.

process of projecting can henceforth be experienced as a process.

With this description, we now have a characterization of the first part of the process of becoming authentic in the domain of understanding. It is the dissolution of an understanding of the being of an entity as *fixed* into an understanding of the being of this entity as *a process of projection*, where this projection is itself of a *possibility*. This dissolution happens when the process that *fixes* and *commits* becomes non-reflexively self-aware (transparent) as being a process of possibility. The starting point of this, what triggers it, may arise internally or come from outside the process of understanding, for example, when it is pointed out to the individual that what appears to them as the fixed being of an entity is actually an iterative process of projecting the being of the entity. In this way, the process begins with something breaking through the repetitive process of projection that fixes one's understanding of the being of an entity. In Chapter 6 we will look in detail at this moment of breaking through.

Seizing the moment

In the previous section we saw how, as Dasein becomes pre-reflectively aware of itself as, among other things, a process of understanding that is based on continual projection, it gives up fixing and committing to the being of entities as it has projected that being. This dual movement of pre-reflective self-awareness (which Heidegger calls transparency) and letting go is also characterized as a process of withdrawing from one's absorption in the entities one finds in the world. This, we saw, corresponds with the aspect of "turning away from the world" which was, in Chapter 2, identified as the first step in the process of becoming authentic. In that chapter a second aspect of authenticity was identified as "turning back" to the world, in the sense that the whole of authenticity is characterized as a "turning away from the world" and "turning back". We will now briefly look at the "turning back" part. This will require less space than our account of "turning away", because it follows naturally out of that first movement.

What happens is that, as Dasein becomes aware of itself as a process of understanding that projects the being of entities as possibility, with every projection there is the possibility of understanding the being of the entity Dasein encounters in that projection. As Dasein is aware of projecting the being of an entity, that projection offers Dasein a way of grasping, understanding, the entity. But the entity, as understood in terms of the being which Dasein has projected, is also still understood against the backdrop of the process of understanding itself (temporality), because that process itself has become transparent (pre-reflectively self-aware). Therefore, while Dasein grasps the entity in a projected understanding, it does not become absorbed in the entity.

This awareness of its own temporality within which the being of the entity is projected Heidegger calls "the situation". We could say that it is a kind of expanded awareness (one that includes an awareness of the entities involves and the process of understanding being pre-reflectively aware itself[7]) within which a narrower context of awareness exists. This narrower context of awareness Heidegger calls "circumstances" [*Lage,*], which is the situation as it is given through tradition and culture, through *das Man*. That is, one's understanding of an entity is based in one's personal experience, culture or tradition (*das Man*), because whenever one projects the being of an actual entity, this being is almost certain to be mediated through *das Man*. But while this is a necessary limitation of any kind of understanding of being one may project, it is still possible to project it within a wider kind of awareness, the awareness of the process of understanding as temporality. Despite the refusal to fix and commit, the entity is now understood as a certain kind of entity (having a certain kind of being), in such a way that there is an actual (as opposed to merely possible) understanding of the entity. This is the moment where Dasein "turns back" to the world, engages with things, acts, takes a stand, and so on.

Heidegger calls this moment of engagement "the instant" [*Augenblick*, also translated as "moment of vision"]. For Heidegger, *Augenblick* signifies both a moment in time (the moment at which one takes an entity as having a certain kind of being) and a certain perspective on the situation (*Augenblick* consists of the German words for "eye" and "view" or "look" and thus signifies a certain view of the situation). It is, therefore, the moment at which the situation is viewed in a certain way. It "is that which, arising from resoluteness [i.e. authenticity], has an eye first of all and solely for what constitutes the situation of action" (Heidegger 1982, 287). But, though a certain perspective has been adopted, the wider pre-reflective awareness of oneself as temporality, as the process of understanding as projection, is

---

7   Note that this is not a contradiction, as pre-reflective awareness can, contrary to reflective awareness, be simultaneously aware of both itself and that which it is aware of.

hereby not relinquished. "It is the mode of resolute [authentic] existence in which the Dasein, as being-in-the-world, holds and keeps the world in view" (Heidegger 1982, 287). And this means that Dasein does not get absorbed in the entities it is dealing with, Dasein does not get lost in *das Man* again, even as it engages with the entity in terms that necessarily involve *das Man*.

As Dasein settles for the being of an entity, it does so in good faith. Heidegger calls this "holding-for-true", and one could say that it is a form of taking something as the entity it is *to the best of one's ability to determine this*. This is not a kind of relativism but an acknowledgement of the fact that at the level of the *being* of entities there is no higher court that one's immediate understanding of that being[8]. But, as has been said before, this understanding does not become fixed: "[t]he certainty of the [authentic understanding] signifies that one *holds oneself free* for the possibility of *taking it back*" (Heidegger 1962, 355). And this in turn means, as we also saw earlier, that the process of projecting an understanding of being continues: "this holding-for-true, as a resolute holding-oneself-free for taking back, is *authentic resoluteness which resolves to keep repeating itself*" (Heidegger 1962, 355).

So we have the situation where Dasein "simply cannot become rigid as regards the situation, but must understand that the resolution, in accordance with its own meaning as disclosure, must be held open and free for the current factical possibility" (Heidegger 1962, 355). This does, however, not mean that Dasein does not take responsibility for its actions. On the contrary, because authentic Dasein has *not* become absorbed in the public, anonymous understanding of the situation as it is given by *das Man*, it can and will take full responsibility, a responsibility it would otherwise quite easily be able to shrug off, as it would be able to pass on the responsibility for understanding the situation by saying that this is "how one tends to understand it" or "how it is always understood".

With regard to the process of learning the authentic "turning back" to the world we have considered in this section, we can conclude that this process is very much the same process as that of the "turning away from the world" we discussed in the previous section: it is the process of *understanding*

---

8 Note that all scientific methods available to determine the truth of something already imply an understanding of the being of the entity the truth of which is being established, which means that it is logically impossible for such methods to establish the being of an entity.

becoming transparent to itself and of *letting go* the understanding of being that is being projected, as a result of which an understanding of being will be projected as *possibility* in a way that one *holds oneself free* for the possibility of *taking it back* and that *resolves to keep repeating itself*. I also mentioned that the very beginning of this involves a moment of "breaking through", which we will look at in more detail in Chapter 6. And I briefly touched on the idea that this kind of pre-reflective awareness is one that is greater than and encompasses the awareness one may have of an object, and we will look at this aspect in more depth in the next chapter. Finally, we saw that this kind of authentic understanding, even though it contains the elements of *taking back* and *repetition*, enables one to be resolute in one's actions and take responsibility for them, specifically because one's understanding is not derived from *das Man* but truly one's own.

Understanding learning to be authentic

Letting go and becoming pre-reflectively self-aware

In order to characterize the process of becoming authentic correctly, we should not posit the existence of a self, in any conventional meaning of the term, because, as we have seen, the authentic mode is in such a state of flux that any notion of a fixed sense of self quickly becomes unintelligible. Learning to be authentic is a unitary, impersonal event. This means that what we are trying to get into focus is not so much the process of Dasein gaining authentic understanding, but of understanding itself becoming authentic. Bearing this in mind, we are now in a position to recap the process of understanding learning to be authentic, and in doing so anticipate some aspects of learning to be authentic that will be discussed in later chapters.

Understanding learning to be authentic begins with inauthentic understanding, when Dasein understands itself pre-reflectively from out of the entities it is engaged with (and does so in terms of the practical and/or theoretical entities found in *das Man*) and understands these entities from out of its understanding of itself: Dasein's self-understanding is projected onto the entities it is engaged with, just as the being of these entities is projected by Dasein itself.

This state of affairs is then "broken through", when understanding finds itself face-to-face with something it notices it cannot possibly resolve, when a certain affective disposition arises (See Chapter 5), or when of a communication by another Dasein (See Chapter 6). This awakens a sense of the limitations of Dasein's current understanding, as well as a sense that these limitations are self-imposed and, as such, may conceal other possible ways of understanding. This begins two, reciprocally related, mutually reinforcing, processes: a "letting go" of existing projections and an increasing pre-reflective awareness of the process of projecting itself.

In terms of letting go of the projections, there is, as a first step, the cessation of the activity of *fixing* and *committing* to the projection of the being of entities. This is a letting go of what is being projected as fixed as soon as it is being projected. As a result, Dasein experiences itself as the on-going process of projection that is not brought to a halt by the fixing of a particular projection in its commitment to it. Also, this process becomes self-aware as being a process of possibility, in that any actual projections are experienced as occurring within a process that is more fundamental than these projections themselves, and that could, therefore, also yield other possible projections.

In terms of Dasein becoming pre-reflectively aware of its projections, there is again a reciprocally related process that drives it (as it were, a sub-process that is part of the overall process). It starts with either Dasein becoming aware of how it tends to understand itself in terms of the activities and the things it is engaged with, or with Dasein becoming aware of how it understands the entities it encounters in the world in terms of itself. Dasein begins to understand that both of these comprise a limitation, and that they are mutually reinforcing. What is more, to the extent that Dasein is more aware of itself as projecting the being of entities, it becomes more aware of how it understands itself in terms of the being of the entities it projects, and vice versa.

The awareness of understanding itself in terms of the entities it finds in the world gives Dasein the notion of the possibility of understanding itself in terms of itself for the first time in an authentic way (before this it will have understood this possibility inauthentically), as a process of projection, with the result that Dasein is *directed* towards itself, gains *access* to itself and is *guided* in its engagement with itself by the process of projecting (temporality), rather than by the projections. This also gives Dasein the notion of understanding the entities it finds in the world in terms of temporality, with the result that Dasein ceases to fix and commit to the projection of the being of itself, in a process of letting go.

With these two, the process of letting go and that of becoming pre-reflectively self-aware, we have the mutually reinforcing process of understanding becoming authentic. Dasein projects its self-understanding onto temporality, it projects it onto its own being, and thus understands itself in terms of its own being and not in terms of the entities it encounters in the world. This temporality discloses understanding itself as a free-floating and finite process of projection: authentic Dasein has a sense of itself as "thrown projection", a process that has no substantial basis, that is limited, and that understands things, including itself, by projecting the thing it understands onto an understanding of the being of that thing. At the same time, authentic Dasein understands that "letting go" of any projection of itself and things in the world is the only way it has to understand things in a true way, where this "letting go" is experienced as a kind of existential death that leaves behind only openness (the possibility of being affected).

When this process is complete, Dasein understands itself and the things in the world in terms of temporality and no longer in terms of ready-to-hand or present-at-hand entities. Temporality projects itself and does not require anything to be projected onto, it temporalizes itself in a kind of impersonal, unitary "*it* is disclosed that", which is a form of disclosure that discloses being-in-the-world as a whole, that discloses both the individual and the world at the same time. This kind of pre-reflective awareness is one that is greater than and encompasses the awareness one may have of an object. It is experienced as an impersonal "there is understanding", which is an experience of the absence of the separation between a subject and an object pole of experience.

As a result, the being of the entities Dasein finds in the world is first projected onto temporality, which constitutes a kind of pure contact with the entities, before there is either a practical or a theoretical engagement with them. When it concerns an entity with the nature of Dasein itself, this results in authentic being-with, a kind of communion where the other is experienced as one with Dasein and as an end in itself (See Chapter 6). This understanding will be different in actuality from the earlier understanding (which was based in inauthentic disclosure) in that the other Dasein will no longer appear as either a practical or theoretical entity. Where it concerns entities other than Dasein itself, these become understood, in so far as it is necessary to engage with them practically of theoretically, in accordance with the situation as a whole.

"Getting the being of an entity right" means taking it as the kind of entity it is appropriate to take it as, relevant to the situation and the entity itself, grasping the being of the entity, as a ready-to-hand entity, a present-at-hand one, or an entity like Dasein, existence. And because understanding is understood in terms of possibility, any actual understanding of a concrete situation is characterized by a readiness to "take back" and by "repetition", resulting in a stance towards entities (both Dasein itself and other entities) that can be full of resolve and that takes full responsibility for itself and the actions that flow from it (because responsibility is not abdicated to *das Man*). The entity will thus be understood in a way that is capable of returning to the entity in itself and of then "taking a stand" on that entity that is authentic in the sense of being genuinely Dasein's own.

In this way, there will be the kind of grasping of the being of entities that is described in conventional accounts of learning at the moment of "turning back" to the world, of seizing the moment, once Dasein has resolved on the kind of situation it is. But the process that makes such authentic seizing the moment possible is that of becoming pre-reflectively self-aware and letting go of any preformed projection of the being of entities. It is this element of pre-reflective self-awareness and letting go that cannot be captured by conventional accounts of learning, and that forms the basis of the process of learning to be authentic.

Relation to theories of conventional learning

If we now return briefly to the presuppositions we said were shared by the theories of learning we considered in Chapter 3, we can recap how the process of understanding becoming transparent and of letting go one's understanding of being relates to these theories of learning. For the currently dominant theories of learning, learning is a process of growth, increased integration and differentiation, which tends towards increased stability, even rigidity, where learning is always a modification of the existing way of being of the learner, which involves an intentional object, with there being a separation between the subject and the object. We will finish this chapter by looking briefly at these in turn, in relation to the process of understanding becoming authentic.

We can reconcile *learning as modification and growth* with the process of letting go, as far as the aspect of understanding itself being a process is concerned. That is, it is not just learning that is a process, but any understanding of an entity is processal in nature. Viewing understanding itself as a process is in line with Piaget's notion of understanding, where understanding does not consist of a representation but of an intentional act which is carried out in a specific way, where the act is "built up", re-constituted, every time the understanding manifests in relation to that specific object. This notion of understanding as process is also compatible with the neurological notion of neurons that fire together wiring together, in that the structure of such neuronal acts as they repeat themselves is also one of a process taking shape. From this perspective, the process of *letting go* would simply mean that an understanding was not re-constituted in relation to the entity in relation to which it was originally constructed. This same process of understanding could then be re-constituted in relation to the entity at a later point, with the result that it would possibly grow and be modified as a result of this renewed engagement. The decision whether or not to re-constitute the understanding would be the initial moment of "decision", Heidegger's "moment of vision" [Augenblick] when the entity was or was not taken as a practical or theoretical object. That is, so long as conventional accounts of learning take understanding to be in essence processal they can exist side by side with the notion of learning to be authentic we are trying to bring into focus.

Where this is a notable difference, though, is that the process of understanding becoming authentic is itself not one of increased integration, differentiation and rigidity. On the contrary, there is a dissolution of any established integration and differentiation and with it of any rigidity that may have built up. It was explained in this chapter that this dissolution is based in a mechanism of increased transparency (pre-reflective self-awareness) and letting go, where the increased transparency discloses the existing integration and differentiation as processal and based in possibility, which leads to a letting go of some of that integration and differentiation, which in turn increases the transparency, which in turn leads to more letting go, and so on. It is, therefore, in many ways the opposite process to the one that is described in the theories of learning we have been looking at. To put it in terms used earlier, where conventional learning leads to increased integration and differentiation of knowledge, to the extent that this leads to ever more stability, a degree of openness is lost. This openness can then be regained via a process of letting go that is based in pre-reflective self-awareness, but this opening up is not a process that can be captured by conventional accounts of learning that think in terms of continuity (opening up is discontinuous) and growth (opening up is about letting go).

As part of this dissolving of the integration and differentiation, which takes place as a result of existing patterns not being repeated, there is in addition an expansion of awareness. As existing patterns of relating to entities lose their fixed nature, the understanding awakens that understanding itself is a process of finite temporality. Such an awakening is an expansion of awareness, because the possibility of repeating and building on (further integrating and differentiating) existing patterns remains, while it is seen as but one possible way of being of Dasein. That is, this possibility of repeating and building on existing understanding is now experienced within the awareness of the wider situation, which includes not only the actual situation in the world (Lage) but also an awareness of the way in which any particular understanding is itself only one possibility among many which all emerge into the openness of Dasein's temporality. And this means that the expansion of awareness that comes with pre-reflective self-awareness goes counter to the continuity that lies at the basis of the increased integration and differentiation that make up conventional learning. Letting go of existing understanding is a discontinuous process, and as such not accounted for in conventional accounts of learning.

It was also said that there is in the main theories of learning the presupposition that learning is always a modification of the existing way of being of the learner. But the process of *understanding learning to become authentic*, as a process of letting go, is not a modification of an existing way of being. Though it begins with inauthentic understanding, the end result (Dasein experiencing itself as openness, process, and possibility) cannot be said to be *a modification of* the initial state of there being a certain understanding of being in terms of *das Man*, no more than letting go can be called a modified form of grasping. What is more, once the individual resolves on the being of an entity after having let go of their previous understanding of it, it is hard to imagine what the way of being of the authentic individual is other than nothingness. As we saw earlier in this chapter, the being of the individual is usually closely connected to the understanding they have of the being of the entity or entities they are engaging with, and in that context it makes sense that learning is based in the existing way of being of the learner. In the case of not yet having decided on the being of the entity involves, as we saw in the previous point, there is, as yet, not a definite way of taking the entity, and with such an absence of a way of taking the entity, the next moment, that of resolving on the being of the entity, cannot be said to be a modification of one's earlier way of being.

Finally, according to the accounts of learning we discussed in Chapter 3, learning always includes an intentional object, with there being some sort of a separation between the subject and the object. It has become clear in this chapter that this is not the case in relation to the process of *understanding learning to be authentic*, which is one of pre-reflective self-awareness, an awareness that does not have an object that is separate from the subject[9] and where the entity that is learning coincides with what it is learning about. What is more, since the process is one of letting go, there is an initial object (at *t1*) but not one or much less so at *t2*. This is different from what happens in the learning as described in the main theories of learning where the initial object (at *t1*) is modified into a second object (at *t2*), as when rain turns from being understood as the angels emptying their watering cans (at *t1*) to it being understood as air cooling off and shedding some of its $H2O$ (at *t2*), in which cases there is something like an aspect shift but not necessarily a transition to authentic understanding. Importantly, the experience of this letting go of an understanding of being is *experienced* as discontinuity and as a falling away rather than the transformation of an existing object. The result is a greater sense of openness to the being of the entities involved, and this openness is itself not a modification of a previously fixed way of taking the being of the entities.

All in all, we have in this section seen that the process of understanding becoming authentic is different in most, if not all, respects from the processes we found in some of the main theories of learning. In Chapter 7 we will consider whether the two accounts are compatible and can be merged so as to provide one account of authentic learning. For now, we have as our first characterization of the process of authentic learning that it involves a moment of becoming pre-reflectively self-aware and letting go of previously established ways of taking the being of the entities involved,

---

9   Other than perhaps in a purely formal sense, if we assume that all awareness is awareness of something and thus has to have a formal object, but this would not invalidate that in the phenomenological sense such pre-reflective self-awareness has no object.

resulting in greater openness to the being of these entities. We saw that this kind of opening up is a reciprocal process, where increased pre-reflective self-awareness makes us let go fixed notions about the being of the entities, while the very process of letting go expands our sense of pre-reflective self-awareness.

Learning to be authentic is, therefore, an iterative process that goes in the opposite direction of the increasing integration and differentiation that builds on the continuity involved in conventional learning. So, if we want the account of authentic learning we are seeking to bring into focus in this book to include a moment of learning to be authentic, we need to include this pre-reflective self-awareness and letting go into our accounts of conventional learning. Where conventional learning is about growth (even if, as was pointed out in Chapter 3, allowance is made for forgetting), authentic learning includes a kind of letting go. Where conventional learning is about modification of existing ways of being, authentic learning includes moments of genuine openness, ones where existing ways of being are let go of. Where conventional learning centres around the subject-object relationship, authentic learning puts a more fundamental pre-reflective sense of awareness at the basis of any subject-object relationship. And where conventional learning is based in processes of association, the letting go of learning to be authentic opens us up to beings in relation to whom no possible kind of association would be able to bring us into contact, such as the examples I have been giving as the origin of experience, those beings who are truly other, and life as a whole.

Authentic attunement

Authentic attunement

The authentic mood of letting the entities be

In Chapter 2 I explained how Heidegger distinguishes three ways in which Dasein is in the world: understanding (both practical and theoretical), attunement, and being-with (the way Dasein is related to other Daseins). Ultimately, Dasein is one, whole, and in this sense its tripartite division is somewhat artificial, even if there is a common-sense plausibility to it, because we do tend to distinguish between, for example, our emotions from our ideas or practical nous from theoretical knowledge. But, as I explained in Chapter 1, whenever we learn something, all these different ways of being-in-the-world play a role, such as when solving a theoretical puzzle still involves certain practical skills (perhaps note-taking) and an emotional dimension as to how we feel about solving the puzzle (even if this feeling is one of indifference). So, as we turn to the way of being-in-the-world that Heidegger calls attunement, we need to bear in mind that it is not strictly separate from the understanding we looked at in the previous chapter or the being-with we will be looking at in the next.

You could perhaps say that understanding, attunement, and being with are three dimensions of any particular moment of learning: whenever there is learning, all three are, at least to some extent, involved. As a result, the authentic mode of each will, in many ways, not be separate from the authentic mode of the others. And this means that there is a certain amount of overlap between the authentic modes. What is more, we will see that the authentic modes support each other, provide the context for each other even. Thus, we will find that pre-reflective self-awareness plays a part in authentic attunement, just as it does in authentic understanding. Openness and letting go are also part of authentic attunement. And it will be easy to see that the openness and pre-reflective self-awareness we find in attunement is in some ways even a precondition for authentic understanding, just as the transparency that is part of authentic understanding supports authentic attunement.

Thus, we will see in this chapter that, in line with what we saw in relation to authentic understanding, the process of coming to find oneself in an authentic mood is one of an increased *pre-reflective self-awareness*. In the case of attunement becoming authentic, we will see that the increase in *pre-reflective self-awareness* is the result of a spreading which starts with "staying with" the beginning of such *pre-reflective self-awareness*. Also in line with authentic understanding, the change involved in attunement becoming authentic is one of moving from experiencing oneself and the entities one encounters in the world in terms of *das Man* to experiencing oneself in terms of oneself and the entities in terms of the nothingness from which the entities emerge. In the case of attunement, the result is the experience of oneself as "transcendence", and of one's relationship with things in the world as one of "letting the entities be", a kind of disconnected openness that allows for immediacy of contact with these entities.

In addition, just as we saw a reciprocal process at the basis of understanding becoming authentic (that of letting go and becoming pre-reflectively self-aware) there is a mutually reinforcing process at the heart of attunement becoming authentic. The mechanism here is that of a reciprocal movement of increased pre-reflective self-awareness of oneself as transcendence and disclosure of the "nothingness" of the world. As we will see, the "nothingness" of the world is linked with the openness to the being of entities we saw in the previous chapter. In this way, there is in attunement becoming authentic the same kind of letting go and openness to the being of entities we saw, in Chapter 1, needs to be part of our notion of learning.

We can thus characterize the importance of authentic attunement, of a mood of pre-reflective self-awareness that is characterised by "letting the entities be" as fourfold. First, attunement becoming authentic is an integral part of the process of learning to be authentic as a whole: authentic attunement brings to awareness the structure of the self; it represents a turning away (disconnecting) from the world; it returns Dasein to the state of being-possible (rather than being absorbed in any *actual* way of finding itself emotionally in the world). Second, attunement becoming authentic entails an openness to the being of entities (living beings as well as material things) at the level of mood and emotion, enabling Dasein to respond adequately to events, because Dasein's experience of itself and the world is not being coloured in advance by a mood that takes it and the things it encounters in any particular way (other than that the *possibility* exists of taking them in certain particular ways). Third, as a mood of "letting the entities be", authentic attunement is pervaded by "a peculiar calm" (Heidegger 1998, 88), which is experienced as having the potential to respond emotionally if necessary, while not identifying with things in the world, so that one does not expend energy responding unnecessarily at an emotional level to what happens, even if one does act practically or theoretically (and this corresponds with authentic understanding not understanding itself in terms of the entities in the world and these entities not in terms of das Man. Fourth, in Chapter 6, we will take this combination of the openness to things as they present themselves, and see how this gives rise to the possibility to respond emotionally in a way that is commensurate with this entity together make possible the emotional experiences of affection, love, and communion in an authentic way.

In the first part of the chapter, I will say a bit more about attunement and give a more practical account of the importance of authentic attunement for the question of learning. In the middle part of the chapter we will look at the nature of authentic attunement in more detail. And in the final sections of the chapter I will construct a notion of attunement learning to be authentic, bringing into focus the process whereby attunement becomes authentic and contrasting this with the kind of conventional learning we looked at in Chapter 3.

The nature of attunement

In Chapter 2 I referred to the "mood" dimension of Dasein's existence, using the word *attunement*, which is a translation of the word "*Befindlichkeit*", the word Heidegger uses and which is sometimes also translated as *state-of-mind* or *sofindingness*. The word *Befindlichkeit*, itself a neologism, comes from the German "finding oneself" in a certain place, situation or emotional state. Thus one may ask, in German, "How are you finding yourself?", which would translate as "How are you doing?", where the notion of "finding oneself" has obvious spatial connotations in terms of being located in a certain place, or one could say, emotional space. The translation "attunement" is based in the fact that mood in German is called "*Stimmung*" which is related to the notion of tuning an instrument and consequently of being in tune with certain things in a certain way.

As we saw in Chapter 2, attunement as mood is not based in a separation between subject and object. Thus, according to Heidegger "[m]ood has already disclosed, in every case, being-in-the-world as a whole, and makes it possible first of all to direct oneself towards something" (Heidegger 1962, 176). This is at once the most important and perhaps most counter-intuitive aspect of a mood, as Heidegger uses the word. A mood, and all other ways in which attunement manifests, is something that permeates the whole of one's experience. In the words of Matthew Ratcliffe, a "mood is not an intentional state directed at either the self or something other than the self and it is not a more encompassing state directed at lots of things." A mood is there *prior to* there being the experience of anything in particular. A mood does not "'colour' some already experienced world. It is what *opens up* a world in the first place; it is through moods that we find ourselves in a world" (Ratcliffe 2008, 48).

The most well-known mood Heidegger describes is that of anxiety (Angst), which we will look at in the next part of this chapter – it is how early Heidegger characterized the mood one is in when authentic. Importantly, in the mood of anxiety there is no separation between the one being anxious and that which they are anxious about. We need to bear in mind here that Heidegger did sometimes attribute the structure of intentionality to anxiety, for example, when he sets out that Dasein is, in anxiety, anxious *about* something as well as anxious in the face of something (the nothingness of the world). Thus at one point Heidegger writes that "Dasein is anxious ... about its ownmost potentiality-for-being," (Heidegger 1962, 321). But at other points Heidegger stresses the absence of a separation between subject and object. And in this I agree with those commentators who have found Heidegger's extension of the structure of intentionality to include attunement contrived. Ratcliffe's (2008) notion of an existential feeling as unitary seems, therefore, more appropriate. To clarify, we can contrast being in a certain mood with having certain feelings *about* something, where the feelings we have *about* something imply a separation between the one having the feelings and the entity we have the feelings about. Being in a certain mood, in contrast, means that one experiences both oneself and the world one finds oneself in as disclosed by this mood. What is more, even a feeling that is directed towards a particular thing, a person, an object, or something like "life itself", is based in attunement as a mode of being that does not separate subject from object. As was explained in Chapter 2, even a feeling that is directed towards a particular entity reveals both oneself (say, as amused) and the entity of is intending (say, as amusing) in a certain light.

Moreover, for Heidegger a basic mood is what makes possible for certain things to come to one's notice rather than other things: "[i]t is a condition of possibility for any specifically directed intentional state" (Ratcliffe 2008, 48). We are familiar with this kind of phenomenon in that we may say that one needs to be in the *right mood* to understand a joke or to be receptive to certain kinds of art; that is, our mood either first makes it possible to hear a joke or be touched by a work of art or we may be brought in the right mood for jokes or art by initially being exposed to "the promise of" a joke or "the promise of" art – something we sometimes call priming. This can then lead to a mutually reinforcing cycle of first being exposed to "the promises of" a joke, to then getting in the mood for jokes, as a result of which one hears the funny side of more things, which increases one's jocular mood, and so on. Thus, we will see in our discussion of the process of attunement learning to be authentic how there too there is such a positive feedback loop (reciprocity) that drives the process of learning to be authentic – just as there is a positive feedback cycle in the process of understanding letting go and becoming pre-reflectively self-aware.

The importance of attunement for the question of learning

To make the question of attunement learning to be authentic more tangible, let us look at an example of how it may play out in learning situations. An example of a basic mood would be that of a learner, let's say an older worker retraining after being made redundant, who generally experiences the world of work as a hostile place, perhaps because previous employers have been exploitative. In such a case the worker *finds* (experiences) *himself*, at a basic level, as being under threat in a world that is potentially hostile. That is, his basic feeling is that of the retraining situation being in some ways threatening, even if this basic feeling is not experienced consciously.

This basic feeling then discloses the retraining setting as inhabited by potentially hostile people, for example the trainers or those who monitor his progress. At the same time, if he is not entirely traumatised, this feeling of threat is counterbalanced by the sense that there are also some people and situations that are safe, like the colleagues he trusts, certain skills and possessions he feels he can fall back on, as well as ways in which he can momentarily escape the unpleasant sense of living in a hostile world, such as focusing of the promise of retirement, or on the weekend when he goes for walks with his granddaughter.

Apart from disclosing the world and the things that fill it in a certain way, this same basic feeling discloses himself as a certain kind of entity, one that is, in this case, essentially vulnerable to exploitation. With this comes the feeling that he needs to look after himself, perhaps build up defences, remain alert to threats, hone his skills of avoidance and attack, and so on. And this mood that belongs to the workplace will in some ways spill over into his sense of life as a whole: he will find the world in some ways both threatening and providing shelter, and himself both vulnerable and to some extent capable of looking after himself. Thus a mood is defined in terms of its possibilities: where threat is a possibility, security also is, where being hurt is a possibility, self-defence also is.

And we see here a link with authentic understanding, where, it was said, authentic Dasein experiences itself as possibility. We can, therefore, see that an authentic mood, which is pre-reflectively self-aware, will disclose itself as having the apriori structure of possibility. Authentic attunement, in this way, discloses that possibility is one of the basic structures of Dasein, in a way that resonates with authentic understanding disclosing itself as possibility.

More practically speaking, there are several ways in which mood, in the way it is used here, is relevant to the question of learning. First, the way of being in the world, of being attuned an individual "picks up" in early life may well persist even if what caused it has disappeared in fact. A tragic example of this phenomenon is that of the child who has been abused and in later life finds it impossible to establish deep, trusting relationships because he or she is stuck in a mood that takes the other human being as a potential abuser, themselves as potentially defenceless to abuse, and the world in general as a place that does not provide protection against abuse from those close to one. This phenomenon is often referred to as "internalisation", where it is believed the circumstances of one's upbringing are internalised, with the result that one structures one's experiences in line with such internalised expectations. And we can see that it can be an important part of learning to dissolve existing moods that are obsolete or dysfunctional so that the learns to open up to the reality of the situations they are in, rather than remain stuck in a mood that was formed earlier and that has become internalized, possibly in an unconscious way. But it is not just in early life that our sense of what kind of place the world is gets shaped – though those are often the deepest and most pervasive ones. To return to our example, even though the actual threats that made the worker feel vulnerable in the first place may have in actual fact disappeared (for example, the retraining setup is genuinely supportive and quite unlike the exploitative work situations that shaped his views on work), the worker may still experience the world as threatening and himself as vulnerable. So in this case too it is important for there to be a letting go of the mood one may have internalized. Here too it is important to be open to the situation.

The second example of the importance of attunement in any kind of learning environment is that of the kind of mood that is conveyed through the learning experience itself, in such a way that the learner adopts it as a more or less permanent one. This is especially relevant for formal educational settings and the overall atmosphere (one could say mood) in which a child grows up. An upbringing that is, for example, pervaded by reward and punishment may well instil in the child, if it is done over a long enough time, a basic sense that "life" punishes or rewards one and that one is oneself subject to such reward and punishment. As a result, the individual's actions may attain a quality of seeking (reward) and avoiding (punishment), where they perceptually structure a situation they enter for the first time in terms of possible reward and punishment, and so on. In formal education we then see this expanded into things like being assessed, competing, being tied to a schedule, deferring to an authoritative figure (the teacher, and later the boss or the priest), being identified with a group (the set), all of which are examples of situational moods that can be instilled into the pupil through education both formal and informal. Such basic moods of the educational experience have been much commented on, for example in discussions of "the hidden curriculum", which point out that some of the deepest influence schooling has on the individual is through aspects of the experience that are not part of the stated curriculum (such as Maths and Science or social and emotional skills), but come with the experience of schooling itself, with its general atmosphere or mood.

So we find that attunement, the basic sense we have of life as a result of (often early) experiences has a lasting effect on the kind of persons we turn out to be: we tend to experience the world as a certain kind of place and ourselves as a certain kind of being, as a result of previous experience. This basic way of being attuned to life in general, and to specific situations in particular, has considerable impact on what can be learned. We also saw that the way learning itself has taken place has just as much an impact on us, because the processes of learning we engage in shape us, affect how we experience the world and ourselves. All this needs to be born in mind, when we want to find a way of learning that is not just about growth and continuity (the moods we internalized early in life restricting any new learning that follows) but also about letting go and opening us (becoming aware of the nature of attunement, so that we can let go of our particular mood and open up to the being of the situation we find ourselves in).

In Chapter 2 we saw how we can make a fundamental distinction between discovery and disclosure: we may discover something (as one possibility among many other given possibilities), and we may disclose something (revealing what kinds of things are possible in the first place). With regard to mood, we would make a similar distinction. On the one hand, one may discover that different moods are possible: thus the victim of abuse may discover that it is possible to trust at least certain adults after all, where before they had experienced real trust only, for example, in the company of animals or when immersed in a novel. This sort of discovery will be important in any healing process, but it is not by itself enough for authentic attunement. Because, and this is the kind of learning we are after in this chapter, the very possibility of mood itself may be disclosed, where this disclosure of mood as such discloses the possibilities of both inauthentic and authentic mood. This will then help the individual being free not only from the particular way of being attuned they tend to find themselves in, but free from all determining ways of being attuned, in such a way that they open up to the very being of the entities they encounter. To return to the example, opening up to the situation they are actually in at the level of attunement will allow the person who in the past suffered abuse, first, let go of the way they tend to feel about themselves and the world and, second, get a sense of the situation they are in that is based in the actual situation, and not in their memory of past experiences. What such a disclosure of authentic attunement involves will become clear in the remainder of this chapter.

Moods of authenticity

Anxiety, boredom, awe, astonishment, and wonder

Before we look at the process of moving from an inauthentic to an authentic mood, we will look in some more depth at Heidegger's description of the mood that comes with authentic existence. This will give us the mood which learning to be authentic should result in. This mood of authenticity has been given different names at different times by Heidegger. In *Being and Time* it is existential angst, usually translated as anxiety, a state where, according to Heidegger, Dasein experiences itself "as it really is", i.e. authentically. It should be noted, though, that other basic moods have been suggested by Heidegger as the defining moods of authentic existence. In the 1929-1930 course *The Fundamental Concepts of Methaphysics* (Heidegger 1995) he singled out boredom (Langeweile). Then, after 1930 "Heidegger became reluctant to identify one fundamental, defining mood; even so, we find that in his later thinking he gave greater attention to 'awe' (*die Scheu*) and 'astonishment' (*das Erstaunen*) in describing the prevailing affective disposition of Dasein's authentic existing, thereby recalling the importance of the mood of "wonder" spoken of long ago by the ancient Greek philosophers" (Capobianco 2007, 1).

It is important to note that Heidegger gave all the concepts that refer to the mood of authenticity their own specific meaning which deviated significantly from their ordinary meaning. For example, with respect to the concept of anxiety, Heidegger writes in *What is Metaphysics?* that "a peculiar calm pervades [anxiety]" (Heidegger 1998, 88), which means that anxiety does not share some of the key characteristics of our common-sense notion of anxiety. Not only is the existential version of anxiety characterized by a notable absence of calm, authentic anxiety is not contradictory to joy.

"Along with the sober anxiety which brings us face to face with [authentic being] there goes an unshakable joy in this possibility" (Heidegger 1962, 358). Also, in the common form of anxiety one is anxious about some, at least in principle, identifiable thing, whereas in the anxiety that is part of authentic existence there is no such determinate thing in the face of which we are anxious. That is, there is "indeterminateness in the face of which and concerning which we become anxious [and this] is no mere lack of determination but rather the essential impossibility of determining it[10]" (Heidegger 1998, 88).

Though over time Heidegger gives different names to this authentic mood, they all have certain common characteristics: they disclose Dasein itself as transcendence, as "encompassing" both self and world; they disclose Dasein as individualized and as nothingness (what this means will be explained presently); they involve both a lack of identification with and an openness towards the things Dasein finds in the world; they disclose Dasein as always being attuned, as things mattering to it, as always being in some kind of mood, and that it can be either inauthentic or authentic in its mood. As has already been suggested, these characteristics of authentic attunement tend to resonate with what we found, when we looked at authentic understanding; there too the subject-object separation was seen to be merely derivative and secondary to a more basic unity; there too authentic Dasein understood itself in essentially negative terms (finitude and facing its own existential death); there Dasein became transparent to its own being as projection and possibility, just as in authentic attunement it discloses itself as always being attuned. To repeat a point made at the beginning of this chapter, as we bring into focus the characteristics of authentic attunement, we need to bear in mind that there is not a clear separation between attunement and other aspects of Dasein, because ultimately Dasein is one and whole.

The authentic mood discloses Dasein as transcendence

As has been indicated, Heidegger believes that "Mood has already disclosed, in every case, being-in-the-world as a whole" (Heidegger 1962, 176). That

---

10 Note that this notion of the impossibility of determining what it is anxiety intends is in line with the notion, mooted earlier, that attunement does not, strictly speaking have an intentional object, but rather stands at the basis of how one experiences both oneself and the world on is in.

is, understood authentically a mood does not only disclose both self and world in a unitary way, thus making it possible for certain kinds of things to be discovered (the meaning of a joke, the artistic merit of a painting), it also discloses being-in-the-world as a unitary entity, one that comprises both self and world. Of course, we may not be aware of the fact that mood discloses being-in-the-world as unitary, because (as we saw in Chapter 4) we are absorbed in the entities that are discovered within the space of being-in-the-world, stuck, as it were, in a sense of subject-object separation. But the fact that we may not notice does not detract from the fact that mood actually discloses the unitary structure of self and world. Dasein itself is this *process* of transcendence, it is "being-in-the-world"[11]. "Transcendence is not instituted by an object coming together with a subject, or a thou with an I, but the Dasein itself, as 'being-a-subject', transcends. The Dasein as such is being-towards-itself, being-with others, and being-among entities handy and extant" (Heidegger 1982, 301). And it is easy to see that authentic Dasein would be (pre-reflectively) aware of this and would not take itself to be a subject that is separate from the objects it engages with, even if it also sees that this subject-object relationship is possible within the wider unity of being-in-the-world. As we saw in Chapter 2, one way of envisaging this notion of Dasein as being-in-the-world (a term that is hyphenated to indicate the unity between self and world) is as openness. This "clearing", this open space where things can manifest, is there prior to there being anything like a subject or an object. This openness is itself transcendence, it is where self and world come together. "Self and world belong together in the single entity" (Heidegger 1982, 297).

Dasein's authentic mood discloses the unitary nature of being-in-the-world to Dasein. But this notion of self and world belonging together goes very much against the common-sense notion of an immanent subject which then needs access to things in the world – giving rise to the question as to how it is possible for an immanent subject to get such access and, ultimately, to scepticism. As we saw in Chapter 3, we also find this subject-object assumed in our conventional learning. But, Heidegger claims, "[e]xactly that which is called immanence in theory of knowledge in a complete inversion of the phenomenal facts, the sphere of the subject, is intrinsically and primarily and alone the transcendent" (Heidegger 1982, 299).

---

11   Note that this does not amount to an Idealist position, as Heidegger denies neither the actual existence of things in the world, nor the possibility of Dasein to have access to such things.

As already indicated, the idea is not that we always experience the unitary nature of our relationship with entities but that the authentic way of being in the world discloses it. And because Dasein is in many ways its self-understanding, the moment it feels itself to be openness and transcendence, it becomes this openness to the world. That is, there is in the authentic mode no difference between understanding, attunement, and being-with on the one hand, and being on the other hand. When Dasein understands itself as openness in a way that is authentic (and not, say, merely theoretical) it becomes this openness. And when Dasein is in a mood of anxiety, astonishment, or wonder, the feeling of there not being a separation between subject and object dissolves this separation. You could say, going back to one of our characterizations of becoming authentic in Chapter 2, that Dasein *awakens* to itself as being-in-the-world. But this awakening happens at the experiential level, which means that the individual body will still be the same biological, self-contained organism it was before. Still, though at the bodily level not much may have changed, the way in which authentic Dasein is in the world will have shifted significantly.

Importantly, the change from understanding oneself as a separate subject in relation to intentional objects to understanding oneself and the objects one is in relation with as unitary is not one that can come about through the kind of conventional learning we looked at in Chapter 3. This is because conventional learning presumes there to be a subject-object separation, as well as subsequent states of the learner being in important ways defined by the initial state of the learner. And this means that conventional learning cannot account for going from a mode where there is a subject-object separation to one where this separation has been dissolved, because the authentic unitary state is incompatible with the subject-object separation in which conventional learning is based. So, if we want to account for the possibility of going from inauthentic to authentic attunement, a different notion of learning is needed.

Authenticity disclosing Dasein as individualized and existing in nothingness

The mood of authenticity discloses Dasein not only as essentially inseparable from the world. It also discloses Dasein (to) itself as it is *in itself*, prior to any involvement it has in *das Man*. Authentic attunement discloses

Dasein, in Heidegger's terminology, as individualized. And it discloses the nothingness that accompanies Dasein: in the mood of authenticity the human being "is brought before the nothing itself" (Heidegger 1998, 88). In line with what I wrote earlier in this chapter about the overlap with authentic understanding, we find in authentic attunement echoes of what in relation to authentic understanding was called Dasein's being towards death (having come face to face with its own finitude), as well as Dasein understanding itself from out of itself and not in terms of *das Man*. In the context of authentic attunement, Heidegger characterises this notion of Dasein *in itself* and *in relation to nothingness* with the concept of *thrown projection*. Thus, authentic Dasein experiences itself as *thrown projection*.

On the one hand, authentic Dasein experiences itself as "thrown", as finding itself in a world (parents, siblings, a place in which it lives, a language it speaks, norms it is required to follow, and so on) that predates it, with its own way of being-in-the-world (things it likes and dislikes, talents and weaknesses, a temperament, and so on) that predates even its awareness of itself as being-in-the-world. So, in the mood of authenticity Dasein experiences itself as not being anything more basic than the way of being-in-the-world it has been thrown into. One could say that, in terms of being a something, Dasein finds that any "something" it is is purely a function of the way of being-in-the-world it has found itself inhabiting, without there being a basis *in Dasein itself* for these. To return to the notion we looked at in Chapter 2 of becoming authentic in terms of "bringing oneself back from lostness in *das Man*" (Heidegger 1962, 312-313), one could say that Dasein finds that it is lost in *das Man* (it finds itself with a way of being-in-the-world that has been appropriated from *das Man* and in a world which is not of its own making) and that apart from *das Man* it is not a "something", but rather openness, a "nothing". This being a nothing, which finds itself with a way of being-in-the-world and in a world, both of which are not of its own making, constitutes Dasein's thrownness.

On the other hand, authentic Dasein experiences itself as projection. It finds that it "exists as thrown Being towards its end" (Heidegger 1962, 295). We saw in Chapter 4 how Dasein's understanding is always based in projection, of the being of entities and ultimately of itself. We also saw that authentic Dasein experiences itself as "thrown towards its end", as irreducibly finite, to the extent that its very being becomes defined by this finitude. Authentic Dasein is, therefore, always face to face with its own existential death, in Heidegger's terms "the possibility of the impossibility of all possibilities". And, just as authentic understanding involves an awareness of the nothingness of death, the mood of authenticity "puts Dasein's being-in-the-world face to face with the 'nothing' of the world" (Heidegger 1962, 321).

The upshot of this is that Dasein experiences itself, in the mood of authenticity, as having nothing substantial to either fall back on (it has no basis in itself) or project itself onto (its own existence is defined by its nothingness). This means that Dasein has to ultimately understand itself as possibility (it is nothing substantial) and as process (temporality) in relation to nothingness, if it wishes to understand itself in terms of itself rather than in terms of *das Man*. Dasein in the mood of authenticity is a Dasein that is denuded of the sense of being something in terms of *das Man*, living in a world that is also no longer understood in terms of *das Man*.

This sense of itself as nothing substantial in a world that is, likewise, characterized by nothingness makes sense in the context of understanding the process of becoming authentic is one of "bringing oneself back from lostness in *das Man*" (Heidegger 1962, 312-313). It is what in Chapter 2 we called the moment of "giving itself up", of "turning away from the world", and brings into focus that the process of letting go we have already seen plays an important role in understanding becoming authentic is equally important here. Again, such coming into contact with the nothingness of oneself and the world is not something that can happen through conventional learning, because, as we have seen, conventional learning contains a sense of continuity and growth and is, in that sense, incapable of bringing the learner to the kind of existential nothingness that characterizes authentic Dasein.

Authentic mood as non-identification and nearness

The idea that authentic attunement "makes manifest the nothing" (Heidegger 1998, 88) means that Dasein experiences itself as individualized and as existing in the nothingness of the world. This experience is sometimes referred to with the word "uncanniness", which is the translation of the German *Unheimlichkeit*, which literally translates as "not-at-home-ness", in that the root of the word, *Heim*, means home. We can see how the meaning of uncanny as "uncomfortably strange or unfamiliar" (SOED 2007) fits with the idea of feeling "not at home" - and this is the pun Heidegger is playing on. Another way Heidegger has of describing this feeling of uncanniness is that of Dasein's experience of itself "as the 'not-at-home' – the bare 'that-it-is' in the 'nothing' of the world" (Heidegger 1962, 321). This corresponds with the notions I discussed in the previous section of Dasein experiencing itself as individualized, in terms of itself (the "bare 'that it is'") and in relation to nothingness (the "'nothing' of the world").

We see how this uncanniness distances the mood of authentic existence from the moods, described in the examples in the first part of this chapter, of, for example, feeling under threat in a potentially hostile world or feeling curious in a world full of things to discover. What the mood of authenticity does is not disclose Dasein as a certain kind of Dasein (for example, being potentially under threat or as the potential discoverer things), but as possibility itself, as something that has the possibility to be affected by mood, where it is the possibility that is the essential characteristic of Dasein, in a way that is more basic than any particular way of being affected. That is, "anxiety discloses Dasein as being-possible, and indeed as the only kind of thing which it can be of its own accord as something individualised in individualisation" (Heidegger 1962, 143). And as we have seen, the mood of authenticity does not disclose the world as a certain kind of world, but as the nothingness, the emptiness, out of which a particular way of being of the entities in that world may emerge. This then, can be said to involve a certain lack of identification with the entities authentic Dasein encounters in the world.

But, apart from this lack of identification with things, where "being affected" emotionally (in terms of a mood) is a possibility but not yet actual, we also find that the mood of authenticity involves a new kind of openness to oneself and things in the world. As Heidegger puts it in *What is Metaphysics?*, "All things and we ourselves sink into indifference. This, however, not in the sense of mere disappearance. Rather, in their very receding, things turn towards us" (Heidegger 1998, 88). Thus we have a combination of non-identification and "things turning towards us". Michael Zimmerman describes this new-found openness to things as one which "allows things and other humans to manifest themselves in more complex, complete, and novel ways, rather than as mere objects or instruments for our ends" (Zimmerman 1993, 245). Thus we have a mood that is characterised by non-identification as well as by a closeness to things. Importantly, such a non-identification is not a separation but an openness to what the things are in themselves, to the being of the entities.

If we now return to some of the concepts that in Heidegger's later philosophy stand for "the prevailing affective disposition of Dasein's authentic existing" (Capobianco 2007, 1), we find the same dual movement of non-identification and openness. In the 1955 lectures *What is Philosophy?*, Heidegger uses the word astonishment: "In astonishment, we hold ourselves back (*être en arrêt*). We step back, as it were, from beings, [astonished] that they are rather than are not [where this stepping back] is at the same time enraptured by and, as it were, held fast by that from which it steps back" (Heidegger 1958, 85, cited in Capobianco 2007). We find here a reference to the issue raised earlier that conventional learning cannot bring us any nearer to life as a whole, because life as a whole is unlike any particular thing we find in the world. The notion of astonishment in relation to beings, astonished that beings "are rather than are no" is exactly such a mode of being in which we come into contact with the bare existence of life itself. Astonishment can bring us into contact with life itself, just because it allows life itself to come to it from out of the nothingness of the world.

And again, writing about awe, in his *Elucidations of Hölderlin's Poetry* of 1943, Heidegger writes about "holding oneself back" and a nearness: "As this primordially firm holding oneself back (*Ansichhalten*) before what is awesome, awe has at the same time the most intimate affection for it ... Awe is that reserved, patient, astonished remembrance of that which abides near in a nearness that consists solely in keeping what is distant in its fullness distant, and thereby keeping it ready for its welling-up emergence from its source" (Heidegger 2000, 153, cited in Capobianco 2007). Here we have a kind of relating that does not take that which we are relating to as an object of use or theoretical reflection but takes it "as it is in itself", something which we saw in Chapter 3 conventional learning cannot do, because it is always based in an initial understanding of the entity and works by way of association, whereas what is disclosed in authentic attunement cannot be associated with anything other than itself.

But there is, I believe, a limitation to this notion of non-identification and nearness. Authentic attunement as a way of being-in-the-world where Dasein has been individualized and experiences the entities it encounters in the world in this mood of non-identification and nearness seems to make sense in relation to practical and theoretical entities: as Dasein no longer projects an understanding of being onto these entities (because it experiences itself in terms of itself and no longer out of the entities it encounters in the world) these entities appear both detached (they are no longer understood from out of Dasein's self-understanding) and near (they are no longer mediated by *das Man*). So we can, indeed, see how this mood of authenticity would be a constituent part of having "being open to the being of entities" I said in Chapter 1 would need to be part of a process of authentic learning. But, as we will see in the next section, the notion of non-identification can easily become one that emphasizes detachment and distance, and in that sense seems to fall short when it comes to our relationships with other Daseins.

The limitation of Heidegger's notion of authentic attunement

One limitation of the description of authentic attunement so far seems to arise when Dasein encounters another Dasein. As this other Dasein is not understood from out of Dasein's self-understanding or mediated by *das Man*, it will appear as it is in itself. But, as we will see in Chapter 6, the other Dasein that is encountered by Dasein is not disconnected from this Dasein. The basic faculty of being-with entails that the communal (any group which Dasein is part of) as well as the interpersonal (the other Dasein that is encountered) are co-constitutive of this Dasein. It is, therefore, possibly incoherent to talk about the mood of authenticity disclosing *everything* as disconnected or detached. Practical and theoretical entities may well appear thus, but how their being is understood is, as we saw in Chapter 4, dependent on Dasein's projection of an understanding of being. This is not the case with another Dasein, who is disclosed to authentic Dasein as existing for its own sake, in terms of itself, and, therefore, not in terms of an understanding of being that is projected by another Dasein, even an authentic Dasein.

There is another way of putting this, which is to say that authentic attunement is a much impoverished one, if the feelings and emotions it brought were to remain restricted to things such as anxiety, astonishment, boredom, awe and wonder, even in their Heideggerian sense of including a sense of calm and joy. One would expect and hope for more human emotions, at least in relation to other Daseins, such as affection and love. In the next chapter I will attempt to rectify this shortcoming in Heidegger's account, by establishing what affective dispositions could be part of authentic being-with, and, as such, be appropriate ones to appear as part of authentic attunement.

Bearing this promissory note in mind, with the characterisation of "the prevailing affective disposition of Dasein's authentic existing" as *non-identification* and *nearness* we have returned in many ways to the idea of Dasein as openness. This is the idea that Dasein has the possibility of being directly affected by something that is other than it, without it being mediated through *das Man* and without it being assimilated into what the individual already knows (as we saw in Chapter 4, authentic understanding keeps it self open to the being of entities and does not restrict its current understanding to a previously established one). In the basic mood of authenticity, of anxiety, astonishment or awe, Dasein experiences itself as transcendence (based in pre-reflective self-awareness), where this transcendence means that Dasein finds itself in a world that predates it and with a way of being-in-the-world that is not of its own making, and where its understanding of the things in the world is one it itself projects and which can be authentic if the projection happens in terms of its own finitude. Authentic Dasein does not feel connected to itself or things in the world in a way that is based in a connection from out of *das Man*. Rather, "things turn towards" Dasein, it is "enraptured by" and "held fast by" these things. These things are "near" to Dasein in their distance. Dasein is "ready for [their] welling-up emergence from [their] source". And they do so as arising within the transcendence of being-in-the-world, where Dasein is experienced as individualized (though, as indicated, it is also in an, as yet, unspecified way connected with other Dasein's) and the entities that it encounters in the world are experienced as arising in the nothingness of the world.

Attunement learning to be authentic

Learning to be authentic happens at the level of pre-reflective self-awareness

The nature of the process that leads to the kind of authentic attunement described above is one that happens at the level of *pre-reflective self-awareness*. Contrary to most terms used in our discussion of the mood of authenticity, this notion of *pre-reflective self-awareness* is not one Heidegger himself used, but it is helpful in constructing an account of attunement learning to be authentic. Such a pre-reflective self-awareness is akin to kinaesthetic or proprioceptive awareness in that there is no reflective sense-perception of oneself as such, as from a distance, but rather an awareness of oneself from the inside, as when, in kinesthesis, the sensory nerves in the muscles themselves are aware of the movement one makes when one moves. But, whereas kinaesthetic awareness is located firmly within the individual's body, the pre-reflective self-awareness that comes with the mood of the individual spans being-in-the-world as a whole, because, as we saw earlier, one's mood discloses both *oneself* and *the world* in a particular way. Thus, Dan Zahavi writes, in relation to a discussion of Heidegger's notion of attunement, that "Heidegger did, in fact, operate with a form of self-acquaintance [self-awareness] that precedes reflection", where "no self-acquaintance can occur independently of, or prior to, our world-disclosure" just as "this world-disclosure ... cannot occur independently of or prior to a disclosure of self" (Zahavi 2005, 84-85).

Note how these remarks pertain to the whole of the being-in-the-world, i.e. also to being-with (see Chapter 6) and understanding (see Chapter 4). Indeed, we already saw in the previous chapter that the transparency that goes with authentic understanding is a kind of pre-reflective awareness of oneself as a being that understands by way of projection. And a similar kind of pre-reflective self-awareness applies to attunement as more akin to proprioceptive or kinaesthetic awareness than to the kind of "sight" that characterizes transparency.

That authentic attunement involves a kind of pre-reflective self-awareness is in itself not surprising, if we consider that moods and emotions are generally experienced in such a pre-reflective way. The way we experience moods and emotions is primarily not by taking a third-person perspective on them, but by simply feeling them. Just as we saw in Chapter 4 that we do not have to "take a step back from ourselves" to know what we are doing (reading or fixing a door), we do not have to envisage ourselves getting red in the face to know that we feel embarrassment (though sometimes a physical sign may alert us to an emotion we be having without noticing it). And, indeed, moods and emotions are often experienced as physical, as when being in a good mood may be located in the pit of the stomach or love in the heart. So, if we are looking for a process that leads to Dasein experiencing itself as having the *possibility* of being attuned (the *possibility* of having a certain mood and emotional disposition) and we want to conceive of that process in terms of attunement itself, we are, in effect, looking for a process that happens *at the level of* pre-reflective awareness.

Inauthentic Dasein is absorbed in *das Man* and, as such, not fully aware of the primordial *pre-reflective self-awareness* that lies at the basis of its moods, because it is absorbed in a mood that colours both it and the entities it encounters in the world. But authentic Dasein is aware (at the level of pre-reflective self-awareness) of the pre-reflective self-awareness that attunes it to itself and the world. This brings us back to the notion, discussed in Chapter 2, of the process of becoming authentic as one of "becoming who one already is", in that becoming authentic consists of beginning to experience oneself as being *pre-reflectively self-aware* and to live accordingly. And this growth in awareness needs to happen within pre-reflective self-awareness itself: you could say that pre-reflective self-awareness itself needs to become pre-reflectively self-aware.

As I explained earlier in this Chapter, when Dasein gives up its absorption in the things in the world, it finds itself in the mood of non-identification and nearness (anxiety, awe or astonishment), which is open to being affected by the things it finds in the world. So, what needs to be brought into view in the process of attunement learning to be authentic is that of a change *away from* the individual being in a mood that connects him or her with the world in a particular way *into the direction of* the individual being in a mood that is characterised by both a sense of non-identification and of openness towards things in the world, where the things are "let be" and the self is disclosed in terms of itself only. And the way of coming to this pre-reflective self-awareness of oneself as open to being affected by things in the world needs to happen at the level of pre-reflective self-awareness itself.

The process of attunement learning to become authentic

Now that we have seen that the process of attunement learning to be authentic happens at the level of pre-reflective awareness itself, we can turn to the process itself. As we saw earlier, one always finds oneself in some mood or other, so the question of learning to be in the mood of authenticity becomes one of going from the mood one finds oneself in (say, being driven to achieve), to the mood of non-identification and nearness, of authenticity. This mood one already finds oneself in discloses oneself and the world in a certain way (in our example, one experiences oneself as badly needing to be fulfilled by some achievement and the world as a field of potential opportunities for achievement as well as failure). We could say that going from such a mood of "needing to achieve" to one of authenticity is a matter of replacing the first with the latter, but that would be a change at the level of what in Chapter 2 I called discovery rather than disclosure. In other words, the change we are after cannot be based in either taking the new mood over from the society one lives in or retrieving the mood from memory (which would constitute a form of continuation). The new mood needs to be found in and of itself, and it needs to be found within the existing, inauthentic mood, because in becoming authentic, we become "what we already are".

The solution to question of how we can become "what we already are" lies in the fact that all moods already contain a level of *pre-reflective awareness*. We are always to some extent aware of the mood we are in, in a pre-reflective way, even if this awareness is minimal or merely implicit. As we saw earlier, we do not need to reflect on ourselves to know, for example, that we feel optimistic (experience ourselves as having plenty of positive opportunities and the world as a place where such opportunities exist). That is, even the inauthentic mood contains a degree of pre-reflective self-awareness; and it is this that provides the starting point for the process of attunement becoming authentic.

But authentic pre-reflective self-awareness is not only aware of the particular mood it is in, but of the very possibility of being in a mood. What is more, this pre-reflective self-awareness of the possibility of being in a mood is characterised by a lack of absorption in either one's particular way of being-in-the-world or the world as it is given in *das Man*. So the first thing is to have a *pre-reflective self-awareness* of the very predisposition to get absorbed in one's way of being-in-the-world and in the world as given in *das Man*. And because every mood we are in (authentic or inauthentic) contains this *pre-reflective self-awareness*, we can take the awareness of it to be already there *potentially* in any mood one may have. In other words, the ability to be affected, to feel oneself to be an individual in a world that affects one, is there in every mood we are in – whether we are aware of it or not.

The direction of change is one going from being affected in actual fact to being aware of the possibility of being affected that underlies ever particular way of being affected. Importantly, it is in this the possibility of being affected that is essential to Dasein, that makes up the being it really is, its authentic being. So, if one now allowed what was *inessential* about the mood one was in to fall away, the result would be a pre-reflective awareness of the capacity to be affected by the world at the level of attunement. That which is inessential about the mood is that part of it which is given by *das Man*, so we come to ourselves as we are from out of ourselves by letting go of that aspect of the mood that is given by *das Man*. What is left, after we have let go of what is given by *das Man* is the possibility of being absorbed by *das Man* in the first place as well as the possibility of being affected by things in the world. This then gives then the direction of the change we need: a shift from being absorbed in an inauthentic mood to being pre-reflectively aware of the possibility of being absorbed.

Such a move from a *pre-reflective awareness* of the inauthentic mood one is in to a *pre-reflective self-awareness* of the possibility of getting absorbed would involve allowing both the moods of authentic existence and the inauthentic moods to exist. One would become aware of one's mood as mood, without getting absorbed in oneself or the things in the world that get co-disclosed in the mood. But this would not happen as a process of exclusion of awareness of oneself or the things in the world, but rather as a process of becoming *pre-reflective self-aware* of the mood as it discloses oneself and the world. One becomes aware of the mood as mood, of the mood as disclosive, and as oneself as possibly affected. But one does so in a way that does not try to change the way the self and the world are given by the inauthentic mood, because such a change would merely bring a different mood and not disclose the possibility of mood itself at the level of the apriori.

First, there is the pre-reflective self-awareness a) of oneself and the world as given in a certain way in the mood one is in b) of being focussed on something in such a mood, c) of responding to what one is focussed on as coloured through the mood. At this point one is still absorbed in *das Man*, in things in the world, but this state of absorption is becoming self-aware in a pre-reflective way, without, as yet, quite reaching a total self-awareness. Importantly, there is at this point no movement away from the mood one is in, there is a "staying with" the mood that is similar to the unconditional acceptance of "how one finds oneself" promoted in some humanistic psychotherapy as the first importance step in the therapeutic process. The mood is, as it were becoming pre-reflectively self-aware of itself. And because the mood itself consists of pre-reflective self-awareness, you could even say that pre-reflective self-awareness is becoming pre-reflectively self-aware of itself.

If we now look at the way pre-reflective self-awareness is experienced, when it is experienced as it is in itself (which it does, in so far as it experiences itself and is not experienced, say by a separate thinker reflecting on it or making representations in language or ideas of it), we find that pre-reflective self-awareness experiences itself as a totality. This means that, second, there is the feeling of the *totality* of the mood, which, at this point, co-discloses the emptiness around the particular mood ("the nothing") one is in, even as the mood encompasses both the self and the world as disclosed by the mood. That is, pre-reflective self-awareness experiences the totality of itself, but because the inauthentic mood is only one of many possible moods, it is experienced as surrounded by that which is not this particular mood – and this Heidegger calls nothingness.

This nothingness can be experienced as empty, but also as mere possibility, and it is accompanied by feelings of longing and curiosity[12] for the otherness of the entities residing in the emptiness, and by feelings of urgency in the face of the possibility of becoming determined once more by a world and self-defining mood. In other words, to the extent that the self-awareness spreads to the point of becoming self-aware of the totality of one's being-in-the-world, it begins to co-disclose the emptiness around itself as emptiness in terms of mood, but, at the same time, as containing things that one can possibly be in contact with in a way that is more direct and revealing than the contact one may have with these entities through a mood that colours them in a certain way (as potentially threatening or discoverable, to take two earlier examples). As Heidegger sometimes put it, one becomes aware of the possibility of nearness, of being "enraptured by" and "held fast by" these entities, as one finds them in the nothingness surrounding the inauthentic mood.

Thus, this pre-reflective disclosure of emptiness co-discloses a longing and curiosity for immediate contact with these entities, which needs to be a kind of longing that one has of oneself if it is to be authentic, one that is not instrumental to fulfilling any other need than the contact with what

---

12 Note that the way curiosity is used here is different from the way Heidegger uses it in *Being and Time*, in relation to *das Man*. The way the word is used here lacks the negative connotations of Heidegger's use of the word.

is other. This sense of longing and curiosity is like the "the essential *openness to values* and *primary love of meaning* of the personally existing being" (Heidegger 2004, 250) we encountered earlier. There is, at this point, also a sense that it is "now or never" in terms of the possibility of establishing such contact, because the process of absorption, where world and self are experienced in terms of each other, is still there, co-given with the emptiness and the otherness of things. This longing and curiosity together with the sense of urgency provide a motivation for Dasein to "stay with" what is currently given in the mood.

Third, as one is "staying with" the inauthentic mood one is in, while the emptiness surrounding it is being disclosed and some of the entities hiding in this emptiness are beginning to emerge, there is the *letting go* of the inauthentic mood one was in, in response to the feelings of urgency, longing and curiosity. As one's pre-reflective self-awareness discloses oneself and the world as consisting of the unity of being-in-the-world, as defined by the possibilities given by the mood one is in, and as the emptiness surrounding this being-in-the-world is co-disclosed, the longing for and curiosity about the entities that are beginning to emerge from within this emptiness serve to enhance one's awareness of oneself as being-in-the-world and as (in part) defined by one's inauthentic mood.

This is a reciprocal illuminating of, on the one hand, the emptiness with its emerging possibilities and, on the other hand, the inauthentic mood as colouring being-in-the-world. And this reciprocal illuminating of mood and emptiness exposes the mood as finite, as based in *das Man* and continuity (previous experience), while one is drawn towards the emptiness, towards leaving the mood behind, as it were, moved by the "primary love of meaning" that is part of Dasein's openness. There is a sense in this of being attracted by the openness that promises a more direct contact with the entities one finds in the world. The directness consists in, on the one hand, a sense of being disconnected (in the sense of not understanding oneself from out of the things or the things from out of oneself) and, on the other hand, a sense of being near to the things (in the sense that *das Man* no longer mediates the relationship).

As I explained in Chapter 1, it is the movement itself of opening up and becoming pre-reflectively aware that we are primarily interested in. this movement, I argued, ought to be part of our concept of learning, because true learning contains such a dimension of letting go of one's existing ways of relating to the object. We are not so much focused on the completion of this movement, but on the processes even where these turn out to be incomplete. So, we find here the reciprocal illumination of the mood and the emptiness that surrounds it, which moves one to leave one's existing inauthentic mood behind, without committing to another mood, but staying with the openness that is essential to Dasein. This process of becoming aware and letting go may well not lead one to complete openness, but even if less than complete, the opening up can make the difference between being stuck in old patterns of experiencing oneself and the world and being open to the newness of both one's own being and the situation one is in.

But, though the completion of the movement of becoming authentic is not of prime importance, complete authenticity does give us the direction of change we are looking for. That is, to the extent that the openness is complete, there is the experience of oneself in terms of oneself and the emergence of entities from out of this emptiness also in terms of themselves. To the extent that one allows the mood one was in to dissolve, there is still the experience of oneself as *capable* of having a mood, as having the possibility to experience oneself and the world in terms of a mood, and as having being-in-the-world permeated by a mood. The possibility of having being-in-the-world permeated by an inauthentic mood and of connecting to the world through *das Man*, is always there, as it needs to be for one to be able to respond to situations that may require to be defined in terms of mood. There is always the *possibility* of, what in Chapter 1 I called "turning back to the world", even if in the moment of disconnection and openness there is as such no defining mood. So, attunement becoming authentic is a change in the direction of a mood where one is experienced in terms of oneself rather than the world, and where things in the world are experienced in one's essential openness, because *das Man* is not mediating the experience, while at the same time an inauthentic mood is present as possibility, because the possibility of "turning back to the world" is always there.

The movement of learning associated with this kind of awareness is one where the pre-reflective self-awareness that was always already part of one's inauthentic mood grows in intensity until it permeates the whole of one's being-in-the-world. Unlike a growth in intensity of an emotion, such as anger or affection, the intensification of authentic attunement does not originate from the individual. The sense of non-identification and nearness does not become more intense "in the person"; just like "night falls" or "silence descends" authentic attunement grows in intensity in being-in-the-world itself. It is, therefore, not a change that is tied to any particular centre, but a unitary change that always concerns the whole of experience. This growth in intensity is one of reciprocation: the pre-reflective self-awareness that is already there in any mood becomes more intense as a result of experiencing oneself as in certain ways individualized and the world as in certain ways detached and near, which discloses some of the emptiness that surrounds things that are detached and near, which in turn intensifies the mood's pre-reflective self-awareness, which then co-discloses more of the emptiness around the mood, and so on.

Note that at any point either a communicative element, in terms of authentic being-with (Chapter 6), or an element of understanding (Chapter 4) may affect these processes of reciprocation and spreading. This is due to the essentially unitary nature of Dasein and of the process of becoming authentic. But in this chapter we have been trying to get into focus the way in which attunement itself learns to be authentic or, as I put it earlier, the way in which pre-reflective self-awareness becomes pre-reflectively self-aware from out of itself.

Relation to theories of conventional learning

If we now briefly revisit the notion of learning as modification and growth we looked at in Chapter 3, we can see that the process of attunement learning to be authentic is in almost all respects different. As we saw, for the currently dominant theories of learning, learning is a process of growth, increased integration and differentiation, which tends towards increased stability, even rigidity, where learning is always a modification of the existing way of being of the learner, which involves an intentional object, with there being a separation between the subject and the object.

The first clear difference is that when attunement becomes authentic, the process is not one that happens in the subject-object relationship, because the mood that becomes authentic is unitary, in that it affects subject and object at the same time. What changes is not the relationship between subject and object but being-in-the-world as a whole. It is a change from one's mood being coloured in a specific (inauthentic) way to it being one where one experiences oneself as capable of being affected and the world as capable of being coloured by a mood. In this way, attunement becoming authentic discloses the authentic nature of attunement, and in doing so discloses to Dasein the possibility of becoming authentically attuned, in a way that is, as it were, at right-angles to the subject-object relationship.

We did see, however, that there is a kind of continuity when attunement becomes authentic, because the pre-reflective self-awareness that is there in every mood is still essential to authentic attunement. But when it comes to the actual mood one is in, it does not become modified in the more usual sense of being coloured differently. For example, a mood of wishing to be liked is not replaced by one that wishes to be admired or one that disregards the opinions of others. Rather, there is a dissolution of the existing mood, which does not lead to indifference in the sense of no longer being able to be affected, but rather to a new-found openness, where no specific way of being attuned has manifested, but which is and remains open to it. This is a kind of emptying out of the mood, which results in openness and the ability to be affected. So while there is continued pre-reflective self-awareness, there is a qualitative difference regarding the content of the mood.

We saw in Chapter 3 that *learning as modification and growth* tends to involve processes of association. But when attunement becomes authentic, this is not based in association, because the authentic mood is not associated with the inauthentic one. There is a dissolution of the inauthentic mood rather than its replacement with one that is associated with it. This dissolution comes as a result of a growing pre-reflective self-awareness and a letting go of the existing mood. But this process of letting go is not driven by association, in the way a mood of wanting to be liked is, for example, associated with one of being afraid of being disliked. It comes from within, from a growing sense of pre-reflective self-awareness becoming pre-reflectively aware of itself. In this way, becoming authentically attuned is qualitatively different from any form of being inauthentically attuned, because it is a return to the possibility of any and all ways of being attuned.

Where in the conventional accounts of learning there is growth, becoming authentically attuned is a process of intensification rather than integration and differentiation. This intensification of one's pre-reflective self-awareness is not something that is differentiated or integrated, because pre-reflective self-awareness is unitary. Authentic attunement's intensification has no distinct centre or parts, it encompasses both self and world. But this intensification is not tied to any particular way of being in the world, and as such there is no continuity of being in the world, but a moment-to-moment sense of being affected, of being open to entities that one does not identify with, even as one senses their presence as near.

Finally, when attunement becomes authentic, there is not an increase in stability, in the sense of the response to events becoming ever more predictable. In learning as modification and growth this predictability is associated with reliability and accompanied by increased integration and differentiation, which allows for more refined and subtle responses as it is perfected, as it becomes more stable, because experience will have consolidated those responses that were found to be more appropriate. This stability and predictability is in many ways the hallmark of expertise, and its importance in the realm of learning as modification and growth is well-established. But it is being argued that, apart from such notions of learning as leading to increased expertise we need a notion of learning as opening up to the being of entities. And here we find another kind of stability, which is not associated with predictability (with the same inputs leading to the same outcomes). The openness that comes with authentic attunement is, if anything, less predictable than when a person associates certain events with certain moods in an ever more stable way, which would happen as a result of conventional learning. When attunement becomes authentic, the situation is allowed to reveal itself in a way that is not based in previous situations: there is an openness to the entities that present themselves, because the way they appear in awareness is not coloured by any particular mood. At the same time, authentic attunement is not unstable in the way a person with, say, a mood disorder would respond to events in ways that are bizarre or erratic. As Heidegger writes, authentic attunement comes with a certain calm, where the openness one finds oneself in allows one to respond to events in a way that is not prefigured by an existing mood or a disposition to respond in particular ways. The openness of authentic attunement is, therefore, not stable in the sense of being predictable or following patterns that have been learned through experience, but stable in the sense of coming from out of a real connection with the entities. We, therefore, see again that the process of becoming authentic is qualitatively different from the process of *learning as modification and growth* that characterizes conventional accounts of learning.

Authentic being-with

Heidegger's account of authentic being-with

Heidegger's account of being-with

Being-with designates that the Dasein who is encountered by another Dasein "is there with them" (Heidegger 1962, 160). Dasein is being-in-the-world (transcendence) and "the world is always the one that [Dasein] share[s] with others" (Heidegger 1962, 155), which means that Dasein's world is a "with-world" (Heidegger 1962, 155) and that "being-with is an existential constituent of being-in-the-world" (Heidegger 1962, 163). Being-with is, therefore, a constituent part of Dasein itself: "So far as Dasein is at all, it has being-with-one-another as its kind of being" (Heidegger 1962, 163). In so far as learning happens in the context of parenting, education, or more generally in collaboration with others, it is in many ways the most important of Dasein's three basic faculties, because it represents the interpersonal and communal dimension of human life, and it is in this dimension that most complex learning is rooted.

As we will see later in this chapter, Being-with is the basis of what Heidegger calls discourse (*die Rede*). Indeed, Heidegger himself usually takes discourse rather than being-with as one of the basic faculties of Dasein (together with understanding and attunement): "*Discourse is existentially equiprimordial with [attunement] and understanding*" (Heidegger 1962, 204).

The reason I am taking being-with rather than discourse as the third basic faculty of Dasein is that in Dasein's authentic mode discourse becomes "silent", and it is difficult to see how this can be articulated in a coherent, positive way. In this chapter I hope to construct a positive account of authentic being-with, where we will on three passages in *Being and Time* in particular: Heidegger's account of being-with in § 26, his account of the authentic community in § 74, and his account of the "call of conscience" in Division Two, Chapter II.

We will begin this chapter by looking at Heidegger's account of being-with in general. Then we will look at ways to conceive of authentic being-with and find that these tend to remain unsatisfactory. We will then look in detail at the notion of the "call of conscience" and at the process of "hearing the call of conscience" as it interrupts Dasein's absorption in *das Man*. Here we find a number of indications as to the kind of learning that could lead to authentic being-with, in that the call of conscience *shows* Dasein the possibility of authentic existence, *appeals* to Dasein to become authentic, *summons* it to being authentic, and *calls it forward* into authentic existence. Though the call of conscience does not in itself give us an account of learning, it gives important indications, on the basis of which I will attempt to construct an account of the actual learning involved in being-with becoming authentic. I will characterise this process of learning in terms of a change from experiencing others in terms of *separateness* and *actuality* to experiencing them in terms of *oneness* and *possibility*; the process involved in this change will be characterized as one of becoming silent, where the beginning of this process is one of spreading as "opening up" and "falling away".

This construction of a coherent account of being-with becoming authentic will be more complex than the notions of understanding and attunement becoming authentic. This is mostly due to the fact that there are a number of holes in Heidegger's discussion of being-with. It is also, as already indicated, because learning happens, more often than not, in relationship with others: caregivers, teachers, or peers. And even where there is learning that the learner does by him or herself, they often invoke language or some other discursive practice to assist them in the learning and these, we will see, are also thought to be rooted in being-with. Finally, learning to be with others in a way that is authentic is also something we would want to engage in for its own sake, because it is by all accounts important to relate to other humans in a way that is open to the being of these others. Being-with learning to be authentic is, therefore, not only important because it is an integral part of becoming authentic, but also in itself, as a way of learning to relate in the right way to others.

Being-with

As we saw in Chapter 2, when we first looked at Heidegger's notion of authenticity, being-with (*Mitsein*) is, according to Heidegger, one of the three basic faculties of Dasein, where Dasein as being-in-the-word "in every case maintains itself in some definite way of concernful Being-with-one-another" (Heidegger 1962, 204). What this means is that Dasein *is* not only the faculties of *understanding* and *attunement* we looked at in Chapters 4 and 5, but also that of *being-with*. Thus William McNeill writes that "my very being-in-the-world is, always and intrinsically, a being-with. In this perspective, the assertion 'I am', notes Heidegger, is incorrect: one should really say: 'I am one', in the sense of 'I am others, I am them'" (McNeill 2006, 82). For many people it may be unusual to think of Dasein, the individual human being, not only as him or herself (as expressed in Dasein's understanding and attunement) but also other people (other individuals as well as the interpersonal and communal).

Most of *Being and Time*, and indeed the writings of most commentators on Heidegger, focuses on the ways in which this being-with is said to manifest inauthentically, which are that of "discourse" (language and other discursive practices) and *das Man* (the ways in which things are done and perceived by the general culture and tradition the individual finds him or herself in). But there has been much less attention for what it means for being-with itself to be authentic, and those accounts of authentic being-with that exists in Heidegger's early writings (that of the authentic community and of the voice of conscience) are, as we will see, in many ways unsatisfactory.

In so far as authentic being-with has been conceptualized, it has been so mainly in negative terms, as it involves Dasein "bringing itself back from lostness in *das Man*" as well as discourse becoming "silent" in the call of conscience (we will look at this in detail later in this chapter). Though this negative approach is in line with the emphasis on *opening up* and *letting go* we have already seen at work in Heidegger's approach to authentic understanding and attunement, what is missing is a convincing positive account of authentic being-with that does justice to it, both in terms of its interpersonal and of its communal aspect.

In this first part of the chapter, we will look at the communal aspect of being-with and then at the interpersonal one, followed by a discussion of some of the shortcomings in Heidegger's account of authentic being-with. In the middle part of the chapter, we will turn to what Heidegger calls "the call of conscience" as a first indication as to how authentic being-with may come about, in order to, in the final part, construct a full account of being-with learning to be authentic. This will then complete the description of all three ways of relating (understanding, attunement, and being-with) becoming authentic, so that in the last chapter of the book we can return to the kind of authentic learning that brings together conventional learning (as modification and growth) with the kind of pre-reflective self-awareness and letting go that leads to authentic openness to the being of entities.

Being-with as existing as part of a common world

In discussions of the being-with faculty of Dasein, the emphasis has usually been on the communal, collective dimension of being-with, rather than on the interpersonal one. As with all the basic faculties, Heidegger posits this faculty as prior to and as the basis of any actual manifestation of it. As William McNeill puts is, "Being-with gives rise to a common world and a common good" (McNeill 2006, 79-82). That is, rather than a common world giving rise to something like communal life, it is, according to Heidegger, the basic faculty of being-with that makes possible for individuals to have anything like a common world.

We experience being-with in the openness of being-in-the-world. Just as every understanding has its attunement and every attunement has its understanding, every understanding and attunement also have their being-with: "Dasein-with is already essentially manifest in a co-attunement and a co-understanding" (Heidegger 1962, 205). For example, with a particular understanding of something, there is a way of being attuned emotionally, as well as a way in which other Daseins are there "with" one in that understanding. In concrete terms, if one, for example, understands a bird as belonging to a certain species (i.e. theoretically), there belongs to this theoretical understanding a kind of detached, objectifying way of being emotionally attuned to the situation. But one is also there *with* others in this, for example with the authors of the textbook in which one first found the name of the species or with one's father who may have introduced one to the joys of bird watching.

Being-with gives rise to a common world (which, according to McNeill's reading, includes a common good, because the world we live in is always one of values), and this common world gives rise to language as well as deliberative practices. Heidegger calls this discourse. "That common world and common good give rise to discourse" (McNeill 2006, 79-82). Discourse gives one the ways of conceptualizing (through articulation) the world and the entities within it, and thus helps one decide in what ways to act in any given situation. "One's deliberations derive from that communal dimension as they are discursive (and this is true for ethical deliberation and phronesis as well)" (McNeill 2006, 79-82). Taking something *as a certain kind of thing* and acting *in certain a kind of way* are, in so far as they are based in being-with, part of the discourse that articulates the common world.

As discourse, being-with articulates the way in which things are understood as well as Dasein's attunement. Articulation refers to the way in which some things are taken as belonging together and some things as belonging apart. As "the articulation of the intelligibility of the 'there', [discourse] is a primordial existentiale of disclosedness" (Heidegger 1962, 204), which is to say that discourse is one of the basic faculties with which Dasein discloses the world and the entities it finds in the world. Discourse is the foundation of language as well as other discursive practices that exist in cultures and traditions, as these articulate the world and the entities in it. "The intelligibility of being-in-the-world – an intelligibility which goes with [attunement] – expresses itself as discourse [*spricht sich als Rede aus*]. This totality-of-significations of intelligibility is put into words" (Heidegger 1962, 204). In other words, language and cultural practices have their basis in being-with.

Because we often act on the basis of deliberations, and because deliberations are discursive and, as such, based in the common world which is itself based in the with-world of being-with, our deliberations are themselves collective in origin. The terms we have, in previous chapters, used for the collective ways of conceiving of and acting in relation to things is *das Man*. "Thus one's deliberations take the form of 'one does ...'". (McNeill 2006, 79-82). "This 'one' [*das Man*], properly understood, is the 'how' of everydayness, of our average, concrete being-with-one-another; from it arise the ways in which human beings 'at first and for the most part' see and are affected by and address the world" (McNeill 2006, 82).

Here we encounter a clear link with what happens in learning, especially when people grow up. That is, some perspectives on things (taking them as certain kinds of things and acting in relation to them in certain ways) that are collective in origin are actualized as concrete perspectives in the individual Dasein, through a process of enculturation. Another way of saying this would be that some perspectives from the collective are "internalized", which is a common way of explaining how a person ends up looking at things in a way that is similar to the way others, especially those close to them during their formative years, look at them.

The Heideggerian way to make sense of such "internalization" is, first, to reject the internal/external dichotomy: Dasein is transcendence and other people are there with it in the world that shows up in the openness. What happens during "internalization" is that, as a result of the individuals concerned being turned towards the same entities in the world and in the same way, this way of being turned towards these entities sticks (note that this is a process that can be explained by the conventional accounts of learning discussed in Chapter 3). The reason we then observe that one individual (e.g., the child) has adopted the ways of being of the other (e.g., the culture they grow up in or the parent) is that what they were turned towards had previously not been articulated (i.e. taking some things as belonging together and some as belonging apart) in as coherent, persuasive or committed a way by the child as it had been by the culture of the parent. And it is this articulation that does the work in "internalization", where the process, from the perspective of the child is one of partaking in the articulation. Thus, the process of enculturation is another apt way of putting the process of internalization, or, as Heidegger would say, entering into *das Man*.

With this we have an account of the collective dimension of *das Man*, including the way in which the individual is enculturated into it. But, as has been argued throughout, becoming authentic involves "bringing oneself back from lostness in *das Man*". We, therefore, need an account of the basic faculty of being-with as it exists for the Dasein that has extracted itself from *das Man*, while retaining what is essential to being-with: authentic being-with. But before we can do so, we need to look at the interpersonal dimension of being-with, at the way two individual Daseins encounter each other. This is an important aspect of being-with, because our interpersonal relationships have a deep impact of our lives, but it has received much less attention that the communal aspect in Heidegger's writings.

Being-with in terms of interpersonal relationships

Heidegger describes how we encounter the other Dasein through our engagement with practical (ready-to-hand) entities. "The structure of the world's worldhood is such that others are not proximally present-at-hand as free-floating subjects along with other things, but show themselves in the world in their special environmental being, and do so in terms of what is ready-to-hand in that world" (Heidegger 1962, 160). We encounter the things in the world as things that other Daseins are also involved with. For example, "along with the equipment to be found when one is at work, those others for whom the 'work' is destined are 'encountered' too". Or when "we walk along the edge of a field [...] the field shows itself as belonging to such-and-such a person" (Heidegger 1962, 153). And we could add that, if, for example, we walked carelessly across the field, we would be shown to ourselves, from the perspective of the farmer, as someone trespassing or trampling their crops.

This is a rather limited account of how we encounter other individuals, in that it is mediated by the entities we encounter in the world and not, as it were, face to face. Sarah Sorial discusses how "the other" (the individual one comes face to face with) fails to become truly another person in Heidegger's analysis. This other person becomes somehow strangely impersonal, like a flat character in a play. "The specificity of the other, that unknowable and evasive aspect of the other expressed in her face and by her speech is something that Heidegger bypasses in his pursuit of Being" (Sorial 2005, 144). That is, "Heideggerian ontology, effaces the alterity of the other by reducing her to the anonymous categories of Being" (Sorial 2005, 144). What this means is that Heidegger loses sight of the "ontic [actual and concrete] differences and multiplicity that exists in concrete relations between Daseins" (Sorial 2005, 144). In other words, Heidegger fails to bring out what is specific about the experience of encountering "another person", their individuality, their specificity and their particularity. Heidegger's descriptions of how we encounter the other person is, almost always, indirect, as when we make something for them or walk along their field.

Another indication of Heidegger's neglect in this area is the lack of discussions of some of the most important interpersonal events in people's lives, such as love and friendship. The word "love", for example, occurs only once in the whole of *Being and Time*, and even then only as a mention in a footnote about anxiety (Heidegger 1962, 492). Similarly, the word "friend" only occurs twice, but never as part of a discussion of friendship itself (Heidegger 1962, 206 & 294). What is more, this friend "has no distinguishing attributes [he or she] appears to have no face, no figure, no sex, no name. It is not man or woman, nor is it an 'I,' a subject or a person. Rather, it is another Dasein that each Dasein *carries* with it, in the form of a voice it hears *in* itself" (Sorial 2005, 103). Contrast this with a concept like truth, which appears dozens of times, and it becomes clear that it was not Heidegger's priority to specify different possibilities with regard to interpersonal relationships. So, given the limitations of Heidegger's account of interpersonal relationships, I will attempt to construct one, using his claim that, from the perspective of being-with, Dasein is "for the sake of others" (Heidegger 1962, 160).

We saw in Chapter 4 that Dasein is properly understood in terms of itself only. So, when an individual Dasein meets another Dasein, how is Dasein to take this other Dasein? If this Dasein (Dasein 1) was to understand the other Dasein (Dasein 2) like it understands ready-to-hand or present-at-hand objects (i.e. in terms of Dasein 1's world, the totality of references Dasein 1 has), then it would not understand this Dasein 2 in an authentic way (in accordance with the being of Dasein 2). This is because Dasein 2 has its own world from out of which it understands itself as well as the entities it encounters. This Dasein 2 understands itself from out of its own world, and this self-understanding from out of its own world is the most fundamental way in which Dasein 2 can be understood (more fundamental than any theoretical or instrumental way). As Heidegger puts it: "Dasein's being [is] that being *for the sake of which* Dasein itself is as it is" (Heidegger 1962, 160). This reasoning lies at the heart of Heidegger's argument that each individual Dasein can only be understood in an authentic way if it is understood in terms of its own experience of the world, as its own *for the sake of which*, its own end as well as totality of references. But in the context of being-with Heidegger brings in another factor, namely, the notion that, when we encounter another Dasein, because that Dasein has its own world, its own *for the sake of*, we also encounter ourselves as existing *for the sake of* (*in terms of* the world of) that other Dasein: "as being-with, Dasein 'is' essentially for the sake of others" (Heidegger 1962, 160).

Such an existing *for the sake of* others does not mean that one exists for the benefit of others, as subordinate to their wishes and needs. Nor does it simply imply that one *means* something to the other person in terms of the other person's world, though that is undoubtedly the case as well. Rather, it means that in oneself, as part of one's own perspective, one exists *as* for the sake of the other person. That is, one is always also who one is in terms of the world of the other person, where this *being in terms of the world of the other person* is fundamental to one's being. There is no self that is more basic than the one that exists *in terms of* the other person (though the communal dimension of being-with as well as other parts of the self - attunement and understanding - are co-original with it). One could, therefore, say that, *from one's own perspective*, one exists *from the perspective* of the other person as well. Or to use Heidegger's phrase, one becomes disclosed in being-with "as the existential 'for the sake of' of others" (Heidegger 1962).

Importantly, this phenomenon of existing *from the perspective* of others is always the case ontologically (at the level of possibility), but only the case in certain ways ontically (in actual, concrete situations). It is, for example, not the case that one necessarily exists *for oneself in terms of the world of* the neurotic person who works in the office canteen. Such an existing in terms of the world of the other person is there always in principle (at the level of possibility), but the actual perspectives of the individuals one is in contact with do not all get actualized in oneself (which in the case of the above example would involve actualizing a neurotic perspective on oneself, which could be quite disturbing). That is, though the phenomenon of existing from the perspective of the other is always there in the form of possibility, not all the perspectives become actualized as concrete (factual) perspectives one has on oneself, though in our formative years much of what we mean to, say, our parents or the community we grow up in tends to become internalized more or less without question.

We can say that the faculty of being-with means that one dimension of the being of the individual it that it exists as *from the perspective of* the other individual. Such existing as *from the perspective of* the other is there first as possibility, where some of the possibilities become actualized, notably those perspectives that are held by those close to the individual (parents, for example, but also the language and culture the individual grows up in). These perspectives themselves consist of articulation, of taking some things as belonging together and some as belonging apart, which manifest as ways of being turned towards entities in the world. And we saw in the discussion of being-with as existing as part of a community how the perspectives others have on the things one finds in the world can become "internalized" by the individual Dasein. To this we can now add that the perspectives others may have on the individual Dasein get "internalized" by that Dasein (where we need to remember that this is not really internalization, because ultimately there is no distinction between inner and outer in Dasein, it being being-in-the-world, transcendence, openness).

Now that we have a sense of the interpersonal dimension of being-with, we can begin to consider what authentic being-with is like. As we saw in the analyses of authentic understanding and authentic attunement, the authentic mode of Dasein is one where Dasein exists as possibility rather than any of the actual ways of being that lie in that possibility. Thus, in authentic understanding Dasein existed as the possibility of having an understanding of being, prior (remember that this prior is neither temporal nor logical, but structural, as phenomenology discloses the structures of experience) to adopting any actual understanding of being. Likewise, in the authentic mood, Dasein existed as the possibility of being affected by the entities it finds in the world, prior to being affected in any actual way. So when we now seek to establish what the mode of authentic being-with is like, we need to look in the direction of Dasein existing as the possibility of existing for itself from the perspective of the interpersonal other (but prior to entering into any such perspective in actuality), as well as existing in a common world (but prior to entering into any actual articulation of that world in *das Man*).

Authenticity is expressed mostly as individuality

One difficulty finding a coherent description of authentic being-with in *Being and Time* is that the authentic mode is portrayed as one where Dasein becomes "individualized". We saw, for example, how in the authentic mode of "anxiety" (the mood of being both "not identifying with" and "near to" the entities one finds in the world) "[t]he 'world' can offer nothing more, and *neither can the Dasein-with* [the being-there-with] *of others*" (Heidegger 1962, 232, emphasis added). Or, "anxiety discloses Dasein as [...] something individualized in individualization" (Heidegger 1962, 232), where the German, "*vereinzelt in der Vereinzelung*", is in fact stronger than the translation, "individualized in individualization", suggests, because it can also be translated as "isolated in isolation" or "separated in separation". Likewise, in the context of authentic understanding, Heidegger writes that "all being-with others, will fail us when our ownmost potentiality-for-Being [the authentic facing of death] is the issue." (Heidegger 1962, 307). It, therefore, seems as if Heidegger claims that in its authentic mode Dasein becomes individualized, to the point where the faculty of being-with either disappears altogether or becomes irrelevant.

We find this kind of critique back in Lambert Zuidervaart's charge that Heidegger "turns the truth of Dasein into a denial of mediation" (Zuidervaart 2007, 94), because for Heidegger "[t]he most primordial truth is an anticipatory resoluteness [i.e. authenticity] whereby Dasein secures its own 'freedom towards death' in disentanglement from the entities, including others, to which Dasein necessarily stands in relation" (Zuidervaart 2007, 91). Though Zuidervaart's critique is well taken, we should beware that his notion of intersubjectivity keeps looking for a connection between separate individuals, where what we need is an account of authenticity that does justice to the fundamental nature of being-with, which goes beyond that of a connection between separate individuals.

One possible solution to the difficulty of reconciling the individuality associated with authenticity with the fundamental character of being-with where we exist "for the sake of others" is suggested by Sorial, who argues that it is the very individuality (note that she tends to use Jean-Luc Nancy's concept of "singularity") that is shared in being-with. "While we are all different in the sense that we have different faces and bodies, mannerisms and gestures, while we have different possibilities and will pursue different projects, there remains a commonality about our experiences. ... What is shared here is our singularity ..." (Sorial 2005, 89-90). Thus, our individuality (singularity) not only divides us but also unites us. "This sharing of singularities are what constitute the 'we.' Singularity refers to both the uniting and dividing phenomenon of being-with; uniting because it is what we all share, but also what divides us because there remains something unique and untransferable about our singularity" (Sorial 2005, 89-90).

One can question whether Sorial's proposal manages to do justice to the nature of being-with, in that it appears to understand the relationships between individuals in present-at-hand terms, in terms analogous to us being divided because, for example, all of us are wearing a different cap, but united because every cap has the quality of being different. This translates into saying that each Dasein is individual, because it is its own "for the sake of which", but all Daseins are united because they all have this "for the sake of which". Thus, she writes that "[d]eath is both a singular and shared experience, in the sense that finitude and mortality is something that we share, but that we also have to assume individually. The experience of death, my death, or the death of the other demonstrates to me that the only thing I can recognise in the death of the other is that there is nothing recognisable" (Sorial 2005, 93).

I believe there is a lot of merit in the emphasis on there being a sense in which we can never in any way assimilate the other into our own understanding of things. What remains missing here, though, is the incorporation of the idea considered earlier that "as being-with, Dasein 'is' essentially for the sake of others" (Heidegger 1962, 160). That is, all Daseins do not only share the fact that they all have their own individualized perspective on the world (their own singularity), but also the fact that each Dasein exists in terms of the perspectives of other Daseins. It is, therefore, not so much a sharing of present-at-hand qualities or characteristics, but a sense of being constituted *by* the other, while retaining one's inalienable individuality, which we are after.

Authentic interpersonal relationships

One place where Heidegger does write something about authentic interpersonal relationships in *Being and Time* is where he writes that authentic Dasein has the possibility to "let the others who are with it 'be' their ownmost potentiality-for-being, and so co-disclose this potentiality in the solitude which leaps forth and liberates" (Heidegger 1962, 344). Authentic Dasein can show other Daseins that they have the possibility to be authentic as well. And it can, according to this citation, be done in a solicitude (*Fuersorge*, the kind of care human beings can have for each other) that "leaps forth and liberates". This particular authentic care is one that is contrasted with inauthentic care, which consists of "taking care of or caring for the other in her place, to spare her from the troubles of care" (Nancy 2008, 6,7). Such inauthentic care "relieves the other of her own care" (Nancy 2008, 6,7) and can be seen along the lines of a kind of care that takes the other's responsibility away, but with that also, in some way, their dignity. In contrast, authentic care, by showing the other the possibility of authentic existence, "hands them" the possibility of taking such responsibility for themselves.

Nancy believes that this notion of authentic care is not fully intelligible, and he asks how we can "leap ahead of the decision and the opening of the other [...] so as to 'hand it over' to her? This is not clearly established" (Nancy 2008, 6,7). As Nancy is well-aware, it is not about the "handing over" between two ready-to-hand entities that exist external to each other (as we would hand a key to another person) but rather one of co-constituting the transcendence that each individual Dasein is. As Heidegger puts it, "[being-with] is already essentially manifest in a co-state-of-mind and a co-understanding" (Heidegger 1962, 205). We could say that such authentic care for the other does justice to the individuality (singularity) of each Dasein (in that responsibility is left with, or even handed back to, the Dasein that is being shown authentic care), while the very possibility of such authentic interpersonal care is based in the shared nature of being-with. This means that the question of how such "handing over" is possible is secondary, because it is only on the basis on an understanding of authentic being-with that such authentic "handing over" can be made intelligible.

The other place where we find Heidegger write about authentic interpersonal relationships is when he writes about working together. But, as Jean-Luc Nancy points out, it is not clear how authentic working together can happen. The contrast is one between inauthentic working together where "we find a common occupation by virtue of an exterior task" and authentic working together where "we find an engagement for the same affair [Sache] in common" (Nancy 2008, 7). Nancy writes that in the case of authentic working together "there must be a common thing or cause" (Nancy 2008, 7). When we look closely at what it says in *Being and Time*, we find that Heidegger writes that people working together authentically are engaged with the same thing, in the sense of being wholeheartedly involved in it (*sich gemeinsam einsetzen fuer dieselbe Sache*), in a way that is determined by, driven by the engagement that each individual (*eigens*) Dasein has (Heidegger 1962, 159). In other words, the cooperation is not external (as in the inauthentic way of working together on the same external task where, for example, for one the task *means* an opportunity for making money, while for the other it *means* a way to get personal satisfaction) but consists of those involved being truly engaged in the same thing, where they have each appropriated the task for themselves in such a way that they can be said to have a common world with a common good. But, again the shortcoming in Heidegger's account seems to be that his concept of authentic working together depends on a notion of authentic being-with which is not given: we cannot determine what authentic working together would mean, because we lack, as yet, a concept of authentic being-with.

So, just as we saw in the discussion of authentic care for the other person, there is a combination of having a shared understanding and attunement (a co-understanding and a co-attunement based in being-with) while retaining the individuality of each Dasein. The shortcoming in each case appears to be the lack of a coherent characterization of authentic being-with. And it is of little help that we find in Heidegger's a description of inauthentic working together, which is characterized by "distance and reserve" as well as "mistrust" (Heidegger 1962, 159). It may be that authentic working together should be associated with their opposites – perhaps something like closeness, giving oneself, and trust. However, a correct working out of such opposites still requires an understanding of authentic being-with, because authenticity is not simply the opposite of inauthenticity but that which makes the inauthentic mode possible in the first place. It cannot, therefore, simply be inferred from the inauthentic state what the authentic one would be like. The order of priority is clear: first we need an account of authentic being-with, and only then does any notion of inauthentic being-with become intelligible.

The authentic community

Apart from the interpersonal dimension of being-with, Jean-Luc Nancy also critiques Heidegger's notion of the authentic community. According to Nancy, Heidegger falls into the trap of privileging the collective in his notion of the people [*das Volk*] as authentic being-with. First he notes that "Heidegger does everything to affirm the essentiality of the with" (Nancy 2008, 3), where this "with" is not "the simple external 'with' of things which are only put together, only contiguous to one another" (Nancy 2008, 3). Though it is coherent to see being-with as not simply the being together of externally related Daseins, Nancy still rejects what he believes to be Heidegger's notion of what we may call the *internal* "with", the one that supposes "a single communal Dasein beyond the singulars" (Nancy 2008, 4). In the case of an internal "with" the individual Dasein is, according to Nancy, but an expression of the collective, and as such subordinate to it. Between these two extremes (of Dasein as externally and internally connected) the right understanding of being-with would, according to Nancy, "require that the openings [that constitute the individual Daseins] intersect each other in some way, that they cross, mix or let their properties interfere with one another, but without merging into a unique Dasein (or else the *mit* [the with] would be lost)" (Nancy 2008, 4).

Again, we can say that what we need is an account of being-with that does justice to, on the one hand, the notions of co-understanding and co-attunement and, on the other hand, the individuality (singularity) of Dasein, the fact that authentic interpersonal relationships need to have some sense in which the other remains truly other. But in his account of the authentic community Heidegger appears to put so much emphasis on the collective dimension that the individual becomes subordinate to the collective. We encounter much the same objection, when Zuidervaart notes that there is a problem with Heidegger's notion of authenticity as implying that "participation in an exclusive community is the proper path to authentic truth" (Zuidervaart 2007, 87). Zuidervaart notes that, while authenticity may in itself not be verifiable in a public way, Heidegger nominates *das Volk*, the people of a specific nationality, as the authentic community, when he argues that a people (*das Volk*) is the site where authentic being-with manifests. This would be so, because, on the one hand, authenticity is the one measure of truth, but is in itself not verifiable in a public way (because that would put the arbiter of authentic being-with in *das Man*), while, on the other hand, a certain kind of community (*das Volk*, the people of a specific nationality) becomes Heidegger's expression of the authentic community, as based in Dasein's being-with. Bearing in mind Heidegger's later involvement with Nazism, Zuidervaart writes that "Adorno had good reason to attack the 'jargon of authenticity' as a 'German ideology'" (Zuidervaart 2007, 86-87).

As a result of this privileging of *das Volk* the individual becomes, in the words of Nancy, subordinate to the collective, thus giving up the individuality that is necessary for authentic being-with: "the community that becomes *a single* thing (body, mind, fatherland, leader …) necessarily loses the *in* of being-*in*-common. Or, it loses the *with* or the *together* that defines it" (Cited in Sorial 2005, 90-91). Heidegger ascribes "to community a *common being*, whereas community is a matter of something quite different, namely, of existence inasmuch as it is *in* common, but without letting itself be absorbed into a common substance" (Cited in Sorial 2005,

90-91). "It is precisely because we are singular beings that the project of fusion or communion is problematic for Nancy" (Sorial 2005, 90-91). But though there are clear shortcomings in Heidegger's notion of authentic being with, as a result of his emphasis on "the people", we can still glean some elements from his writing to help us form a coherent, positive account.

Thus, Benjamin Crowe takes a more positive view of Heidegger's notion of the authentic community. As we saw when we looked at authentic interpersonal relationships in terms of working together, "authentic individuals participate in one way or another in the resolution of common problems or in the realization of common goals" (Crowe 2006, 203). This is expanded in Heidegger's notion of the "generation", where individuals growing up in the same culture, as part of the same generation, share certain ways of looking at things (for example, the inter-war generation in Germany that had to come to terms with both an inhumane war and with what they considered an unfair defeat in 1918) as well as challenges (for example, restoring Germany's sense of dignity). Thus, Crowe writes, "an authentic individual inevitably incorporates shared ideals and projects into her overall pattern of vocational commitment, simply by virtue of belonging to a 'generation'" (Crowe 2006, 203).

Thus Heidegger writes in § 74 of *Being and Time* how the moment of authentic understanding is one that always occurs as a collective event as well as an individual one: "if fateful Dasein, as Being-in-the-world, exists essentially in Being-with others, its historizing [*Geschehen*, similar to what in Chapter 4 we called *seizing the moment* but happening at the collective rather than individual level] is a co-historizing [*Mitgeschehen*], and is determinative for it as *destiny (Geschick)*" (Heidegger 1962, 436). That is, the event of "historizing", the authentic seizing of the moment, happens in the context of a collective phenomenon, the generation. Thus Heidegger writes about "the historizing of the community, of a people" (Heidegger 1962, 436) and that "Dasein's fateful destiny in and with its 'generation' goes to make up the full authentic historizing of Dasein" (Heidegger 1962, 436). This, as we saw earlier, is where Nancy maintains that Heidegger makes the individual subordinate to the collective.

Though it is true that Heidegger does, at certain points, emphasize how the individual Daseins become authentic in a way that is in some ways irreducibly collective, it goes, I think, too far to say that he subordinates the individual to the collective in any systematic way. It is true that he writes, for example, that "[o]ur fates have already been guided in advance, in our Being-with-one-another in the same world and in our resoluteness for definite possibilities" (Heidegger 1962, 436), but this does not mean that we can find in *Being and Time* anything like a systematic subordination of the individual to the collective. Indeed, the criticism we discussed earlier that the collective dimension tends to be lost in his account of authenticity, because there is too much emphasis on individuality (what Nancy calls singularity), is easier to defend, simply on the basis of the weight of the textual evidence, and it is hard to see how the two can be true at the same time.

Rather, the difficulty again appears to stems from the fact that Heidegger has not worked out the concept of authentic being-with in a way that can accommodate the different demands such a concept raises: the preservation of both the individual and the collective dimensions of Dasein, as well as the notion that Dasein exists both "for the sake of" the other Dasein and "for its own sake". Benjamin Crowe comes closer to a satisfactory, if still limited, account of authentic being-with, drawing on Heidegger's writings that precede *Being and Time* and that draw more explicitly on religious sources. Crowe combines the notions of sharing membership of a generation with the interpersonal commitment to authentic individuality: "we find Heidegger elaborating the idea of a generational 'community of struggle' [Kampfgemeinschaft]. Here individuals are united not only through a common culture or a shared historical situation, but also through a commitment on the part of each person to the value of an authentic way of life" (Crowe 2006, 203) – where this authentic way of life would, needless to say, do justice to Dasein as existing "for its own sake".

Importantly, the collective dimension of the authentic community as Crowe finds it in Heidegger's early writings is a far cry from the kinds notion of subordinating individuals to the collective. "This commitment seems to entail the rejection of paternalistic relationships of a sort that ultimately subjugate other people by encouraging the innate drive of self-abdication. In place of this, Heidegger envisions the possibility of a community in which each individual exemplifies what it means to be authentic in his or her own unique way" (Crowe 2006, 203). Crowe does not elaborate on this notion of the authentic community in enough detail for it to yield the kind of notion of authentic being-with that we require, but he does point in a direction that can be taken up to construct a notion of authentic being-with that allows for authentic community and authentic interpersonal relationships, while doing justice to Dasein as existing "for its own sake".

The call of conscience

We saw in the previous section that Heidegger's account of authentic being-with will have to do justice to both Dasein's individuality and to the ways in which the communal as well as the interpersonal are co-constitutive of this Dasein. The elements of authentic being-with that we have been able to glean from Heidegger's writings are that of a care for the other person which shows the other the possibility of authentic existence and "hands them" the possibility of taking responsibility for themselves; a working together from out of a common world and a common good; and a generation which shares a common culture or a shared historical situation, in a way that is not in contradiction to a commitment to an authentic way of life that steers clear of subordinating the individual to the collective. In this part of the chapter I will attempt to bring these together in a coherent concept of authentic being-with with the help of Heidegger's notion of the "call of conscience", which is, as a form of discourse, part of being-with, and which plays an important part in Heidegger's account of the process of becoming authentic.

The nature of the call of conscience

It has been stated throughout this discussion that for Dasein to become authentic, it needs to be brought back from lostness in *das Man*. That is, "because Dasein is lost in *das Man*, it must first find itself. In order to find itself at all, it must be 'shown' to itself in its possible authenticity" (Heidegger 1962, 313). Because Dasein has tended to understand itself in terms of *das Man* it is not aware of its possibility of authentic existence, and as such it needs to have this possibility pointed out to it. What Dasein needs to be shown is that it is already authentic in potential: "[i]n terms of its possibility, Dasein is already a potentiality-for-being-its-self [for being authentic], but it needs to have this possibility attested" (Heidegger 1962, 313).

The English "attestation" is the translation of the German *Bezeugung*, which also means testimony, as in *giving testimony of, confirming the truth of* something by saying something about it; as well as expressing one's respect, sympathy, or mercy to someone. The root word in *Bezeugung* is

Zeuge, which means witness, and which is etymologically related to the word *zeigen*, which means to show. This notion of "being shown what one already is" is very much in line with the perfectionism we looked at in Chapter 2, with "becoming who one is". And, Heidegger continues, "this potentiality [for-being-itself] is attested [*bezeugt*] by that which is familiar to us as the 'voice of conscience'" (Heidegger 1962, 313). As such, the call of conscience is that which, more than anything else in *Being and Time*, can be said to *bring* Dasein back from lostness in *das Man*.

The call of conscience is itself a phenomenon with the nature of Dasein. This means that the call is neither a practical nor a theoretical entity. The call is located both "in" oneself and somewhere "beyond" oneself. Thus Heidegger writes that "we must ... hold fast .... to the phenomenal finding that I receive the call as coming both from me and beyond me, but also to the implication that this phenomenon here is delineated ontologically as a phenomenon of Dasein" (Heidegger 1962). Another way of putting it could be to say that the call is located in Dasein, but that at the level of the call Dasein is undifferentiated as to the individual and other Dasein. This is very much in line with the notion that authentic being-with has to be able to accommodate the individual as well as the interpersonal and the communal dimensions of human existence. The voice of conscience is neither a voice that comes from outside the person (as in a literal "hearing" the call of conscience) nor is it an internal dialogue taking place in the individual – it is somehow prior to the separation between self and other.

Therefore, when Heidegger writes that "[i]*n conscience Dasein calls itself*" (Heidegger 1962, 320), we have to take "Dasein" as a generic term. Practically, the call of conscience can come, for example, from another person or through the reading of poetry – just as we sometimes say that a poem speaks for the whole of humanity, we could say that the call speaks for the whole of humanity. This undifferentiated element of the call of conscience is further accentuated when Heidegger writes about the call that "'It' calls" (Heidegger 1962, 320). This phrase, "it calls" [*es ruft*], has the grammatical structure, sometimes called the middle voice, which we find in phrases like "*it* rains" or "*it* sometimes happens that". This "middle voice" indicates that there is no grammatical subject in the sense of an agent who or that does the "raining" or the "happening". Another way of saying the same thing, contrived though this may sound in English, is that "*there is* a calling of the voice of conscience".

The call of conscience exists prior to there being a separate subject. This is similar to what I said about authentic understanding in Chapter 4 which, we saw, occurs prior to the separation of subject and object at the moment when "Temporality […] *temporalises* itself" (Heidegger 1962, 376-377) prior to an engagement with entities in terms of action and perception, where there is no separation between the subject and object moments in the intentional act. And we saw in our discussion of authentic attunement that the intensification of attunement's pre-reflective self-awareness also happens in this way of there not being a clear separation between what is inner and outer. Similarly, prior to the differentiation between individual Daseins or between the individual and the collective, there is no separation between the one calling and the one hearing. There can still be calling and hearing, it's just that now this process is best characterized with the phrase "it calls", where this call comes from both the person hearing it and from beyond them.

The caller of the call is "Dasein in its uncanniness", and "[c]onscience is the call of care from the uncanniness of being-in-the-world" (Heidegger 1962, 335). This brings us back to, when, in Chapter 5, we saw that uncanniness literally means "not-at-home-ness" or being in a place that feels "uncomfortably strange or unfamiliar". The caller is experienced as "Dasein ... as the 'not-at-home' – the bare 'that-it-is' in the 'nothing' of the world" (Heidegger 1962, 321). But this Dasein is, in terms of attunement, authentic Dasein, who experiences the entities it encounters in the world in a way that it is at once *disconnected* from them and *near* to them. As such, this Dasein is fully individualized, because it has not identified with anything, but at the same time it is open to being affected by the entities in the world. This is also the Dasein that is able to exist prior to a differentiation between subject and object, because authentic attunement is unitary. And it is able to communicate with other Daseins, because it is near to them, open to them, the more so because it has not become absorbed in the (practical and theoretical) entities it finds in the world (in *das Man*).

We can, therefore, in the call of conscience arising from Dasein in the mood of authenticity, see the beginnings of a Dasein that can resolve in itself the ostensible contradiction between authentic being-with involving individuality and it involving those communal and interpersonal ways of being that are co-constitutive of this Dasein. But, as I pointed out in Chapter 5 on authentic attunement, this characterization of authentic Dasein as "the bare 'that-it-is' in the 'nothing' of the world" lacks an affective disposition that is appropriate for authentic inter-human relationships: it may experience nearness and openness towards inanimate things, but this is not quite the same as feeling the kinds of emotions we associate with deep interpersonal connectedness. We will return to this towards the end of the chapter, but for now note that there is a clear overlap between authentic understanding having a unitary experience of subject and object, authentic attunement having a unitary mood of disconnection and nearness, and authentic being-with as hearing the voice of conscience.

Authentic Dasein is the Dasein that has brought itself "back from lostness in *das Man*" (Heidegger 1962, 312-313). As all language is part of *das Man*, there is, therefore, the implication that the call of conscience is a kind of communication that is prior to language. Such a communication that is not based in language is one that does not take things *as* certain things, either practically (when, for example, a pupil takes a window as a way of exiting the classroom) or theoretically (when, for example, the teacher takes the pupil's behaviour as meriting a sticker with a disapproving face on their report card), because language articulates, and taking things *as* certain things is a form of articulation. The call of conscience does not take Dasein *as* anything, because Dasein can be understood in terms of itself only, having its own "for the sake of". Yet the call of conscience plays an important part in bringing Dasein "back from lostness in *das Man*" (Heidegger 1962, 312-313), as we will see shortly, in that it *shows* Dasein that it has the possibility of authentic existence, *appeals* to Dasein to become authentic, *summons* it to being authentic, and *calls Dasein forward* into authentic existence.

Characteristics of the call of conscience

We are trying to arrive at an account of authentic being-with that does justice to Dasein's individuality as well as to the ways in which the communal and the interpersonal are co-constitutive of this Dasein, where there is a concern for the other person's authentic existence, where working together occurs from out of a common world and a common good, where the communal is combined with a commitment on the part of each to the value of an authentic way of life, that does not subordinate the individual to the collective. With regard to the call of conscience, we are beginning to see that the voice of conscience, as it calls Dasein back from lostness in *das Man*, originates in authentic Dasein in such a way that it is prior to a differentiation into someone calling and someone hearing, thus allowing for the co-existence of individuality and the interconnection that is part of authentic being-with. What is more, the call shows Dasein its possibility of being authentic in such a way that it does not take Dasein as either something practical or theoretical. I will now elaborate on these characteristics by considering some of the further characterizations of the call of conscience we find in Heidegger's writings.

First, the call of conscience communicates in such a way that, though the message is communicated, there are no specifics about how this is done, that is, "the 'voice' is taken ... as a giving-to-understand" (Heidegger 1962, 316), where "giving to understand" (*zuverstehengeben*) is a very general expression which says that something is communicated, without being at all specific about the means of communication. This is the "middle voice" we encountered in the previous section. Saying that something is "given to understand" is, therefore, similar to saying, for example, that one's attention was drawn to something, without specifying how this is done, thus avoiding the need to take recourse to the language of *das Man*. Another way of putting this is, therefore, to say that Dasein is made aware of something (of itself as an entity with the nature of Dasein), in such a way that the awareness is not mediated by anything to do with *das Man*.

Second, the call is reticent[13] in the sense of "being silent". "The call does not say anything, it remains silent, in its appeal to Dasein's authentic self to come to the fore" (Heidegger 1962, 318). That is, "[t]he call [of conscience] asserts nothing, gives no information about world events, has nothing to tell" (Heidegger 1962, 318). This is a claim Heidegger justifies phenomenologically, by writing that this reticent "giving to understand" is already there in our common-sense understanding of the voice of conscience, for if "the everyday interpretation knows a 'voice' of conscience, then one is not so much thinking of an utterance (for this is something which factically one never comes across)" (Heidegger 1962, 316). In this way, the silence of the call of conscience serves as a way of distancing it from anything to do with *das Man*, because all actual language, any kind of conventional sign, is of necessity part of *das Man*. Again, the phrase "becoming aware

---

13   Reticence is the customary translation of the German Schweigen as it is used by Heidegger in *Being and Time*, but it should be noted that Schweigen can also be translated as remaining silent, and that it, importantly, does not allow for "saying little", as the English word reticence does, but insists on no words being said at all.

of" is apt, as this too can occur in silence, pointing towards something in a way that is unmediated by language or convention.

Third, Heidegger states that "[t]he call is indeed not, and can never be, planned, prepared for, or voluntarily enacted from ourselves" (Heidegger 1962, 320). This is an essential part of any call that does not originate in *das Man*, as all planning, preparation or purposeful action would either require language in which the plan is formulated or some kind of task grammar that was of necessity part of *das Man*. What is more, planning and preparation involved a crucial continuity, one that, as we will see shortly, is antithetical to the interruption that characterizes the voice of conscience, which is essentially an interruption, a "turning away from the world" before a "turning back".

Finally, as the voice of conscience is a voice which does not belong to any of the other voices that come to us from *das Man*, it stands out: "[t]he caller is unfamiliar to the everyday they-self [the self of *das Man*]; it is something like an alien voice" (Heidegger 1962, 321). This notion of "a different voice", one that is unlike all the others (and is recognized as such), is not unfamiliar, for instance, in the world of art, where an artist may stand out because they are different from the others and where the different quality of their work "interrupts" the way we tend to look at art. The same can be true for other situations, such as "a different voice" in a discussion about an issue, a voice that seems to "come from a different place" and that makes us take a different stance towards the issue under discussion. Thus, the voice of conscience is unlike any voice that would come from *das Man*, and is, as such, capable of bringing something genuinely different to our attention.

As a result, we see that the call of conscience is a silent, un-planned-for "giving to understand" that is different from any call that may come from *das Man*. This description allows the call to exist prior to any differentiation into a call and someone being called, while at the same time enabling it to affect Dasein, so that it can play its role in bringing Dasein "back from lostness in *das Man*" (Heidegger 1962, 312-313). To put it in schematically, there is a communication ("the call") that originates in authentic Dasein ("uncanniness"), arising ("it calls") in a way that is prior to a differentiation between the caller and a listener ("the call as coming both from me and beyond me"), and that brings to Dasein's awareness ("giving to understand") in an unspecified ("silent"), yet unmistakable way ("alien voice") what kind of entity Dasein really (authentically) is and has the potential to be (becoming "who one is") and it brings this to Dasein's awareness purely in terms of Dasein itself ("for the sake of") and not in terms of anything else (there is neither the practical nor a theoretical "as" of *das Man*).

As such the call gives expression to the authentic being-with we are after, given that it does justice to Dasein's individuality as well as its communal and the interpersonal aspects, that it shows the other the possibility of authentic existence, and calls them forth into taking responsibility for themselves. An account of authentic being-with in terms of the communal, collective, dimension is missing in this account, as the communal element that is present, *das Man*, still has only a negative function, in that it is what Dasein needs to be liberated from. It, therefore, remains to be seen if we can pick up a positive characterization of the communal dimension of authentic being-with later in the chapter. Before that, however, we will press on with our search for an account of being-with learning to be authentic, and then to see if an account of this learning process can shed more light on authentic being-with itself, including its communal dimension that still needs to be filled out.

What happens when "it calls"

As we have seen, the call of conscience plays an important role in bringing Dasein back from lostness in *das Man*. More precisely, the call of conscience *shows*, points out to, Dasein that it has the possibility of authentic existence, it *appeals* to Dasein to become authentic, it *summons* it to being authentic, and it *calls Dasein forward* into authentic existence. This is where the "silent", "un-planned-for" "giving to understand" which is different from any call that may come from *das Man* brings Dasein "back from lostness in *das Man*" (Heidegger 1962, 312-313). As Benjamin Crowe writes: "The 'voice of conscience' is a way of capturing the power of the unexpected to make possible a new future for an individual, a future that has been set free for the possibility of living one's own life in one's own unique [authentic] way" (Crowe 2006, 187).

We could say that Dasein needs to be shown the possibility in itself which is already there, but which it does not yet know itself to have. However, for such a communication to *get through* to Dasein is difficult, because Dasein normally (in its inauthentic mode) hears everything through *das Man*.

Therefore, being "brought back from lostness in *das Man*" involves an interruption in this listening to, being absorbed in, *das Man*: Dasein's "listening-away [to *das Man*] must get broken off" (Heidegger 1962, 316). Only then can Dasein be shown the potential it has for being authentic.

But what must be interrupted is in this case not a certain kind of information but rather the *way in which* one understands things; it is not that new facts about oneself are called for but a radically different way of relating to oneself. Heidegger refers to this different way of relating to oneself as "another kind of hearing", as he writes that "the possibility of another kind of hearing which will interrupt [the listening away to *das Man*] must be given by Dasein itself. The possibility of its thus getting broken off lies in its being appealed to without mediation [of *das Man*]" (Heidegger 1962, 316).

The way this new kind of hearing is awakened is that "only the self of the they-self gets appealed to [*anrufen*[14]] and brought to listen" (Heidegger 1962, 317). In this way, Dasein is *appealed to* in its authentic self, Dasein is being *called on* to be its authentic self, "it has been summoned [*aufgerufen*] to itself, to its ownmost potentiality-for-being [i.e. its potential for being authentic] (Heidegger 1962, 318). In other words, the call summons Dasein to be authentic. What Heidegger does here is take the ability of language to "get someone to be in a certain way", by reminding them of who they are and pointing out the implications of that, as, for example, one would by appealing to someone's goodness and in doing so call forth the good person in them. That is, the voice "calls Dasein forth (and 'forward') [*nachvornerufen*] into its ownmost possibilities, as a summons to its ownmost potentiality-for-being-its-self" (Heidegger 1962, 318).

As we know, this appealing, summoning, and calling forward needs to happen in a way that does not involve *das Man*. And this is possible because the call of conscience is in every way unlike a call coming from *das Man*, with the result that "[t]he sort of Dasein which is understood after the manner of the world [*das Man*] ... gets passed over ...; this is something of which the call to the self takes not the slightest cognizance" (Heidegger 1962, 317). The call appeals to (*anrufen*) something in Dasein that is not shaped by *das Man*. "Precisely in passing over *das Man* [...] the call pushes it into insignificance" (Heidegger 1962, 317).

As the call gets through, as it by-passes *das Man*, it reaches and as a

---

14   Note that Heidegger's play on the common root *rufen* (to call) in the words "appeal", "summon", and "call forward" is lost in translation.

result touches Dasein in its authentic mode. This is a shaking up, as part of the awakening we encountered in Chapter 2. Heidegger writes, "[i]n the tendency to disclosure which belongs to the call, lies the momentum of a push – of an abrupt arousal" (Heidegger 1962, 316). Here the call, having by-passed *das Man*, having appealed to authentic Dasein, summons Dasein to itself, which involves having a different kind of hearing and a different kind of understanding itself.

As we just saw, it is with a slightly confusing dual use of the word "self", that Heidegger explains this moment of Dasein finding a different kind of hearing, and understanding itself not in terms of *das Man*. The breakthrough moment is one where Dasein's "self" is being addressed, but this "self" is different from the "they self[15]" [the self of *das Man*] which has been by-passed and pushed into insignificance. This we could say is the moment of Dasein "giving itself up", where the self that is given up is the self of the "they self" [*das Man*]. And it is in this context that he writes that "because only the self of the they-self gets appealed [*anrufen*] to and brought to listen, *das Man* collapses" (Heidegger 1962, 317).

Then, after the initial awakening and the subsequent "giving up" of the *das Man*, there is the moment of Dasein finding its authentic self. As the *das Man* is "passed over", "pushed into insignificance" and caused to "collapse", "the [authentic] self, which the appeal has robbed of its lodgement and hiding-place [in *das Man*], gets brought to itself by the call" (Heidegger 1962, 317). Here we find a description of something that begins to point into the direction of a rebirth, in which the self is robbed of its hiding place – note that the word hiding place implies that for Dasein understanding itself in terms of *das Man* is a kind of hiding away from its true self.

By seeing it does have this potentiality-for-being-its-self (and seeing how it tends to constantly take itself to be something it is not – i.e. understanding itself out of *das Man*) Dasein drops its inauthentic way of being and begins to live according to this potentiality-for-being-its-self, according to its own true nature. Because, as we saw earlier, part of the structure of Dasein is such that it *is* what it *takes* itself to be, a change in the way it *takes* itself signifies a change in the way it actually *is*. This is based in the notion that when a person understands themselves suddenly as very different from how they had seen themselves before, this will affect how they act, and that

---

15   Note that "the they" is one of the ways *das Man* has been translated into English.

if a person sees and does things very differently, we could say that they are a different person. And this means that seeing its potentiality-for-being-its-self brings out Dasein's authentic way of being-in-the-world.

To set out the sequence once more, the call appeals to Dasein's authentic self, "passing over" the self of *das Man*, where this involves interrupting the way Dasein usually listens (interrupting Dasein's listening away to *das Man*), in order to awakening another kind of hearing (one that does not get mediated by *das Man*), so that the call can reach Dasein's authentic self and summon it to being its own authentic self. In this the call passes over *das Man*, so that *das Man* is pushed into insignificance and collapses, which exposes Dasein's authentic self, which then sees itself as it really is, as a result of which it takes itself as it really is and becomes this authentic self, because it is what it takes itself to be.

As we can see there is circularity in the above sequence: Dasein only *hears* the call of conscience in so far as the call itself has awakened the kind of *hearing* that is receptive to the call. Or, to say the same thing, for the call to be able to appeal to Dasein's authentic self, it needs to pass over the self of *das Man*, which it can only do in so far as it manages to appeal to Dasein's authentic self in a way that is unmediated by *das Man* in the first place. This would constitute a real paradox for an account of the process of becoming authentic, if this process was conceived in terms of the kind of communication that occurs between entities that are externally related, because then it would be analogous to saying that the only way to enter a particular empty house is through a door that can be opened only from the inside. In the case of the process of becoming authentic, however, the circularity does not present a problem, though it requires explication: because the process does not occur between entities that are externally related, but at the level where there is no distinction between self and other, the call getting through and the new kind of hearing awakening can happen at the same time. What is more, the characteristic of being-with of allowing for individuality to coexist with what is completely other means that both self and other are experienced as increasingly individual, at the same time that they are experienced as connected ever more deeply. This then becomes a benevolent cycle of increasing authenticity, where we become one with what remains inalienably other, to the point where there can be said to be authentic being-with. Such authentic being-with does justice to the individuality of all those involved, as well as to the way in which they constitute each other.

The richness of authentic being-with

The authentic personal relationships

As indicated at different points in this book, Heidegger's account of authentic being-with leaves a lot to be desired, and it has been necessary to both supplement and modify it in certain places. At the same time, the faculty of being-with is perhaps even more important than those of understanding and attunement when it comes to questions of learning, because so much learning happens in relationships with other humans and more often than not involves language, discourse, and culture. So, before we look at the way being-with learning to be authentic relates to conventional accounts of learning, we use the processes described in the previous section, to look at a few examples of the way in which being-with can be said to be authentic. The first of these examples will be of a personal relationship within a typical learning context, the school; a second example will be of an authentic community; third will concern the being-with relationship with animals and plants in the natural world; and, fourth, we will return to the question of authentic attunement we looked at in Chapter 5, to consider what the affective disposition would be like within the context of human relationships. Together these examples should give us a taste of the very richness of authentic being-with.

The first example concerns a disaffected youth, who has a history of not functioning well at school and is now in danger of being expelled. We find the youth in conversation with their teacher. In so far as this is an example of authentic being-with, the youth is approached as an equal in value, without labelling or categorizing him as being a member of a category of, say, trouble makers. In other words, the youth would not be approached as having certain (fixed) characteristics (properties and relations) or a fixed essence (being this or that kind of person). On the contrary, they are approached as "possibility", as open to being in many possible ways, and it would be left up to them to appropriate the actual possibility of being such a person who does not "come under" a certain fixed category of person. The communication would itself be characterized by open-endedness, where it is not decided in advance by the teacher what will be communicated, giving space for both the individuals involved (youth and teacher alike) to "become who they are" in this particular situation.

There will, indeed, be a "shared historical situation" of sorts, in our example the youth's misconduct has raised the possibility of expulsion, which will, if it is appropriated jointly and authentically, give rise to a common world (both youth and teacher understanding the severity of the situation). But it is understood that it is not just the threat of expulsion but, more importantly, the issue of authentic being that is at stake. And this means that there is also a common good in the shared understanding of the value of authentic being and of staying in school – if the latter is, indeed, the preferred option. This "shared historical situation" would transcend the conflicting discourses of the inauthentic teacher (representing, for example, middle-class values and government policy) and the inauthentic youth (representing, say, working-class culture and a conceptualization of schooling as alienating and repressive) and, though the actual vocabulary of each may still be rooted in their different cultural background, the *spirit* of their communication would reflect the "shared historical situation" of authentic being-with.

In so far as the relationship is authentic, the youth's habitual ways of understanding things and feeling about things will not immediately manifest themselves in relation to what is being communicated: using the terminology of the call of conscience, "the call" somehow gets through. For this the youth will need to suspend listening in terms of the way in which their world is usually articulated (e.g. teachers will never fully understand my world), and will need to do so "all the way down", in the sense that a mere suspending of one's consciously-held prejudices is not good enough (doing so may be good enough for reaching an accommodation with the teacher but not for authentic being-with). This means that they will need to listen without taking anything that is being communicated *as* articulating either an understanding of themselves or an emotional colouring of their world: the youth will need to be truly open in the way they listen, both cognitively and emotionally – and this resonates with the notion we have that there needs to be trust for this kind of conversation to work.

Such a way of listening may resemble a detached theoretical one, in that those involved do not allow themselves to identify with the person who is being addressed or to identify emotionally by the way their predicament is looking, but this is not quite accurate. Rather, it is a listening without articulation of their own self or their affective world *in terms of actuality* (thus the listening needs to happen in the authentic mood of disconnection and nearness and the authentic understanding of oneself as possibility or temporality). This will allow for their own self and the affective world they find themselves in to exist in terms of themselves only, which is *in terms of possibility*. With this comes a kind of objectivity (a preverbal kind of "yes, what is being said is about me, but I am going to suspend my reaction to what is being said, because I have understood myself to be possibility and openness rather than a fixed entity") and calm (a kind of preverbal "yes, there may be all kinds of reactions that arise in me, but these should be allowed to come and go, because I experience myself as inescapably tied to a past that makes me react to events in certain ways"). Of course, the youth is very unlikely to verbalize it in anywhere near these terms, but, as has been said, this is about a silent way of being, which is a way of being related to other Daseins, and though articulating it thus yields complex ideas, the reality is unitary and simple: it is the voice of conscience getting through. And the fact that there is a real stillness in the listening (not identifying with oneself or reacting from out of established patterns and habits) the factual content of the communication need not be missed. Rather, the listener, the youth, does not get lost in the factual content, but remains open to being addressed as authentic Dasein throughout.

This openness on the part of the youth may come about as a result of what is being communicated taking them by surprise (a teacher who approaches them in a way which is unlike anything they have encountered before), thus circumventing the habitual ways of being received. Or it is because there is something in what is being said that makes these habitual ways fall into abeyance (their initial stance dissolves gradually as the youth is persistently being addressed in their authentic self). Or it is because the youth has already, in themselves, connected with some of what is being communicated and recognises it as something they need to approach without these habitual ways of receiving it (they have, perhaps unconsciously, been waiting for a teacher to address them as they know themselves to be in their real self, and latch on to any hint of being addressed in this way, thus reinforcing any tendency there may be in the teacher to address them in their authentic self).

Whatever it is that broke through the youth's inauthentic listening, the result is a sense of oneness that is not in contradiction with the individuality of those involved. Thus, the youth may be listening in a way that is so open that they no longer make an effort to distinguish between their own thoughts and feelings and those of the teacher. Likewise, the teacher may be talking and listening in a way that is best described as "there is talking" and "there is listening". Such a dissolution of subject and object should, needless to say, not be confused with some kind of hypnosis or charismatic manipulation of the other, because the unique individuality of the other and their being fully responsible for themselves is not taken away from them. Youth and teacher do, in that sense, not loose themselves in each other, but remain firmly rooted in their own individuality; and this is possible, because there is a high sense of pre-reflective self-awareness that keeps them grounded. So we find that authentic being-with resolves the contradiction we tend to feel is there between being individual and being connected at the level of oneness, where each co-constitutes the other.

Once this initial connection has been made and provided the habitual ways of receiving the communication are not reactivated, the recipient of the communication will increasingly listen in a way that does not take what is being communicated in terms of anything they already know, feel, believe, like or dislike. Here the youth (and the teacher too, as it, per definition, takes two to move into new territory *together*) has moved out of the world as is has hitherto been articulated and is ready to disclose both the world (in attunement) and themselves (in understanding) in new and different ways. That is, the world is ready to take on a new colour, a different mood, and the self is ready to be experienced as a new kind of entity (as process rather than substance, as transcendence rather than immanence, as possibility rather than actuality). This is experienced as an awakening, an expansion of awareness and a silencing of the inner voices that would normally articulate what was being communicated in terms of a known world and a familiar self. Finally, the youth as well as the teacher may inwardly change in such a way that the way they experience their own being and that of the world (prior to any action or any particular conception) is transformed, in that they experience themselves as authentic and have become able to act, perceive, feel and communicate from out of this newly-found, authentic mode of being.

And here we are beginning to see that, when the above process of one individual communicating to another individual is met with an appropriate reception, it may well be the case that, rather than one Dasein showing another the possibility of authentic existence, it is the interaction itself that provides the impetus for change in both interlocutors. The silent communication of authenticity arises from out of the relationship itself, where the interactive movement for change is greater than the sum of the parts. Provided they each have something to start with, something that draws their attention to the possibility of authentic existence (a sense of deep connection with the other, a sudden insight into themselves, an abiding sense that a truer way of being is possible, a new-found openness due to having let go of certain convictions and identification, to name a few), the individuals involved may well enter into a shared dynamic that goes beyond what any of the individuals involved may have come to on their own. This is what the process of being-with learning to be authentic in interpersonal relationships may look like, using certain key concepts from Heidegger's incomplete account, in a way that is coherent with the rest of the notion of becoming authentic that is coming into focus.

The authentic community

As an example of the process of going from inauthentic to authentic communal existence, we will look at how this communal existence is expressed in the culture of a school. Though we could take any kind of organization, say, a law firm or a government department, as our example, the school is apt, because schools have learning as part of their core function, and it is, therefore, especially important that schools have cultures that allow for being-with learning to be authentic. In order to consider the school community becoming authentic, we will first look at the nature of such relatively small-scale communities and what it means for them to be authentic.

As part of the dimension of being-with, the culture of a school can be taken as the articulation of the ways things are conceptualized and of the way things "are done" in the school community – the *das Man* of the school community –and it can be taken as involving the atmosphere, the prevalent moods that exist in the organization. More formally, the culture of a school can be thought of as consisting in the school's values, practices, and narratives. As in the previous example of the authentic interpersonal relationship, I will focus on processes of communication, to illustrate the process of being-with becoming authentic, because, according to Heidegger, it is through in call of conscience that authentic being-with begins.

In the inauthentic community the part-whole differentiation will mean that communication articulates differences between the part and the whole. Thus, there will be a boundary between those individuals who are part of the community and those who are not, there will be an articulation of the individual as a (subordinate) part of the whole or of the whole as being no more than an aggregate of individuals, where the former could be called collectivist and the latter individualist. In such an inauthentic school culture, neither of the two would allow for communication to be framed simultaneously in terms of the individual existing for the sake of itself and of the communal and the interpersonal being co-constitutive of this individual, because in terms of *das Man* this would be internally contradictory.

This means that if the individual is articulated as subordinate to the whole (as Heidegger himself can be said to have done in his discussion of "the people" as the site of authentic being-with mentioned earlier in this chapter), there is no authentic concern for the flourishing of the individual. Where, for example, there is much pressure for the individual teacher and student to conform to school norms and values, for example, because exam results are taken to be of prime importance, the individual ceases to be valued for their own sake. Similarly, if the concern was with the individual without acknowledging how the communal was co-original to this individual and, as a result, one looked at the collective as a mere collection of individuals, there would be no authentic concern for the flourishing of the communal dimension. As a result, the individual, being articulated in terms of an essence with certain properties and relations, would not be given the possibility of the kinds of articulations that allow for their individuality being thought of as inseparable from the collective.

For example, a pupil who, in the basis of their experience of life, may have a sense of being connected with other human beings will have certain avenues articulated to give expression to such a sense of being connected, such as that of doing community service or being involved in charity work, both of which depend on the articulation of the individual who acts in relation to a collective whole which they articulate as separate from themselves (even if they subsequently discover that the people they are helping "are just like themselves"). But this relation to the communal is itself thought of as an isolated instance (for instance, once a week on a Friday afternoon), because their life is mostly articulated in terms of themselves as individual (being assessed individually for their school work, being told to worry about their own future, and so on) who stands in certain relationships to certain communal wholes. Therefore, though the experience of communal involvement will go some way to answering the pupil's inner-felt connection with the collective, this very connection will be articulated in a way that is inauthentic, because there is no genuine sense of oneness.

What is more, in such an inauthentic articulation of the relationship between the individual and the collective, there will be not only a continual tension between the individual and the collective, but also a tension between who is considered inside and outside of a given collective, where the relation to those outside the collective is framed in terms of separation and differentiation (articulating similarities and differences). This kind of us-and-them thinking is often seen as highly problematic in the case of, for example, gangs, where the family, the school, or the state all object to the individual subordinating their individuality to membership of the gang. But in essence other ways of sacrificing one's individuality are just as problematic, for example, sacrificing one's sense of self-worth for the sake of domestic peace (when, for example, placating an aggressive parent), sacrificing one's independence of mind for the sake of one's school (when, for example, uncritically going along with the world-view that holds together life at one's school) or sacrificing one's life for one's country. All these are just as inauthentic as is having one's head tattooed.

As we just saw with the example of the pupil doing some community service, what tends to happen in the context of such a separatist and differentiating articulation of the relationship of one collective to another is that, in order to offset some of the isolating effects, there are initiatives of *reaching out* to other groups: inter-faith conferences, coalition governments, the United Nations, inter-cultural exchanges of various kinds, and so on, are all examples of such inauthentic attempts to bring together what has first been articulated as apart. In the context of a school, inauthentic attempts to bring into contact collectives that have previously been articulated as separate happen between the school as a whole and other schools (for example when a privileged school gets involved with a neighbouring under-privileged one), between staff and students (at social occasions that try to bring the whole school together) and between different groups of students within the school. Note that such meetings of collectives *can* be done authentically, when collectives get together that have been separated purely on practical grounds (age, geographical location, function, and so on), but where the spirit has not been one of separation at the level of being-with itself. Similarly, community service can be a valuable learning experience, provided it is done authentically.

If we now turn to the question of how an inauthentic school community may become authentic, we can say that we are looking for a change from the community being articulated in terms of a tension between the individual and the collective to one where there is a listening as well as a voicing of the communal and the individual which lies beyond the communal-individual differentiation. We are, therefore, not looking for a mere change in discourse (though that may come as a consequence) but a change that happens in the way individuals experience themselves, others, and the collective. This change is, as indicated, not primarily at the level of language, culture, and das Man, but at an unspoken level (where one needs to make sure reticence does not become an excuse for inaction).

Similarly, we are looking for a change from the community being articulated as separate from other communities (as including and excluding certain classes of individuals), to one where there is a listening and a voicing of that which lies beyond such differentiations. And, as we will see in the next section, we may as well include the natural world in these other communities, with which the authentic school community feels itself connected at the level of oneness. So, we are again not primarily looking for a change in discourse but a sense of inclusion that knows no outer boundaries other than those excluding those entities that do not have the nature of Dasein: the boundary lies at the existential level, but in relation to Dasein (and I will argue, animals and plants) there is a sense of oneness.

Note that there can be a sense of oneness that includes all forms of Dasein, because the connection is prior to any discursive articulation as either together or apart. In other words, the sense of the individual being co-constitutive of the collective and vice versa is authentically given at a level that is more fundamental than any ideas or practices we may have. In the same way, the sense we may have, authentically, of the inalienable individuality of each Dasein is also based in a preverbal sense of the individual as existing for the sake of themselves. So, we are looking for a situation where a culture goes from a part-whole relationship that is (inauthentically) based in language and discourse, to a part-whole relationship that is based (authentically) in a silent sense of togetherness – where there is a sense of being part of a shared historical situation even as the main point of being together is to enable the individual to come to an authentic way of being-in-the-world. This is not so much a literal falling silent of the community (though actual silence may well play a role) but an sense of there being a silent coming-together underneath the ongoing articulations of language and discourse.

The way this process is experienced may be as the manifestation of a spirit, of an atmosphere, which has an energy that is felt to originate both from within the group and from beyond the group, as explained in Heidegger's notion of the voice of consciousness. This spirit of authentic being-with may be experienced as something that is both open to those not present and protective of those who are present. It may be experienced as facilitating the flourishing of the individual in their individuality, while at the same time bringing out the underlying unity in the actual, concrete, manifestation of an individual's individuality, in so far as this particular individuality does not impede the manifestation of the spirit of authentic community. That is, the individual can and needs to be open to both individual others and the collective without the defences of status, position, strength, cleverness, and so on, keeping up a persona in terms of a theoretical or practical entity. This means that the individual, though their individuality manifests, is appealed to in their openness, the emptiness of the core of their being – where this empty core is co-constituted by the possibility of communication and thus experienced by the individual in question as a deep and rich connectedness to the others.

The process from the community being based in the part/whole and inside/outside tensions to being based in the possibility of communication from out of emptiness is one of a falling silent of articulation, an expanded awareness of the beings one is connected with, and a "being touched by", "filled by", "hearing of" the presence, the energy, the spirit that manifests as both coming from and belonging beyond the actual group of individuals present and as existing as a manifestation of that group itself, where the spirit touches the individual (is experienced by the individual as touching them) and affects the dynamic of the group (where individuals notice how the dynamic in the group changes, even if they cannot construct a clear causal account of the change) in a way that makes the group both amenable to individual flourishing and to communal coherence in the form of mutual affection, solidarity, concern for the other person's authenticity and so on.

Nature and the animal world

Now that we have seen how the relationship between individuals and between the individual and the collective may become authentic, we will turn to the special case of authentic being-with in relation to the natural world. Though we do not have the space to do justice to so vast and important a topic, I will indicate how a process of being-with learning to be authentic may be the very process that enables us to have an authentic relationship with animals and the natural world (plants, rivers, landscapes, and so on). And in line with the overall concern with processes rather than states, I will consider the learning that may lead to such an authentic relationship, rather than prescribing one. For the sake of brevity, I will take the relationship of the individual with animals and the natural world rather than that of humanity as a collective, but a similar case can be constructed around the latter relationship.

What was said in the previous sections is that authentic being-with, conceived of in terms of communication, is a movement away from articulation (taking certain things as belonging together and other things as belonging apart) towards a preverbal experience of being-with (which, we saw, refers to the individual existing "for its own sake" even as their interpersonal relationships and the collective are understood to be co-constitutive of this individual). So, to the extent that our relationship with animals and plants is also one of being-with, our relationship with nature will be authentic only if it is based in a connection that is not articulated in terms of *das Man*, but merely brought to one's awareness in a way that is silent.

But this raises the question whether we really ought to think of our relationship with nature in terms of being-with. To what extent is our being-with not only being-with other Daseins but also being-with animals and the natural world? And this translates into two further questions. First, to what extent are the individual's relationship with animals and plants co-constitutive of this individual, and to what extent is the whole of the natural world co-constitutive of this individual? Second, to what extent do animals and plants exist for their own sake (individually and collectively as the natural world).

It seems to me that the answer to the first question is neither "totally" nor "not at all": the basic faculty of being-with extends beyond human Daseins but, where it does, the relationship is different from that with other Daseins. Our relationships with nature and animals are, I believe, co-constitutive of our individuality, but to a lesser extent than our relationships with other human beings (which is not to say that our relationship with other Daseins does not occur on the basis of a substratum that is very much part of the natural world: cells, neurons, minerals, and the like). Likewise, we exist as part of the animal kingdom and the natural world, though not as fully as we are part of the human world (which is not to say that we are at a physical level independent of the natural world, but this physical level is a different one from the communicative being-with dimension we are considering here). We can therefore say that the co-constitutive side of being-with refers not only to the faculty of being-with the human world but also animals and the natural world, even if the latter form is different, and in some ways less complete.

But when it comes to the question whether animals and plants exist for their own sake, it seems to me to be unequivocally the case that they do. To some humans the natural world may be no more than that which we are related to practically (as ready-to-hand) or theoretically (as present-at-hand), but this is most likely not the way it looks from the perspective of the animals and plants themselves. Especially in the case of animals it seems clear that we exist from their point of view, in that what we do matters to them (they may, for example, be afraid of humans or dislike their natural habitat disappearing). And to the extent that we accept that plants too have their own forms of flourishing, we also need to accept that this flourishing is something they do for their own sake, and that it matters whether or not the flourishing succeeds. Again, there will be those who disagree, but many people will, I believe, feel that the natural world is valuable in its own right and not a mere resource for the benefit of humans, if only because we ourselves are part of the natural world, and, taking into account, for example, the story of evolution, it will be hard to maintain that of all the animals that have evolved only one has intrinsic value.

So it seems to be the case that, in terms of being-with, animals and plants exist as much for their own sake as humans, but that most of us tend not to experience the same degree of oneness with animals and plants as we do with our own species. Note, however, that the fact that we may feel more part of the human world than of the rest of nature in the way just set out does not mean that our relationship with the rest of nature is any less important: precisely because our bodily survival depends on the natural world, we can never ignore what happens to it, even if we somehow ceased to care. What is more, the fact that we may feel more part of the human world than of the world of animals and plants does not mean that the latter may not ultimately be more important and valuable in themselves than the human species. So the simple observation that the faculty of being-with tends for most people to be strongest in relation to human beings says little about how much we should care about and for the natural world. And this relationship of care, I have argued, ought to be based in the faculty of being-with.

Just as authentic being-with in relation to other Daseins (individually and collectively) requires a suspension of the articulation of that relationship (especially in so far as this is in terms of differentiation and separation, part and whole), we can say that authentic being-with the natural world requires a similar suspension of articulation. This is so, because authentic being-with is a mode which itself does not admit of degree, and even where the relationship is not as close, the state of authenticity remains the same: inauthentic being-with may articulate itself in terms of degrees, but authentic being-with is silent, because it contains a sense of unconditional openness. Indeed, one could argue that only from out of state of being-with are we in a position to judge just how close our relationship is with any particular living being. This means that we do not even need to articulate in advance the character of our being-with nature and animals, but need to be able to suspend such an articulation until after an authentic being-with has been established in much the same way as that happens for being-with in relation to other Daseins: silently and based in a sense of oneness with respect for the individuality of all those involved.

And, indeed, a description of being-with learning to be authentic in relation to the natural world yields a familiar picture. We can take as our example the experience of an individual walking through a forest. For their relationship with the forest to become authentic, there needs to be an initial connection that is made with the natural surroundings. Perhaps the individual comes with an openness to the forest; perhaps something (a sudden silence when the wind drops) interrupts the individual's ability to articulate the things they experience in terms of *das Man*; perhaps a prolonged stay wears away some of their habitual ways of articulating the experience of being in the forest. After such an initial interruption of their habitual way of articulating their relationship with the forest, the individual will increasingly look and listen in ways that do not take what they experience in terms of anything they already know, feel, believe, like or dislike. This enables them to disclose both the world around them and themselves in new and different ways: the forest takes on a new colour, a different mood (Chapter 5), and the self is experienced in new ways (Chapter 4). This is like an awakening, an expansion of awareness and a falling silent of the inner voices that would normally articulate what was being experienced in terms of a known world and a familiar self.

We could say that in this experience the forest begins to come alive, the natural surroundings are beginning to be experienced as a live entity, something that senses and communicates. In some sense this may not be the full sense of being-with we may find in relation to other human beings (provided we experience the latter in an authentic way), but we still experience Dasein-like elements in nature (in a forest, but all the more so in animals). But in some ways, there may be a sense in which the authentic relationship with the natural world is deeper than that with human individuals or the human community, because in the whole of nature the story of evolution speaks to us as a whole. And the miracle of there being life at all is, in many ways, greater in the forest than in human life as we tend to have isolated it from its natural context. So, again we find that, though the relationship with animals and plants is different from the relationship with humans, the former is not necessarily less important, and both are authentically based in being-with.

This process of being-with learning to be authentic in relation to the forest is experienced as, to repeat a phrase that was used earlier in connection with authentic community, a falling silent of articulation, an expanded awareness of the beings one is connected with the forest. It is about the individual 'being touched by', 'filled by', 'hearing of the presence of', the energy, the atmosphere that manifests in the forest. The forest comes alive around us and we come alive in the forest. The result is, more often than not (provided the forest does not suddenly become a threatening place, for example, if one gets lost when night falls and it is cold) that one feels one's authentic self is being given the space to flourish, because it is part of nature. There is in this an indifference on the part of the forest to one's position in the world in terms of, say, status, knowledge, position, strength, guile, and so on. So, the individual needs to be open to the forest without staying identified with a persona, which means that the individual can be appealed to in the openness (the nothingness in terms of *das Man*) at the core of their being, which enables a deep and rich connectedness to the forest, one that merits being designated as communion with nature.

We need to remember in this that such an experience of being-with becoming authentic in relation to nature, one that may result in the experience of communion with nature, is, as an authentic experience, one which happens at the level of the apriori, which means that it does not primarily happen at the level of verbal communication, or at the level of actual a practical or theoretical understanding of the natural world, or at the level of an actual emotional reaction to the natural world – though any of these may happen in a way that remains authentic. That is, though it does not make up the essence of authentic being-with nature, there is no contradiction in the fact that much of the time we may engage with the natural world in practical (building a log cabin) and theoretical (counting plant species) ways and have emotional reactions to it (being afraid of a thunder storm or moved by the sight of a duck and its ducklings).

What the authentic mode of being-with in relation to animals and the natural world does is allow us to understand our relationship with them in an authentic way, where the authentic relationship is that which originally enabled the inauthentic one (it is likely, for example, that we have the ability to tame animals, exactly because we share a large measure of being-with with them), and where the "right" kind of inauthentic relationship is the one that does not deny or forget the authentic one but where the authentic relationship embeds the inauthentic one, with the authentic relationship having temporal priority in the sense that the "right" kind of inauthentic relationship needs to have been preceded by or transformed by an authentic one. This "right" kind of relationship is ultimately a matter of ethics, and it is implied in the above account that the ethical relationship to other human beings as well as the natural world and animals is based in being-with. As always, given that the authentic relationship is one that in actual reality (Heidegger would say "factually") needs to be arrived at through a process of learning to be authentic, it is this process of learning to be authentic that has the actual priority.

The affective disposition of authentic being-with

At several points in this book, it has been noted that Heidegger's notion of being-with contains a number of shortcomings. Some of these shortcomings were addressed, when we looked at authentic interpersonal relationships and the authentic community, but one important one remains, and I will turn to it now. As I indicated in Chapter 5, Heidegger's description of Dasein having been individualized and experiencing the entities it encounters in the world in a mood of disconnection and nearness makes sense in relation to theoretical and practical entities but not necessarily in relation to other Daseins, including creatures with some degree of the nature of Dasein, such as animals and the natural world. Now that we have looked in detail at the process of being-with becoming authentic, we can ask what kind of "affective disposition" would correspond with such a process.

As we saw earlier in this chapter, authentic being-with is to be thought of not only in terms of the relationship between individuals but also in terms of a communal being together, and such authentic communal being-with will also have its own affective dispositions. In this section, however, I will restrict my focus to the relationship between two individuals. This is for convenience only and examples of communal relationships or relationships with nature could have equally been given, with similar results. To bring out the emotional dimension of authentic being-with, I will take as an example a mother listening to what her six-year-old daughter has to say, as they are standing next to a river, having come to see if there are any ducks present that day.

Let us say that the mother has been having some problems with discipline at home (bed-time, tidiness - the usual stuff), but the mother has also noticed that her daughter has become less cheerful recently and is wondering whether the pressures she is being put under at school, combined with the daily struggles at home, are beginning to dull the spark of enthusiasm and originality she has known her daughter to have always had. That is, the mother is concerned for the authenticity of her daughter, concerned that she should be able to be "who she really is" as well as flourish, grow into "who she can possibly be". And in this the mother is not taking herself out of the picture, as she is leaving open the possibility that her own ways of dealing with the discipline issues at home may be contributing to her daughter's increasing sombreness.

While they are both turned towards the river, waiting to see if any ducks will appear, the girl begins to talk about what is on her mind. She is not directly addressing her mother, more thinking aloud, and begins to talk about school, her teacher, some of her class mates, and about herself. The mother senses that she is hearing some of the voices in her daughter that do not normally come out. As the mother listens, there is an increasing, a spreading, of her attention. This is experienced as a gradual spreading of silence, to the point where it appears to "envelop" both the girl and the mother herself, even as there is talking going on. With the spreading of this listening, which is also a spreading of the experience of silence, the separation between the mother and her daughter seems to disappear. "The mother is listening" becomes a "there is listening", which is the event of listening before there is a listener who articulates what is being said by the other person. At this level of listening the mother experiences "being one" with her daughter, which is really a feeling of unity, of her and her daughter co-constituting each other, even as they continue to be individuals in their own right. But this oneness is not of two separate entities being welded together, which might feel comforting and secure, but also restricting and suffocating. Rather it is a feeling of being oneself in being one with the other, a feeling of freedom in being one.

Every now and then, while the girl is talking, the mother asks, in a few words only, a question, to encourage her daughter to keep talking. But even her own voice, asking her daughter to elaborate or continue, sounds different to her now, in that it too seems to come out of a silence and to never break that silence. Yet, while there is this feeling of unity, the very same silence brings out the "otherness" of the voice that is being heard. Less and less of what the mother hears is incorporated (assimilated and accommodated, to use constructivist terminology) into her existing ways of articulating things. She is listening to her daughter as if it is the first time she has ever heard her speak. More and more of what is unknown about her daughter is being disclosed, but it is not disclosed as facts pertaining to an actual being, but as possible ways of being which her daughter has and which manifest now, but which may well manifest very differently next time. It becomes clear to the mother (something which she experiences emotionally as a wish "to give" to the daughter) that what the girl needs, in order for her to be "who she really is" as well as "who she can possibly be", is to be allowed to be "openness and possibility" rather than an "actual" person (one with fixed characteristics and predictable ways of behaving).

And the mother also understands that as "openness and possibility" her daughter will always be unknowable, unassimilable and essentially "other". At this point the mother wonders whether she herself is not putting pressure on her daughter to be in a certain way, to become a person whose actuality makes her more predictable and easier to deal with. The silence the mother is experiencing appears to have affected her daughter too, who appears to become more thoughtful and articulate, even as her sentences become more fragmentary, some of them left unfinished. At this point a deep and at the same time completely transparent feeling comes over the mother: it is this "otherness", this *being always unknown* (not because her actual nature has not yet been discovered, but because she is essentially "openness and possibility", rather than a fixed actuality) that the mother wishes to give to her daughter. And this "wishing to give" is the emotion she feels: it is a "wishing to give" the other her "otherness as openness and possibility". All through this simple conversation on the bank of the river neither the mother not the daughter have lost contact with the river, and the mother begins to feel that the silence she has been experiencing is there in the trees as well and in the river. Then the girl points towards the top end of the river: "look ducks!"

In general terms, what we see the mother go through is the double movement of a dying towards the world (her old articulation of the being of her daughter is left behind) and a turning back ("wishing to give" her daughter the otherness which she already is but which she needs to recover), where the moment of *dying towards* is a falling silent and the *turning back* is the coming alive of the living being from who she is not separate. The affective disposition of authentic being-with can, therefore, be described (where such a description is never more than a gesture in the direction of a possibility that becomes meaningful only in its appropriation) as a feeling of oneness in silence (which is a feeling of attentive calm that is experienced as enveloping both the speaker and the listener and which takes away the separation between them), of "wishing to give the other their otherness" (which is a reaching out to the other person in a way that makes one forgets one's own concerns and interests in order for the other one to be able to "be", where this "being" is felt to be all the other needs to do in order to be worthy of existence), of the other person as openness and possibility (which is a feeling of humility in the face of the unknowability of the other).

If we wanted to reduce the above description of the affective disposition of authentic being-with to a few terms, we could consider Nancy's suggestion that the answer is to be found in Heidegger's correspondence with Hannah Arendt in the years 1925–28, where, according to Nancy, the notion of love is the one that captures the affective disposition of authentic being-with: "In the correspondence, love is, indeed, qualified as the genuine space of a 'we' and of a world that can be 'ours,' and represents the genuine 'taking care' of the other" (Nancy 2008, 14). As in the case of the mother and daughter in our example, this love entails being there *with* and *for* the other as they go through life, as well as grasping, *with* the other, what their possibilities are. "Thus, love is a *mitglauben*, a shared faith in the 'story of the other' and a mitergreifen, a shared grasp of the 'potential of the other'" (Nancy 2008, 14).

Though I think it is important to point out that, if we think through the notion of authentic being-with, words such as love and affection need to be considered, it is not our main concern to define the affective disposition of authentic being-with. As has been argued throughout, the important moment is when we come to a relationship with another living being, and do so in a way that is authentic; what we feel, say, and do then will be its own testimony. And even in this it is not so much the perfect state that needs to be understood, but the way of getting there, of going from inauthentic to authentic being-with. From this perspective the suggestion that the affective disposition of authentic Dasein centres on feelings of oneness, generosity, humility, concern, and love is less important than the characterization of the process itself, which we now see can lead to emotions which many people already understand as central to any kind of deeply meaningful learning, as it can happen in intimate relationships.

Relation to theories of conventional learning

To end this chapter, we will once more try to characterize the process of being-with learning to be authentic, but do so in contrast with the process of learning as we encountered it in the main theories of learning we looked at in Chapter 3. There we saw that learning is thought of as a process of growth, increased integration and differentiation, which tends towards increased stability, where learning is always a modification the existing way of being of the learner, which involves an intentional object.

As with the processes of understanding and attunement becoming authentic, we have seen in this chapter that the process of being-with becoming authentic is one that involves a particular kind of growth, but not one that involves increased integration and differentiation. We find a spreading of the spirit of authentic being-with, where the individual may come to feel they have ever more space to be themselves, and where the sense of oneness is ever deeper. But this does not involve increased integration and differentiation with regard to an existing articulation of the world (of oneself and one's relationships with other individuals and the collective). Such articulations "dissolve"; this aspect of the process is often experienced as a falling silent, where a network of discursive articulation goes into abeyance. As Heidegger puts it in relation to hearing the call of conscience, "Dasein which [the call] summons is called back into the stillness of itself, and called back as something that is to become still. ... It takes the words away from the common-sense idle talk of *das Man*" (Heidegger 1962, 343). Rather than the increased integration and differentiation we associate with the individual's articulation of more and more aspects of the world (if only by way of a growing vocabulary and linguistic sophistication), the process of being-with becoming authentic dissolves any articulation that has been arrived at, while at the same time a communal or interpersonal sense of being connected grows and gets deeper.

The increased stability associated with growing integration and differentiation is also not part of authentic being-with. It is the ability to relate authentically to entities as based in the openness of Dasein that is liberated by the dissolution of the articulation, where, as we saw in Chapter 2, the openness of Dasein has to be understood as an openness towards the *being* of the entity encountered rather than towards the actual ready-to-hand or present-at-hand entity. Importantly, this openness understands the Dasein it encounters in being-with as process, and the process of being-with becoming authentic can, therefore, be further characterized as one of letting go of a fixed, actual, articulation to an experience of a process which contains only possible articulations. This part of the process may well be experienced as a coming alive of the other person, the community or nature, and oneself as being-in-the-world, where this coming alive is a continuous movement. Rather than one's articulation of the being of the other person, the community, oneself or nature becoming more and more stable over time, they are all experienced as processal in nature, as being "alive" in a way that allows for novelty and creativity to come into the relationship.

With regard to the notion that learning is always a *modification of* and, therefore, *based in* the existing way of being of the learner, there is the first difference in the fact that the openness, the silence that is the result of learning to be authentic is not based in the initial articulation, because it constitutes a dissolution of that articulation. What is more, we can say that being-with learning to be authentic is rather *based in* the relationship between the individuals, between the individual and the collective, and between the individual and nature. The location where the process of learning originates is the relationship itself, rather than the individual as it stands in relationship to something or other. Consequently, it is the relationship (which I have characterized as one of co-constitution and otherness) that is the locus of the learning process. Seen from this perspective, we could say that the relationship which learns "contains" an individuality which exists "for its own sake". This is another way of saying that, for this relationship-learning to happen in the right way, it needs to allow for the individuality "contained" in it to become itself in terms of itself. In addition, any collective processes of learning need to accommodate processes of individuals becoming truly individual in their own terms, where the individual learning process is based in the learning relationship.

With regard to the idea that learning always includes an intentional object, we are, in the case of being-with learning to be authentic, dealing with a process that is essentially prior to any separation between subject and object. Even so, we can say that being-with learning to be authentic is a learning that occurs in relation to other Daseins, the collective, and the natural world of animals and plants. These are, however, not the intentional objects of learning in the sense that conventional learning is *about* what is separate from the learner. In becoming authentic, Dasein does not learn *about* the other person, the communal or nature, even if its being changes as a result of the process. The other person, the communal, and nature do not appear as separate (ready-to-hand or present-at-hand) entities as a result of the learning, rather the structure of Dasein's experience has changed and, as a result, the world as a whole appears different in a way that means that Dasein experiences the other person, the communal, and nature in a different way, even as they appear in more or less the same ready-to-hand and present-at-hand way in that experience. That is to say, the notion of an intentional object only makes sense in the context of the ready-to-hand or present-at-hand but not in the context of authentic being-with. This is not to say that, as a result of authentic being-with, Dasein's practical and theoretical engagement will not change – after all, its practical and theoretical engagement will now be rooted in authentic being-with. Dasein will, for example, not lightly subordinate the other person, the communal or nature to practical instrumentality or theoretical categorization without being highly mindful to preserve their way of being for their own sake – but such an eminently ethical stance would come out of a form of authentic being-with that is itself not a subject-object relationship, even if it allows for the individuality of all those involved. We, therefore, again see that the process of learning to be authentic differs in essential ways from the process of *learning as modification and growth*.

Authentic Learning

Learning to be authentic and conventional learning

Making a beginning in learning to be authentic

In this final chapter we will look at the way in which the process of *learning to be authentic*, as described in Chapters 4 – 6, can be combined with *conventional learning*, to produce the kind of learning that combines genuine openness to the being of the entities one learns about with the kind of continuity and growth we find in conventional learning. Such *authentic learning* would lead to actual change in attitudes, skills, and knowledge, even as it remained open to what is other and unknowable. It would be a weaving together of the process of "grasping" we find in *conventional learning* with the "letting go" that characterizes *learning to be authentic*. In the final part of this chapter, we will then see how the linear temporality of *conventional learning* interweaves with the momentary temporality of *learning to be authentic*, resulting in a kind of tapestry of *authentic learning*.

Before we look at the tapestry of *authentic learning*, it bears reminding once more that the notion of learning I am using includes much, if not most, of the person we become over time – it is not just skills and knowledge come out of authentic learning, but more or less the whole person, including those processes that are more commonly designated as cognitive and emotional development. As we saw in Chapter 1, *human learning* is increasingly thought of as involving "the whole person - body (genetic, physical and biological) and mind (knowledge, skills, attitudes, values, emotions, beliefs and senses)" where there is a social dimension, all of which is then "integrated into the person's individual biography resulting in a changed (or more experienced) person" (Jarvis, 2006, p. 13). *Authentic learning* is, therefore, a process that changes us in concrete ways, as a result of which the person is not only (as Jarvis would have it) "*more* experienced" but also, in some ways, *less* guided by experience, because a genuine sense of openness also belongs to authentic learning, which involves a degree of letting go.

Importantly, such integrated process of *authentic learning* takes us away from the predominantly sequential notion of authenticity we found in our discussion of educational thinking about the topic in Chapter 2 and implied in Chapters 4 to 6. There we saw the idea of authenticity and inauthenticity being essentially two different ways of being-in-the-world in Thomson's notion, cited earlier, of authenticity as a movement in which we "turn away from the world, recover ourselves, and then turn back to the world" (Thomson 2004, 443). In Bonnett's notion of authenticity as "an achievement" where we "extricate ourselves from the frame of mind that constitutes [*das Man*]" (Bonnett 2002, 232) we find a similar sequential emphasis on *first* letting go of *das Man* and then, *subsequently*, returning to the "authoritative principles, rules, values, and norms that are expressive of the socially prevalent conception of the good life" (Bonnett 2002, 233). In authentic learning, however, there is no such clear-cut sequence, because it integrates *conventional learning* and *learning to be authentic* into a single movement of learning.

Such an integration of *learning to be authentic* and *conventional learning* does not make it incoherent to think of authenticity as comprising of an initial moment of learning to be authentic, followed by a subsequent re-appropriation of the ways of *das Man* in a way that is still authentic, and thus allows for *authentic learning*. We can see that this is so, when we look once more at the notion of becoming authentic. Thus, the process of learning to be authentic begins when Dasein's inauthentic way of being is left as possibility (so that it is not committed to), left as prior to either the subject or object pole of intentionality (so that it is not moved away from or acted upon), and left as open to the possibility of being affected from without it (so that it is ready to be appealed to). This initial opening up is then followed by a process of, on the one hand, growing pre-reflective self-awareness (transparency of understanding, pre-reflective self-awareness of mood, and the voice of conscience calling) and, on the other hand, the awakening of a more authentic way of being (projecting the being of entities onto temporality, encountering entities from out of the nothing of the world, listening in a way that is not mediated by the cultural and linguistic practices of *das Man*). With this comes a "dying towards" one's inauthentic way of being, a "turning away", a "letting go" of the existing structures of experience (of the projections of understanding so that things can be understood in terms of temporality; of one's defining moods, so that things can "let be"; of the linguistic and cultural practices, to make way for a silent "giving to understand"). The result of this is a self-understanding that understands Dasein in terms of itself (as process, transcendence and co-constituted by being-with) and as existing prior to there being either a self or a world (as temporality, attunement and a voice, all of which are self-arising). The result is also a newfound openness (within which authentic learning can subsequently take place), which is expressed as an understanding of the entities Dasein encounters in the world in terms of their being (theoretical, practical, or with the nature of Dasein), in terms of an affective disposition that is non-identifying and near to the entities in the world, and in terms of a way of being-with that takes every Dasein as potentially authentic. In this way, learning to be authentic can be thought of very much as a "turning away from the world", which needs to take place before there can be a "turning back" in the shape of *authentic learning*.

The point of this chapter is, therefore, not to argue that such a sequential notion of authentic learning has no validity. It is entirely in line with Heidegger's writings to think of authenticity in terms of such a sequence when there is, for example, first a conversion, to use a word that resonates with early Heidegger's Christian inspiration (See Crowe 2006), followed by a return to the world. And taken in this manner, the process of learning to be authentic can be seen as valid in itself, in that it would result in a transformed way of being-in-the-world. So, if in this chapter we concentrate on establishing a notion of *authentic learning* that does not require an initial moment of authenticity, this is not to discard that possibility. Rather, we are looking for an account of learning that is whole, in the sense of complete, and this means that there need to be in learning both moments of grasping and moments of letting go, because openness is part of any true form of learning.

So, rather than limit ourselves to saying that authentic learning can only happen when Dasein is in a mode of complete authenticity, we are looking for a form of *authentic learning* that combines moments of *learning to be authentic* with moments of *conventional learning*. In other words, we do not need to be authentic all the way down for there to be authentic learning. But this does mean that, for there to be this kind of authentic learning, the two movements of conventional learning and learning to be authentic need to happen in the same situation, though neither of them needs to happen in a way that is perfect: just as conventional learning does not need to lead to perfect skill or knowledge to qualify as conventional learning, learning to be authentic does not need to reach a state of perfect openness for there to be a moment of opening up to the being of entities. To make this kind of learning intelligible, I will try to identify a process that contains both a moment of opening up towards authentic being and the kind of modification and growth we associate with conventional learning. Ultimately, I hope to show, a true dissolution of the moments of *conventional learning* and *learning to be authentic* will result in a kind of *authentic learning*.

In preparation for such a full integration of *learning to be authentic* with *conventional learning* as a process of *authentic learning*, we will consider what it looks like, when conventional learning occurs in the context of learning to be authentic: as we open up to the kind of authentic understanding, attunement, and being-with described in the preceding chapters, can there still be the kind of conventional learning that is characterized by modification and growth? For the purpose of this, we will start with summaries of the outcomes of Chapters 4 to 6, as a way of reminding ourselves what exactly is involved in learning to be authentic. And it will help us establish that it is indeed possible for learning to be authentic and conventional learning to exist side-by-side. We will then, in the second part of the chapter, look at a characterization of *authentic learning*, as it happens in Dasein taken as a whole, rather than with regard to the three faculties. This will be a general account of authentic learning that merges conventional learning with learning to be authentic in a way that is both authentic and capable of producing the learning of actual, real-world attitudes, skills, and knowledge. And it will be the final answer, as far as this book is concerned, to the challenge put in Chapter 1. There I suggested that there is a deep contradiction at the base of our notion of learning, one that is sometimes referred to as the learning paradox. On the one hand, learning involves the modification of existing ways of understanding, feeling, acting, thinking and relating, in a way that involves continuity, where what is learned always builds on something that is either innate or learned previously. On the other hand, learning involves openness to what is new, to that which we do not already understand, feel, do, and think, in a way that involves discontinuity, because that which is being learned is different from what was already innate or learned previously.

In the chapters preceding this one, I suggested that the kind of openness we can have to what is new and other can be brought into focus with the help of Heidegger's notion of authenticity, and I have tried to tease out of Heidegger's writings the kind of learning process that would lead to such authentic openness. Now, in the final chapter of the book, we will see if this notion of opening up and letting go can be combined with the kind of conventional learning we saw, in Chapter 3, can account for learning as continuity, modification, and growth, but not for the kind of opening up to what is new and other we find in the process of learning to be authentic. As indicated, this authentic learning would then be an answer to the learning paradox, but more than solve a theoretical puzzle about learning, it would bring us closer to the mode of being-in-the-world that is essentially open to life and capable of truly connecting us with ourselves, others, and life as a whole. To return to the earlier phrase, authentic learning would be an integral part of the conversion that led to an authentic way of being-in-the-world, at the same time that it would allow us to learn in a way that combined openness to the being of entities with the acquisition of knowledge and skills that is based in continuity, modification, and growth. It would allow for true learning and for there to be actual learning outcomes that made a tangible difference in our lives. But, as indicated, we will begin by making plausible the possibility of conventional learning happening within a wider authentic way of being in the world.

Conventional learning in the context of authentic understanding

In this section we will look at understanding, and in the two subsequent ones at attunement and being-with. We will recap the arguments made in Chapters 4 to 6, as to how these different faculties can become authentic, and then consider ways in which conventional learning can take place within such wider authentic being-in-the-world. As we saw in Chapter 4, understanding refers to the way in which Dasein is *directed* towards things, the way it gains *access* to things and the way its engagement with things is *guided*. It can be said to comprise both action and perception. The process of understanding learning to be authentic begins with inauthentic understanding, when Dasein understands itself pre-reflectively from out of the entities it is engaged with and does so in terms of practical and/or theoretical entities. That is, the entity that inauthentic Dasein is engaged with "gives" it its self-understanding, just as Dasein "gives" the entity its being. Dasein has, of course, also a reflective, explicit, self-understanding, but this is a present-at-hand or ready-to-hand self-understanding and, as such, not the starting point for the process of becoming authentic.

The beginning of the process of understanding becoming authentic involves a moment of "breaking through", which can occur because understanding finds itself face-to-face with something it cannot possibly resolve; because a certain affective disposition arises; or because of a communication by another Dasein. All these may awaken a sense of the limitations of Dasein's current understanding (of itself and of the entities it finds in the world) as well as a sense that these limitations are self-imposed and, as such, may conceal possible other ways of understanding. This marks the beginning of the process where Dasein's inauthentic understanding of itself becomes transparent, is awakened to itself.

In general terms, the process of understanding becoming authentic can be described as one of a mutually reinforcing process of understanding becoming transparent to itself as projection and letting go of existing projections. This returns it to a point where understanding is itself understood as arising out of openness and any actual understanding is understood as possibility. When Dasein understands this, it *is* openness and possibility, because Dasein *is* in many ways its own self-understanding. Within this openness and possibility understanding may arise (quite impersonally) of another Dasein as one with the Dasein who engages with it and yet as an end in itself. Likewise, understanding of a practical or a theoretical entity may arise within this that is based in an openness towards that entity that is prior to any practical or theoretical concern, and that genuinely constitutes Dasein's own understanding (for which it can then genuinely take responsibility) rather than an understanding that originates in *das Man*.

So, what was at first experienced as the whole of understanding becomes transparent (becomes pre-reflectively self-aware) while this particular understanding quietens down (lets go of its projections), to the point where it may become completely silent (experiencing that its own utmost possibility consists in giving itself up), at which point there is just openness and possibility, from which understanding may arise again (impersonally), but then as only a part of the greater transparency of experience as a whole, always leaving some of the openness empty (so that communion with other Dasein's may occur), and always temporarily (being ready to both take back and repeat), before quieting down again (so that Dasein may genuinely reconnect with the entity).

In contrast to the conventional accounts of learning we looked at in Chapter 3, this process of understanding becoming authentic is not one of increased integration, differentiation and rigidity, but one of dissolving (quieting down) of what has been constituted; the process is essentially discontinuous, in that the end result (openness) cannot be said to be *based in* the initial state of there being a certain understanding of being; the process is prior to there being a subject or an object moment in the intentional act, in that it happens at a level that is prior to action and perception, so that the entity that is learning coincides with what it is learning about. But though the two processes are not the same process, they can be said to be compatible and able to exist at the same time. This is because the process of understanding opening up and quieting down is able to accommodate a process of conventional learning.

The process of opening up and quieting down liberates, awakens a wider pre-reflective self-awareness, *within which* the processes of integration and differentiation described by conventional theories of learning can occur. The process of letting go of an understanding can be thought of in terms of a dissolution of this understanding, where it remains possible to reconstitute the understanding on the basis of the notion that understanding does not consist of a representation but of an intentional act, which is built up again every time the understanding manifests. In the case of an understanding having dissolved, it could be said that the dissolution consisted in the understanding becoming transparent to itself and remaining open to the *being* of the entity involved in the situation. Then, once the understanding has resolved on the being of the entity, Dasein's attitudes, knowledge, ways of acting, and so on, would *re-constitute* themselves in accordance with that resolution.

This notion of an understanding re-constituting itself after it has been allowed to dissolve is compatible with the notion, first encountered in

Chapter 3, that association is the main mechanism driving conventional learning, in the sense that once events occur together – two events happening simultaneously or following each other chronologically – they are more likely to occur together again in the future. Based on this principle, even a complex way of being may be built up out of many simple associations occurring together or in sequence. For example, when a sequence of movements (for example, drawing short lines on paper) constitutes one action (writing a word) that is made up out of those smaller movements, the larger action may be dissolved, without preventing a future re-constitution of this action out of the smaller movements. What would happen in such a re-constitution would be that one small movement would call up, by way of association, another one, which would, in turn call up yet another movement, and so on. And this "bottom-up" reconstitution is likely to happen under a "top-down" guidance of the larger context, in this case, for example, the sentence, the paragraph, and the thing one is writing as a whole. Note that this would not only be a process that took place "internal" to the person, but also in relation to the environment, in the sense that elements of the entity one was engaging with (for example, pen and paper) and the situation in which one found oneself (for example, a classroom) would help call up, by way of association, certain ways of acting, feeling, and thinking. In this way, there is no contradiction between ways of being dissolving and their later reconstitution at different levels of generality.

With the dissolution of the understanding of an entity, two things would happen. First, the actual way of understanding would go into (temporary) abeyance and, second, the existing understanding of the being of the entity would make place for openness to its being. If then, because the situation demanded, Dasein would decide (resolve) on the being of the entity, the actual ways of relating (linguistically, emotionally, practically, or theoretically) would reconstitute themselves in the light of Dasein's understanding of the being of the entity. But in doing so, Dasein would remain open to the being of the entity, would, as we put it in Chapter 4, be ready to either take back or repeat its understanding of the being of the entity. For example, a teacher could allow her understanding of a certain pupil to dissolve, with the result of opening up towards the being of the pupil as an entity with the nature of Dasein. This would constitute the dissolution (letting go) of the act of being towards the pupil in a certain way, with the result that the pupil was understood as openness and possibility. The impetus for this dissolution could come from a sense in the teacher that their existing ways of relating to the pupil were getting in the way of an authentic connection. But if, after the openness has come into being, a certain action was then called for (for example, a report about the pupil had to be written), the theoretical way of taking the pupil would re-constitute itself (the teacher would remember that certain forms needed filling in, that a certain kind of language needed to be used in that form, that certain events needed to be reported, and so on).

Importantly, such a theoretical or practical reconstitution of the way of taking the pupil would occur within a wider field of openness which would never be fully taken over by the actual way of being towards the entity theoretically or practically: authentic transparency would remain as openness to the being of entities. This would allow for the re-constitution of an understanding to take place within transparency, where the effect of the openness was never completely absent. To repeat, because such a process of re-constitution was subject to modification as described by the conventional theories of learning, there could, indeed be conventional learning within the openness of authentic existence. This would mean that any subsequent learning (in the sense of the further construction of an actual way of being via the mechanism of association) could happen in a way that was "informed by" the openness or transparency. This would constitute authentic learning, a learning according to the mechanisms described in Chapter 3, but within the context of authentically transparent understanding, that is, always informed by the openness that characterizes authentic existence.

For example, a pupil in a gardening project who had hitherto handled (which represents a practical understanding) plants much as tools or toys, as inanimate objects, may have previously learned to prune a climbing plant in the school yard. Because the pupil tended to handle plants as if they were things, the skill they had showed, to the experienced gardener, a lack of sensitivity: the boy did not have green fingers. Then the boy, perhaps because he was made aware by the teacher of his mechanical way of approaching the climber, has a moment in which his understanding of the plant as a practical object dissolves. There is a moment in which his movements fall silent and he just stands there and looks at the plant, even as his habitual way of handling the climber is transparent to him. Then, instead of cutting, he begins to feel the stems and the leaves, as if noticing the plant for the first time. At this moment the practical understanding of pruning he had acquired dissolves and he opens up towards the plant but also to his own being, the world around him, in a way that is pre-reflective. Though it may well look like he is fully absorbed in the plant, because that is where his eyes and body are turned towards, he is, nevertheless, opening up towards the whole of life as this ways of engaging with the plant become transparent to him. He begins to get a feel for the climber as a being with, to some extent, the nature of Dasein. So, as he takes up the activity of pruning again, the skill he had acquired earlier re-constitutes itself, but in a way that is now slightly different; for example, he still cuts in the same place, as he has been taught, but with more care and awareness of the plant: the same cut acquires a different meaning. Then, as the teacher notices the boy's increased sensitivity, he decides to show him how to prune a rosebush, something with which he entrusts only the most careful pupils. Now the boy needs to learn a new skill, one that builds upon what he has learned in the context of pruning the climber. As he looks on as the teacher shows him how to prune the rosebush, his whole way of looking is informed by, occurs within, the openness he has found. The new skills involved (for example, how to hold a thorny stem) are then developed in a way that is authentic and, as such, constitute authentic learning. And, in so far as the learning remained authentic, there are likely to be moments when the boy notices within himself that inauthentic ways of being towards the plant reassert themselves (perhaps the mechanical way of handling the plant returns), and he experiences these inauthentic ways as standing in the way between him and the plant, so that from out of this awareness he is able to let go of the inauthentic way that has reasserted itself. And this ability to notice (in pre-reflective self-awareness) the inauthentic way and let go of it ensures the continuity of authentic learning.

To recap, the full development of this learning would, as said, begin when the way in which the boy approaches the climber becomes transparent to him. This pre-reflective awareness would spread and be accompanied by a letting go of the way he used to approach the plant, to the point where he was just open towards the being of the plant. Then, as his pruning skills re-constitute themselves in relation to the plant, they do so in such a way that the re-constituted way of handling the climber is affected by the openness towards the plant itself. And even as the skill is re-constituted, it never absorbs him completely, because some of the transparent openness remains – and this is so, even as he once more applies himself to the task at hand. Indeed, this openness remains even as he turns towards the rosebush. Perhaps at this point all his understanding of pruning again dissolves, leaving him in complete openness towards the bush. At any rate, as he first observes his teacher prune and then applies the secateurs himself, the new skill remains "within" and informed by the openness towards the being of things. There will also be moments when the boy notices, probably at an intuitive level, that a way of being in the world that reconstitutes itself is getting in the way of his connection with the plant, and as a result of this awareness is able to let go of it, because the inauthentic way of being is seen for what it is. And as the afternoon progresses, the openness towards the being of things only grows and what started as the pre-reflective awareness of his way of pruning expands so as to become a field of transparency much greater than any of his ways of acting, and within this field all his ways of understanding the things around him, other Daseins, and himself rise up and die down again, without the underlying transparency of the being of entities ever going away. In this way the conventional learning of attitudes, skills, and knowledge may happen within a wider authentic understanding of the being of entities.

Conventional learning in the context of authentic attunement

We saw in Chapter 5 how the process of attunement learning to be authentic takes place, where attunement refers to the way moods and emotions disclose the world as a certain kind of world and Dasein as a certain kind of individual Dasein. Attunement learning to be authentic begins with Dasein being in a mood that connects it with the world, after which there is a moment of "staying with", where one finds oneself in a world that predates one and with a personality that is not of one's own making, and where one's understanding of the things in the world is ultimately in terms of one's own existential death. This involves a reciprocal movement of increased pre-reflective self-awareness of oneself as individualized transcendence and the disclosure of the nothingness of the world from which the entities one encounters emerge. In response to the feelings of urgency, longing and curiosity that are awakened by the increasing contact with the things one is engaging with, one lets go of the mood one was in. As a result, one's relationship with the things and people one encounters is that of "letting things be" and immediacy: practical and theoretical things in the world are experienced as detached and near, and one's relationship with other individuals is, as we saw in Chapter 6, one of oneness in silence, of "wishing to give the other their otherness", and humility in the face of the otherness of the other. This movement of learning is experienced as one of spreading, where the awareness one has of one's mood grows until it encompasses the whole of one's being-in-the-world.

This process of attunement becoming authentic differs from the process of learning as it is found in some of the conventional theories of learning: the process of attunement becoming authentic is not one of increased integration, differentiation and rigidity, but one of letting go of the mood one found oneself in; the process is essentially discontinuous, in that the end result (emptiness) cannot be said to be a modification of a previous way of being attuned emotionally; the process is prior to there being a subject or an object moment in the intentional act, in that it happens at a level that is prior there being a separation between the individual having certain feelings and that towards which the individual has the feeling, which is in line with the non-dualist nature of authentic attunement, which gives both the subject and the object as disclosed by a certain emotional content.

But having an account of the process of attunement learning to be authentic, and knowing that it does not develop along the lines of conventional learning, does not mean that it is straightforward to construct an account of an authentic process of learning to be attuned. Whereas in the previous section we saw that it was relatively easy to come up with a notion of authentic learning to understand, based on the processes of learning as modification and growth, there appears to be a general lack of accounts of emotional learning that take emotion itself as that which learns, rather than postulating a self which has emotions, and which learns to deal with them in an intelligent way. For example, *The Encyclopaedic Dictionary of Psychology* defines emotional intelligence as the way in which "people attend to, process and utilize affect-laden information" and as "the ability to understand the emotions and mental states in one's own self and in other people" (Davey 2005). Paraphrasing from Daniel Goleman's 1995 book Emotional Intelligence, we find that his kind of emotional intelligence involves learning to read one's emotions and recognize their impact, to use gut feelings to guide decisions, to control one's emotions and impulses, to adapt to changing circumstances, to sense, understand, and react to others' emotions, to inspire and influence others. What stands out in these descriptions of emotional intelligence is that it is in many ways what we have been calling "understanding" that learns, rather than the faculty of attunement itself. That is, learning to read, recognize, control, sense, and understand emotions are all processes take the emotion as the object of learning and thus represent what we have been calling understanding *learning as modification and growth* in relation to one's emotions. Though not all approaches to emotional intelligence may take such an exclusively "understanding" perspective (for example, by focussing on character traits and the personality aspect of emotional intelligence), the examples above serve to show that an account of emotions learning is by no means easily found. I will, therefore, present in broad terms certain aspects of what could become a phenomenological account of emotional learning, so that we can then take these as a starting point to see how it can be integrated with the account of attunement learning to be authentic summarized at the beginning of this section. To construct this account, I will make use of the assumptions about learning shared by the main theories of *learning as modification and growth* we discussed in Chapter 3. It is, however, not claimed that the resulting account of emotional learning is comprehensive or, indeed, the only possible one, but rather that it has enough face-validity to serve as a starting point for a discussion of authentic learning to be attuned.

Taking emotion as a moving force that arises in the individual as transcendence (thus disclosing both self and world in a particular way), we can begin to suggest ways in which such a moving force itself may become more and more mature as a result of the right kind of experience (experience that leads to greater maturity). In doing this, I will take the process of emotion learning as a process of emotional maturation, which gives us the "emotionally mature person" as a guiding concept with regard to the direction into which emotional learning needs to be seen to move. I will take as my unit of analysis the individual who finds him or herself in a certain situation, where emotions arise "in" the individual, meaning that their sense of self and world is coloured emotionally in a certain way, and where this "arising" of the emotions is itself a movement on the part of the individual. I will take, as my examples, emotions that are directed at certain events, entities or situations, on the assumption that what holds true for these holds true *a fortiori* for moods and atmospheres that do not have an intentional structure. Further, it will be taken as one of the basic characteristic of emotions that they communicate themselves by resonating in the person who "receives" the communication (for example, the sadness the pupil is feeling at having received a bad mark is experienced as sadness "in" the teacher by the teacher, even though the teacher is well aware that this is not her own but the pupil's sadness, with the result that the teacher experiences the pupil as sad). Because of this last point and because of the general nature of our discussion, the following examples will not always distinguish between the emotion arising in a certain person and the same emotion being picked up by another person.

In general terms, I am taking the notion of emotion as that which constitutes either the actual movement the individual makes (for example, raising their hands to protect their face against an approaching projectile or "shrinking" with fear) or as that in response to which the individual is moved to act in a certain way (for example, feeling indignation at a television programme and subsequently writing a letter to the BBC). The experience of having an emotional feeling is, therefore, either an integral but secondary part of the emotional response (when the emotion itself is the action) or that in response to which one is moved to act (even if one does not act but allows the emotion to abate un-responded to). As with the distinction between the individual in whom the emotion arises and the one who picks up the emotion, the distinction between the emotion as in itself an act and the emotion as an inner experience (a feeling) that may move one to act will remain blurred in these examples, because both distinctions are thought to be secondary and not directly relevant in the context of the account of emotions themselves learning we are trying to bring to light.

The first aspect of emotions themselves learning is that of a movement towards the emotions being attuned to more and more different situations. This is a clearly cumulative aspect of such learning, where, as a result of the right kind of experience, one's emotional responses have become attuned to more and more situations. This being attuned means that one is able to anticipate probable or possible ramifications of a situation at the level of emotion. For example, having told different patients over the years their prognosis when cancer has been detected may have attuned the doctor to that kind of situation, in that he or she has developed a feel for the emotions that are likely to come up for the patient. This will enable the doctor to not only follow what is happening for the patient in a way that appreciates the meaning of their emotions better (as similar experiences will have enriched their sense of the *possible* meaning the situation may have for the patient) but also to open up possibilities for these patient, say, by showing them ways of feeling that they had not yet discovered for themselves (for example, that adopting a positive rather than defeatist attitude in the face of a negative diagnosis can help one cope).

This aspect of emotional learning has clear similarities with the notion of growth we encountered in Chapter 3, but, rather than the word growth, the word "depth" may be the more appropriate one. That is, this increased sense of the possible meaning of situations is not a kind of practical or theoretical knowledge but rather a "depth" of meaning that is experienced, where the possible meanings of the situation that may be anticipated or opened up are experienced as emotional depth. The emotion that is there at a given moment is able to resonate through the individual in ways that have been opened up as a result of previous experience (when there was a *temporal* unfolding of the emotional meaning of a similar situation), where this resonance is now experienced in more of a *spatial* sense, as the potential development of the given situation as it is experienced emotionally. This resonance is experienced as the potential emotional meaning of the situation and as an openness for the individuals involved to discover this meaning for themselves. We could say that the increased sense of the possible emotional meaning of a situation allows for the actual emotion to manifest that would otherwise perhaps remain hidden or be slow to spread out into possible emotional space. It should be noted that it is not always the case that an individual who has experienced many different kinds of emotional situations is able to allow for emotions to manifest as they are. Indeed, the individual may have certain fears or dislikes, may find pleasure in the experience of certain emotions, or may be committed to certain emotions in ways that distort what emotions can manifest and the depth at which they are allowed to be felt. This is not only a case of blocking certain emotions but also of prioritizing some over others. So, we can say that the above description of an increase in the awareness of the possible emotional ramifications of a given situation as a result of experience does not automatically imply that emotions are, to return to a phrase we used in the context of authentic attunement, "let be".

This then gives us the first element of authentic learning to be attuned, where the process of the increase in the depth of emotional experience can occur in a way that is authentic, when the emotions arising are held with a sense of non-identification and nearness. And there is the reverse, when emotions arise in a way that is inauthentic, emerging in an inauthentic mood (revealing these emotions as, for example, attractive or threatening, good or bad). As a result of inauthentic emotional learning the depth of emotional experience will resist some and promote other emotions in a way that may be both sophisticated (for example, by ostensibly allowing a particular emotion to manifest but actually shielding oneself from it) and resilient, as these resistances and preferences will have been reinforced many times and in many different ways, leading to a web of responses that is not easy to circumvent. Authentic emotional depth, however, involves, as we saw in Chapter 5, combination of openness to things as they present themselves and the ability to respond emotionally in a way that is commensurate with this entity involved – and this, we could say, is the combination of non-identification and nearness we find when there is authentic learning to be attuned.

The second aspect of emotions themselves learning is that of a movement away from emotions manifesting in a way that is "blatant", when the emotion comes out fully, to one where emotions manifest in a way that is measured, proportionate and discriminating, in a way that is commensurate with the situation and with the cues that set it off. In its blatant form the emotion comes out in such a way that, once it has been triggered, the emotion loses its link with the situation and simply manifests fully. In its measured form the emotion, rather than taking the cue and becoming self-absorbed, comes out in a way that retains the relationship with the situation that triggered it. This is not to say that the measured emotional response is necessarily less intense, but that it is clearly directed (for example, it does not spread its anger indiscriminately to whoever happens to be at hand) and proportionate (for example, a child's minor rule-infringement does not elicit a fire and brimstone sermon from the parent. And though the description of a "proportionate response" may suggest that we are talking about control, this is not the case so long as it is authentic, as it is the emotion itself that responds in a way that is measured, by remaining in touch with the situation that triggered it. Similarly, the notion of discrimination may suggest that there is a self that directs the emotion towards its target, but, again, it is the emotion itself that remains in touch with both itself (note that pre-reflective self-awareness is necessary here) and the situation that triggered it, so that, in case it began to spill over into other situations (for example, the parent has been angry with one child and this anger is now threatening to be directed at another) the emotion itself will awaken to the fact that it is, as it were, "barking up the wrong tree".

The inauthentic form of such measured emotional responses is one that is not the result of the emotion remaining itself open to the situation as it changes but, rather, the result of the response being controlled in a way that is reflective, where the faculty of understanding takes the emotion that is experienced and acts in a way that is calculating and measuring. This is a case of critical rationality taking the emotion under its control (for example, by deciding to vent one's anger at the pupil who "deserves it" but present a smiling face to the one who has been good). Though the attempt to take control of one's emotions is probably usually well-intentioned, it is deeply self-contradictory, as it is not really possible to take control of an emotion in a way that is authentic, because, as we saw in Chapter 5, the emotion is that which first gives us the possibility of the experience of the things we experience in the way we do; what can be controlled is one's actions or the expression of the emotion. To say that the attempt to control one's emotions is inauthentic is not to suggest that people should not sometimes control their actions and expressions, for example, in the case of a teacher who gets angry and ready to lash out at a pupil. But it should be understood that the control of one's actions and expressions in the face of an emotion is at best a temporary solution (however necessary it may be), and that, if the emotion itself does not subside, it will frame future situations in such ways that the emotion will transpire in some way or other, purely as a function of its characteristic of disclosing both the self and the world one finds oneself in in a particular way.

The authentic version of the emotional response being measured (proportionate and discriminate) happens as a result of the individual having remained in contact with the situation, because the individual has not become absorbed in the emotion as it was first triggered, where this is not the result of the individual separating themselves from the emotion in such a way that the emotion becomes a practical or theoretical object. Rather, such a lack of absorption is there in the affective disposition of *non-identification and nearness* we encountered earlier in this section. We thus have a mode of being in which the individual is pre-reflectively self-aware of themselves as capable of being emotionally attuned while there is an actual way of being emotionally attuned in operation. What happens in this situation is that the active emotion is first allowed to simply be what it is, but that it is then likely to quieten down, especially in so far as it is experienced in relation to another person (as we saw in Chapter 6 the affective disposition of authentic being-with tends towards an openness in silence) and to "want to give the other their otherness". The result of this will be that the other person is allowed to manifest as themselves anew, which means that the individual experiencing the emotion in relation to them will keep contact with them in the sense that the emotion is allowed to arise but also subside again. Note that this is true of both unpleasant feelings (for example, getting angry with one of one's children) and pleasant ones (for example, being proud of one's child).

The second aspect of emotions themselves learning is that of a movement away from emotions arising in response to clear cues to the arising in response to ever subtler cues, as the individual is being increasingly able to pick up emotionally salient information in a situation. It represents the sensitivity and subtlety that mature people may display where their less mature counterparts are only responsive to more overt cues. Again, this is not a function of the development of a more acute perceptual or cognitive apparatus, though one is unlikely to develop without the other, but a genuine maturation of the emotional faculty itself. The meaning of emotional cues (for example, a pupil is observed as they receive a bad mark) is picked up in a way that is subtler, because they resonate, in the individual, with a more diversified (differentiated and integrated) inner experience. This ability to read subtle emotional cues is sometimes experienced as being able to read the whole of how another person is feeling from their face and posture. It is based in the basic characteristic of emotional communication, mentioned earlier, that emotions communicate themselves by resonating in the person who receives the communication. This ability becomes increasingly mature, to the extent that the emotion is allowed to resonate with ever deeper experience in a way that is proportionate to the situation (for example, the pupil is sad, but it is not the end of the world for her) and discriminate (the pupil is sad, but the sadness seems to be about more than just the grade).

In the case of the emotion revealing the meaning of the situation, the emotion unfolds but the automatic (physical) actions that may have defined the emotions in the evolutionary past do not arise with the emotion unless this is what is called for (as when there is the projectile flying towards one and one ducks, or when the door in the burning house is stuck and anger gives one the strength to open it), where the ability to sense if and when an actual physical response is called for resides in the totality of the situation as it involves a sense of the situation as well as a way of being connected with others through being-with (knowing when to act in response to what the other person is feeling). But in either case (regardless whether one needs to actually respond or not) the emotion one experiences needs to come out, manifest, less and less, and one can stay increasingly close to equanimity: one does not need to pick up the full force of despair the other person is feeling in order to know what to do, just a hint of it is enough; to take a more mundane example, one does not need to feel full-blown boredom, in order for one to know that it is time to switch off the television. This means that one does not "go through" the whole of the emotion, but is touched by it, enough for one to either act in response (quickly picking up that the pupil is depressed and requires one to act by, for example, referring them to the school counsellor), allow the emotion to take one with it (as when the father needs but to see the look in the eyes of his son to be drawn into the emotion of celebrating in jubilant terms that his son has passed the exam), or simply take in the meaning of the situation without, as yet, doing anything (as when the way a parent sighs while they are explaining how the home situation of the pupil has recently changed is enough for the teacher to grasp much of its meaning). That this ability to respond to increasingly subtle emotional cues develops does not mean that one begins to jump to conclusions, after all one may be wrong, but simply that the emotion itself does not need to manifest fully for it to do its work. This does, likewise, not lead to a flattened experience of life, as it happens authentically within the emptiness of possible emotional experience, which is in itself much fuller than any actual emotional experience and which (as the experience of wonder in relation to practical or theoretical entities and the emotion of affection, solidarity and love in relation to living creatures) still has its own experience of being authentically attuned.

So, we now have three aspects of emotional learning as modification and growth. First, the individual will have more emotional depth, an enriched sense of the possible meaning the situation may have, so that they can anticipate and open up these meanings, where this will occur in a way that is authentic, so long as the emotions arising themselves are held in a wider mood of non-identification and nearness. Second, emotional response is increasingly measured (proportionate and directed) by retaining contact with the situation and the cues that triggered it. Third, the emotional meaning of a situation is picked up with increasing subtlety, leaving the individual ever closer to emotional equilibrium, even if they sometimes still respond with full emotion where this is appropriate. There may be more aspects to emotional learning, but these three suffice to give us a sense of what emotional learning is like, when it is thought of in terms of emotions themselves, rather than in terms of learning to read, recognize, control, sense, and understand, which really refer to understanding learning to manage, control, and act on emotions as intentional objects.

Taking the limitations of the description into account, we now find that, as a result of such emotional learning, associations between emotions, situations, events, people and practical or theoretical entities are increasingly experienced in terms of possibility. On the one hand, this manifests as tentativeness and represents an emotional tentativeness that corresponds with the understanding that the associations one has learned to make (for example, between school and the feeling of being repressed) may turn out invalid in a new situation (after having moved to a different school) or for different people (the other pupil may experience the same school as liberating). On the other hand, this very same tentativeness, so long as it is authentically emotional and not merely based in understanding, also brings with it a clear decisiveness, as emotional cues that require a response will be taken as such and not be drowned out by a general noise of confused emotional responses that shoot off in all directions. This combination of tentativeness and decisiveness corresponds with the aspect of authentic attunement we encountered in Chapter 5 of the individual having the potential to respond emotionally if necessary, but, doing so in a way that does not remain identified with that response, or that expends energy unnecessary, even if they act practically or theoretically.

What is more, the space which the emotions created for themselves when they arose but then subsided remains (in a way that is similar to the way in which the possible ramification of emotional situations remained after their moment had passed) as openness and possibility. This openness and possibility strengthens one's ability to remain in contact with a situation even as an emotion arises. It increasingly allows the emotion to let go of itself, if it senses that it has become disproportionate or indiscriminate. What allows the emotion to subside is the emptiness that has built up around it, which is experienced by the individual as being "themselves" more authentically than the emotion itself, where otherwise the absorption in the emotion may have involved identification and an accompanying unwillingness to let go of it as itself. The fact that, as a result of authentic experience (which involves *letting be* as well as *letting go of* the emotion as it arises within the nothingness of self and world), the individual is increasingly able to respond in a way that is measured is, therefore, the result of a steady expansion of the openness of authentic attunement.

This expanding sense of inner space within which emotions come and go, but where the space is experienced as more genuinely oneself than the emotions, is a form of growth that is experiential and yet not represented in accounts of *learning as modification and growth*. The importance of the growth of this sense of inner space over the years is that it comes to anchor the sense of self that arises when the individual "turns back" to the world after having "turned away". This sense of self is then rooted ever more solidly in the emptiness left behind by the emotions that have come and gone. In this emptiness also lies the depth of emotional experience in the form of the possible meanings of the situation that may be anticipated or opened up. The self that grows over the years is then one of openness and possibility, where both gain in strength, as the growing openness can accommodate more and different emotions and the growing ramifications of possible emotions represent more possible ways of responding. The individual will, as a result, have inner strength and resourcefulness combined with genuine openness and humility, as well as the capacity to relate to other *living beings*, which require the individual to take them as openness and possibility. And this means that it is possible for there to be a kind of emotional learning that involves modification and growth, within a wider sense of attunement learning to be authentic.

To summarize, authentic learning to be attuned happens in a mood of non-identification and nearness, where the emotion that arises is let be, and there is an openness to things as they present themselves. This non-identification and nearness also means that the emotional response is measured (proportionate and discriminate) as a result of the individual having remained in contact with the situation, without becoming absorbed in the emotion, even as they remain emotionally open to the meaning of the situation and do not retreat into a theoretical or practical more of being – both of which would be inauthentic from the perspective of attunement. Over time, we then find that the emotional meaning of situations is picked up with increasing subtlety, leaving the individual ever closer to emotional equilibrium, even if they sometimes still respond with full emotion where this is appropriate. And if all this happens in a mood of authentic attunement, the connection with the situation in terms of non-identification and nearness, it constitutes authentic emotional learning. As a result, the way one feels about the situations one is in is held tentatively, in the understanding that other meanings may be possible, even as one is decisive in the way one responds emotionally, because this response is based in a genuine connection with the situation and not, say, a conditioned response.

All this involves the ability of an existential *letting be* as well as *letting go of* the emotion as it arises within the nothingness of self and world, and it is increasingly the emptiness within which emotions arise and subside that becomes the ground of the self. This emptiness is openness, and as the individual's emotional responses become over time more responsive, appropriate, measured, and tentative, they also become more precise and self-aware, as they are rooted in genuine openness to the situation.

Conventional learning in the context of authentic being-with

In the previous chapter we saw how the communal as well as the interpersonal are co-constitutive of Dasein. Heidegger calls this faculty of being connected with other Daseins being-with and, in the context of the question of learning to be authentic, I have taken being-with to be expressed in the faculty of communication, which, as inauthentic, consists in the articulation of experience in terms of *das Man*. In this way, being-with is the basis from which both language and culture spring, where Heidegger calls the state of "being lost" in *das Man* "falling", which he contrasts with being grounded in authentic being-with. But, as has been said before, after the movement of "turning away" from the world (from *das Man*, language and culture) there is a "turning back", and the question I will try to answer in this section is whether such "turning back" can occur in a way that is authentic.

As we saw in Chapter 6, the process of being-with becoming authentic begins with a communication, "a call" that originates in authentic Dasein. It is itself not a communication about practical or theoretical things, even if such communication may also take place. The call is directed at Dasein and appeals to Dasein to become authentic. It communicates in such a way that it is prior to a differentiation into someone calling and someone hearing. It is itself not based in (reducible to) either propositional language or culturally determined ways of behaving towards individuals or collectives. The call does not articulate, because articulation involves taking things *as* certain things, as being either similar or dissimilar to something else, and Dasein can be understood in terms of itself only, having its own "for the sake of". The call brings to Dasein's awareness what kind of entity Dasein really is, that it has the potential to becoming "who it really is", and it does this purely in terms of Dasein itself and not in terms of anything else (there is neither a practical nor a theoretical "as"). This kind of communication then allows for the co-existence of individuality and the interconnection between individuals (interpersonally or collectively).

The process of being-with learning to be authentic is, therefore, one of Dasein going from hearing the call in terms of articulation (as indicating how certain things belong together and other things belong apart) to hearing it as a pure pointing out of the possibility of authentic existence as it is already there in Dasein itself. This is a reciprocal process of the call breaking through and awakening of a new kind of hearing (which does not hear in terms of articulation). One way in which this has been put is to say that the call, "passes over" the self of *das Man*, where this involves interrupting the way Dasein usually listens (so that the habitual ways of receiving the communication are not reactivated), which awakens another kind of listening (one that does not take what is being communicated in terms of anything they already know, feel, believe, like or dislike), so that the call can get through to Dasein's authentic self and appeal to it to be its own authentic self (without the appeal being mediated by *das Man*), with the result that *das Man* is pushed into insignificance and dissolves, exposing Dasein's authentic self, which then experiences itself and the other Dasein as they really are (individualized as well as one with the other and the collective), as a result of which it takes itself as it really is and becomes this authentic self. This process of being-with becoming authentic is experienced as an awakening, an expansion of awareness, and a silencing of those inner voices that would normally articulate what was being communicated in terms of a known world and a familiar self.

If we now want to see if inauthentic learning to be-with (articulating the being of Dasein in terms of *das Man*) can happen within a wider atmosphere of authentic being-with, the first thing is to get clear about the processes involved in inauthentic learning to be-with. Such an inauthentic process of learning to articulate experience in terms of language and cultural practices is, I believe, best described as one of growing participation and enculturation (other factors play a role, but for simplicity sake, we will stick to enculturation as the driving force behind our becoming part of *das Man*). This growing participation leads to an increasingly integrated and differentiated articulation of the experience one is participating in. If we put it in terms of the faculty of understanding, we would say that the individual has an increasingly detailed and generalizable understanding of the way things are perceived and done in a particular cultural setting and of how this understanding is expressed in way that are appropriate. If we put it in terms of the faculty of attunement, we would say that the individual had an increasingly sophisticated feel for the affective significance of the different elements that made up the situation and of the situation as a whole, helping them respond in ways that are appropriate. Taken purely in terms of being-with, we could say that such enculturation consists in articulating the being of entities with ever increasing precision (linguistically and discursively), in a way that is coherent with ever more aspects of *das Man*.

If we now try to capture this process of enculturation in such a way that it happens within a wider sense of authentic being-with, we will not (at least initially) distinguish between the novice (the one being enculturated) and the expert (the one structuring, modelling and bridging the discursive practices the novice is being enculturated into), because the process is, for the purpose of this discussion, the same for both parties. It begins with a moment where the other person (whether that be the novice or the expert) is simply there, where the focus is on the other person without locating that person in any kind of practice. Here the person is, to borrow from our discussion of attunement, "the bare 'that it is' in the nothing of the world", the person is who they are in terms of themselves only. In terms of the experience of being-with, we saw in Chapter 6 that this meant that the person was experienced as "other", as existing in terms of him or herself only. But this otherness is not in contradiction with experiencing the person as "one with oneself", as co-constituting oneself, or, again borrowing from attunement, with a sense of affection and solidarity. Put in common-sense terms, this is the moment at the beginning of enculturation, where those involved may just take a moment to connect and acknowledge each other prior to positioning themselves and the other in the discursive practice (say as novice and expert).

Once the actual process of enculturation gets underway it will need to be guided by, articulated in line with, or done in an atmosphere that is attuned to authentic existence. This means that all throughout one takes every Dasein (oneself and the other) in the spirit of oneness and otherness first, even if at certain points this Dasein needs to become assimilated in terms of the relevant discourse, in terms of the cultural practice one is participating in. Here we again encounter the principle that the authentic way of engaging with an entity or a situation can embed the inauthentic one, in the sense that the former is larger than the latter and able to guide it. This is true even in relation to theoretical or practical entities, such as material objects, in that the non-articulating contact with the entity embeds the process of increasingly detailed and generalizable articulation. But this ability to stay connected with the other as never to be fully assimilated in terms of *das Man* is all the more important in relation to other Daseins.

What this means is that, whenever one's engagement with a Dasein is being articulated there is a voice that discloses the Dasein in terms of itself only and appeals to the authentic being in oneself to respect the authentic being of that Dasein. Let us take as our example a certain psychological research project, where we attempt to learn about certain psychological conditions, say, by linking certain symptoms to a certain neurotic tendency. Here we remain open to the call that reminds us, over and over again, that the ones that the research is about are essentially other, so that no diagnostic instrument, however sophisticated, can ever articulate their true being. And this is true even if, to stay with the example, it concerns psychological research where there is no live Dasein who is being studied, but merely a hypothetical patient and a list of symptoms; in such a case it is still authentic Dasein who is the intentional object of the learning as modification and growth, notwithstanding the fact that it involves what in phenomenology is called "empty intending". Or, to put it in common-sense terms, even if we are dealing purely with theoretical constructs, we still need to remember that it is ultimately about real people.

The result of this holding the inauthentic articulation as embedded in authentic being-with is that, to stay with our example, the profile of the neurotic individual and the knowledge of how and when to apply the symptoms is held in a way that is highly tentative, and ready to take back the articulation. At the same time this very tentativeness is the ground from which decisiveness can grow, because one can take full responsibility for the inauthentic articulation, rather than having to refer to some authority or tradition, because one does not fully understand the inauthentic articulation – after all, we can only really understand an inauthentic articulation of Dasein if there is authentic being-with. So, once the decision has been made as to what the inauthentic way of taking the Dasein in question should be, many of the dilemmas that would otherwise have to be dealt with are resolved. For example, if, after having been very tentative in one's theoretical and practical articulations of a certain patient, one decides that a situation involving the patient has to be dealt with in a way that takes them as a practical entity (for example, because the patient has become a threat to themselves and needs to be constrained), one simply acts in accordance, albeit in such a way that still keeps in mind the nature of the individual as a Dasein, and in a way that is open to revising itself if it turns out that another approach is asked for.

A Dasein cannot be articulated in a way that is commensurate with their nature, because they exist both as "other" and as "one" with oneself and all other Daseins. Dasein exists in terms of itself only. So, if the being of a Dasein is articulated at all, it should be done tentatively in terms of possibility, with a readiness to drop the articulation once there is once again the space for authentic being-with, and in a way that only becomes actual, when the whole of one's being understands, feels and is called by the circumstances to make the decisive leap into articulating their being. Note that such inauthentic articulation may not be as dramatic as it sounds here, as when, for example, one plans a public health campaign, which requires large scale planning in a way that deals with individuals statistically (for example, the aim of a policy is to save 10000 lives, where it is unimportant from a policy perspective whose lives these are within a given population). Such planning would be done in the context of impersonal discourses, practices and institutions, and the people who are the intentional object of this intervention will need to be articulated in a way that is decisively theoretical. That is, to do such planning, one has no option but to treat those involved inauthentically (as mere statistics). But even this can be done within a wider authentic relationship with them, which always understands that these "mere statistics" are in themselves essentially "other", and which tries to represent as much of this otherness in, say, the data that are being used. In this way, it is possible for us to relate to Daseins in a way that is inauthentic, while still retaining an underlying sense of their otherness, of the fact that the true being of Dasein can never be captured in language, discourse, or *das Man*, even if our daily life requires us to do so.

But authentic being-with not only relates to other Daseins as truly "other", it also takes the other and the community as co-constitutive of itself. At the same time that one exists for oneself, one also exists for the sake of other Daseins. And because who we are in not only who we are for ourselves but also who we are for other Daseins, this dimension of co-constitution needs to be part of authentic being-with. It is a kind of co-constituency of oneself in terms of the other that loses its paradoxical nature only in the individual who no longer articulates him or herself in terms of the culture and language he or she is part of. This is because, if one takes oneself in cultural and linguistic terms (articulates who one is) and the other is co-constitutive of one, this other becomes articulated in these same terms. Likewise, if one takes oneself as existing for the sake of the other Dasein, and takes the other Dasein in terms of its cultural and linguistic terms, one becomes oneself articulated in the terms of the other. It is not possible for both to be articulated in terms of the other at the same time without the articulation becoming self-contradictory. This problem does, however, not arise if the articulation is left silent, because two silences can each be taken as being part of the other without this becoming a contradiction.

But a *learning as modification and growth* that occurs for an individual who is in themselves not articulated is possible only if the functional existence of that individual, their role, their persona as defined in terms of the language and culture they are being enculturated into, is appropriated in a way that does not identify the individual with the persona. Such a non-identifying way of being can happen, if the individual enters a situation where the role they have been enculturated into is called for, while the voice that articulates the situation in line with the relevant language and cultural practices arises in the same impersonal way as does the voice that calls Dasein to its authentic existence. The place from which this voice originates is Dasein as openness, as possibility. The *learning as modification and growth* happens, as a result within a context of the nothingness of the individual, where there is no self that learns but rather a process of *learning as modification and growth* that creates a self at the same time as it creates the intentional object of that learning, where the self that is created is merely a functional self, a role and profile that exists within a larger absence of identification. Here we, therefore, have the kind of "giving up oneself" Heidegger writes is Dasein's utmost possibility, expressed in terms of being-with, where the articulation of self and other happens in the impersonal voice of conscience that addresses Dasein's potential for being authentic. Here too we find a tentativeness, but now in relation to the very self that makes up one's identity within the cultural practices and language, where, again, there may be a decisive appropriation of the role when that is called for, but in such a way that is not personal, merely functional. This is, in some ways, the very picture of the impartial practitioner or functionary. But in the case of having learned in an authentic way to fulfil the function, the functional identity is embedded in a larger, authentic silence which articulates neither the self of oneself, nor that of the other one engages with, but communicates with them in a way that expresses the authentic affective dispositions of oneness and otherness, of affection and solidarity, of wanting to give the other their authentic being.

The result of this learning being embedded in the silence of authentic being-with is that the articulations that are appropriated and later applied are informed by authentic being-with. Initially this will mean that there is considerable tension between the way the culture and language articulate experiences (entities, events and situations), because the culture and language reflect the extent to which the individuals and groups involved are inauthentic. For example, the individual may be articulated as in substantive terms rather than as a process, and all learning may be articulated in terms of modification and growth. This tension will make it more difficult for the individual in their functional capacity to retain contact with their authentic understanding of the situation. What this tension highlights, therefore, is the importance of authentic learning cultures, the local cultures in families, schools and other learning organizations, in enabling the individual to establish their ways of articulating experience in such a way that the tension between the actual articulation as constrained by culture and language and the way experience would be articulated in a world where all articulation occurred under the auspices of authentic awareness are kept to a minimum. A context where the practices individuals have appropriated are looked upon as arising in an impersonal way from within the silence of the authentic individual is very different from one where these practices are taken as constituting the whole individual, and where the individual is identified with the way in which they are articulated in *das Man*. Apart from the role of cultures in learning organizations, to help enable authentic being-with take root in the individual, by minimizing the tension between authentic existence and the inauthentic articulation of experience, these learning organizations also have a role in changing the culture and language itself. Such change is necessarily gradual and on-going, but nevertheless an important part of human existence, because it is the way in which *das Man* itself changes over time. As individuals become firmly rooted in authentic existence, they will eventually be in a position to partake in a transformation of the cultural and linguistic practices of a community. As parents, colleagues, teachers, managers, academics, politicians, and so on, they will be able to reform one or two bits of the culture or language so that it may facilitate rather than obstruct individuals discovering authentic ways of being. Such a process could then lead to an authentic collective learning to be-with.

We are thus seeing that the inauthentic being-with we find in language, discourse, culture, and *das Man* can be embedded within a wider, authentic being-with. This requires, on the one hand, that the otherness of Dasein is respected, even if this Dasein is described in terms of *das Man* and their being articulated in a practical or theoretical way, for functional purposes. On the other hand, the essential co-constitution of all Daseins needs to be respected, even if we sometimes need make clear distinctions between individuals. Such a combination of *otherness* and *oneness* begins with openness to the authentic being of those involved, suspending for the time being any articulation of their being. Any articulation that one settles on is held tentatively, as one knows that it will never capture what is essential to the individual. Similarly, one will always remain open to a connection that is authentic, ready to allow moments of being-with that are not articulated in terms of das Man, where one, as it were, returns to the initial relationship of openness, simply meeting the other as other. And where all of one's communication is mediated by das Man, for example, when one is implementing a policy from one's office, there is still the understanding that one is dealing with real Daseins, even as one is, say, manipulating numbers on a computer screen. This, further, needs to happen with a sense that one is not separate from the other Daseins, but that there is an underlying oneness that is most clearly expressed in terms of us being co-constituted by others, at the same time that these others are co-constituted by us. This then brings with it an impersonal sense of responsibility, one that is authentic only in so far as we refrain from identifying with our role, our persona within the culture, because any such identification articulates us as separate. There needs to be a real sense of connectedness with others, in the way we articulate our relationships, if we want this articulation to happen in the spirit of authentic being-with. And such connectedness can only come, if we are willing to "give ourselves up", our status, our cherished opinions, our ideas about ourselves and others. And, because our being-with necessarily happens within communities and shared cultures, there is the need to bring these collective expressions of *das Man* as much as possible in line with an authentic way of being-with. As has been explained, the way we articulate the being of Dasein can itself never be authentic, but some language and discourse leaves more room for authentic relationships than others, for example, where a discourse that articulates all human races as essentially equal is more in line with authentic being-with than a racist one. In this way, a collective learning process is part of inauthentic learning to be with within the context of a wider authentic being-with.

The tapestry of authentic learning

The tapestry of authentic learning

Now that we have seen how conventional learning can take place within a wider authentic being-in-the-world, it is time to construct a notion of authentic learning where the processes of learning to be authentic and conventional learning are woven together into one. As explained at the start of this chapter, such a unifying notion of authentic learning would both solve the learning paradox of how we can ever learn something new (given that all conventional learning includes continuity with previous learning), and bring the promise of authentic being-in-the-world more within reach: *authentic learning* would be a way of learning that helped open up the possibility of a life where the day-to-day of learning was integrated with a genuine openness to the being of entities (including we ourselves, others, and life as a whole).

As a first way of, in this part of the chapter, weaving such a tapestry of authentic learning, we will look at the way in which *conventional learning* and *learning to be authentic* can form part of each other – though there is not complete symmetry. Put schematically, within each moment of conventional learning there can be a moment of learning to be authentic, at the same time that each moment of conventional learning can take place within a wider process of learning to be authentic.

To make the discussion a little less cumbersome, I will refer to *conventional learning* as "grasping" and to learning to be authentic as "letting go". The word grasping is chosen, because all *conventional learning* end up with a new-found grasp of the intentional object – in the sense that when conventional learning is successful, the intentional object is understood in a new way, experienced in a way that is appropriate, related to in a way that does justice to it. The process of *learning to be authentic* will be referred to as letting go, because, as we have seen, the process of opening up to the being of the entity involves a moment of letting go which is based in a pre-reflective awareness of Dasein's way of being. Put in this new shorthand, we can then say that, in authentic learning, there is a moment of letting go whenever there is grasping, and vice versa.

After we have looked at the way in which grasping and letting go interweave, we will turn to the way in which such a process of authentic learning then allows for the being of entities to be grasped in a moment of openness. Here we find the openness to the being of entities that, we saw in Chapter 2, is an essential part of authentic existence, and thus of authentic learning. And we end this part of the chapter by looking at the way in which the linear temporality of conventional learning can coexist with the momentary temporality of learning to be authentic. This will then give us a coherent temporal characterization of authentic learning as a process that takes at once momentarily, in the instant, and over time in a way that is linear and thus capable of being cumulative in the way conventional learning is cumulative.

Grasping and letting go

In authentic learning the moments of grasping and letting go interweave in the sense that grasping happens within a wider sense of pre-reflective self-awareness, while within each moment of grasping there is also a sense of letting go.

This happens when within the very process of grasping an opening appears in the intentional relationship where subject and object would otherwise keep each other fixed in place: for understanding this is the moment one does not commit to a projection of the being of an entity; for attunement this is the moment one "stays with" the mood one is in, even as one is moved to act in response; for being-with this is an interruption in the way one has been listening to things by way of *das Man*. The result of this opening up is then a wider sense of pre-reflective self-awareness that, as it were, embeds the process of grasping that occurs in relation to the intentional object.

This starting point then sets in motion a movement that is reciprocal, a virtuous cycle towards increased openness, where there is a mutual reinforcement of two different elements. For understanding there is an increase in the "transparency" of understanding, which combines with a letting go of Dasein's projection of itself onto the things it finds in the world, all of which results in increased openness to the intentional object one is trying to grasp. For attunement the increase in pre-reflective self-awareness is coupled with letting the entities one is directed towards be encountered from within the nothing of the world, which means that the intentional object of learning is increasingly taken in terms of itself. For being-with there is an increasing awareness of the voice of conscience calling both from oneself and from beyond oneself coupled with Dasein hearing this call increasingly in terms of the call itself rather than in terms of *das Man*, which again involves an increase in openness to the being of the call, that is, the being of Dasein itself.

So, there is both an opening up, in the sense of letting go of existing ways of relating to the intentional object, and a spreading of a wider, authentic, pre-reflective sense of being-in-the-world. This is a mutually reinforcing process is which Dasein comes to a more direct relationship with these entities. It sets aside, as it were, the ways in which the intentional relationship had been structured at the level of the apriori. That is, rather than understanding these entities in terms of its own projections, Dasein begins to understand them in terms of temporality, of the process that projects itself, and this opens Dasein up to the being of the entities it is trying to grasp. At the same time, having let go of the moods that were defining both itself and the world in certain emotional terms, Dasein allows the entities to emerge from out of the nothing of the world in a way that is immediate, allowing the entities to disclose themselves as they are in themselves. And with regard to the faculty of being-with, having let go of the linguistic and cultural practices that were mediating its contact and communication, Dasein begins to re-establish a direct relationship with itself and other Daseins, in a way that connects it at the level of oneness, while remaining open to the otherness of the other, by way of a silent communication.

In this way, the moment of authentic learning opens the intentional relationship from within, even as it provides the wider, pre-reflective sense of being-in-the-world that allows these entities to exist in their own right, without Dasein projecting its own self-understanding onto them, without its mood colouring the relationship, without denying Dasein (both itself and the other) their unique otherness within a wider sense of oneness.

The way in which Dasein then grasps the entity it is learning about will, as we saw in Chapter 2, need to return to, make use of the ways of relating that are given in *das Man*, through language, practices, concepts. But this re-appropriation of the concrete ways of relating that is necessary for there to be the continuity of conventional learning does not need to imply a return to being absorbed in *das Man*. Because the letting go of learning to be authentic happens *within* and *beyond* the intentional relationship of conventional learning, it does not need to end when Dasein once more enters the intentional relationship of grasping. Rather, what is likely to happen is that there is an alternation of attention, going from grasping to letting go, and from letting go to grasping. Here we have the notion of learning as breathing out as well as in, which we looked at in Chapter 3. And we see that the kind of learning that breathes out (learning to be authentic) is qualitatively different from the learning that breathes in (conventional learning).

Importantly, the breathing in and out are not in contradiction with each other. This is because the pre-reflective self-awareness and openness to the being of the entities involved can keep on growing, even as Dasein's attention shifts back to the intentional relationship. There can be an ever-stronger sense of pre-reflective awareness that envelops the intentional relationship. This is experienced as awakeness and being-there in the present, because, as we will see shortly, the movement of letting go brings us to the moment of the here and now. And this sense of awakeness in the present does not need to diminish, as Dasein focuses on the intentional object, because the awakeness spreads beyond its focus on the object. There can also be an ever-stronger sense of openness to the intentional object, one that is the result of letting go in such a way that the object is allowed to show itself from out of itself. And both of these are not in contradiction to there being an ever-clearer, more precise grasp of the intentional object.

Thus the process of grasping can have its continuity, its moments of modification and growth, its integration with and differentiation from other intentional objects, even as the authentic sense of openness grows. What is more, the way in which the intentional object changes for Dasein (as part of its learning to take the object in an ever more truthful, effective, appropriate way), will be affected by the authentic openness that is likewise growing. You could say that Dasein's intentional grasp will be more objective, when it comes to forming ideas and representations of the object, because its understanding will be ever less distorted by it projecting its understanding of its own being onto the entity, allowing it to stand for itself instead. You could, likewise, say that Dasein's learning to be attuned to the situation it is in will happen in a way that displays ever more depth and maturity, because it can stay with the emotions and moods that arise without identifying with them. This will allow Dasein to truly learn emotionally, because it is able to remain in touch with the situation, even as its emotional responses come and go, as a result of which it will increasingly be able to respond in a way that is appropriate and proportionate. Finally, in learning to relate to itself and other Daseins, the sense of oneness and otherness that pervades authentic learning will enable Dasein to learn what things mean, what is and is not important, what to say and not say, in a way that takes Dasein as neither a ready-to-hand nor a present-at-hand entity, thus doing justice to the being of Dasein as an entity that exists in terms of itself and for its own sake. In this way, the process of grasping, of conventional learning, is enriched by the process of letting go that comes with learning to be authentic.

At the same time, the process of learning to be authentic itself requires for its full development there to be a process of grasping in which it can manifest. That the letting go and opening up of learning to be authentic needs there to be the grasping of conventional learning is in some ways the logical consequence of the fact that we are always already involved in intentional relationships. In that sense, every learning to be authentic takes place in the context of a prior intentional engagement with entities. There is, to say the same thing differently, no way of relating to become pre-reflectively aware of or let go of, and no entity to open up towards, if there is not an intentional relationship to start with: you cannot breathe out, if you have not first breathed in. But there is a further reason why learning to be authentic needs to happen in a way that is integrated with conventional learning in a single movement of authentic learning. This is because only then can the truth of authentic being-in-the-world manifest in Dasein's actual relationships. That is, the openness that comes with learning to be authentic is not a mere absence, the way an open window would be the mere absence of glass between us and the world outside. Rather, that which is disclosed in authenticity has its own positive way of being. We saw for example, in Chapter 6, that the affective disposition of authentic being-with really needs to be thought of in terms of things like love and affection. So when we think about authentic openness becoming part of conventional learning, we now see that this means, for example, in relation to ourselves and other Daseins, that this learning can now happen in a way that is informed by love and affection.

If we now anticipate the deepening of the authentic mode we will look at in the last part of this chapter, we can say that there is a further way in which authentic openness is important. This is because that which is disclosed in authentic openness is, in Heidegger's terms, being itself. But being is, at least in the sense we will take it later in the chapter, not here a mere empty-denominator, some abstract category that we apply to those entities that exist. There is a sense in which Dasein opening itself to being in Heidegger's writings is analogous to the soul opening itself to God in the Christian tradition, as it is found, for example, in the sermons of Meister Eckhart. That is, "the relationship, the dialectic, the interchange, between God and the soul in Meister Eckhart is similar to the relationship between Being and Dasein in Heidegger. As God takes the initiative in Meister Eckhart, so Being takes the initiative in Heidegger. As the soul must stay open and receptive to God, so Dasein must stay open to Being" (Caputo 1986, 144). In this sense, openness to being is a much more meaningful event that a mere formal openness to an abstract category of thought. We do, of course, not have to subscribe to the idea that there is something divine about being, with which authentic openness then brings us into contact. But we can say that the openness is not a sterile absence, in the sense that it becomes openness to life itself, and as such meaningful. And because of this, it matters that there should be authentic understanding of being. More than just allowing us to relate to entities in a way that is correct and appropriate, being open to the being of entities entails being open to being itself, and this is important in its own right. Some of this becomes clear to us in a tangible way, when we see that the openness of authentic being-with brings with it feelings of love and affection, which manifest in the world, through our actual relationships with Dasein in ourselves and others. And for this, Dasein needs to be intentionally related to entities, which is why it is important that the openness to being also manifests in the context of conventional learning, because only then can being manifest in the actuality of human existence.

All these, then, mean that when in authentic learning, conventional learning happens together with learning to be authentic, the quality of the conventional learning is enhanced as a result of being embedded in and informed by authentic openness to the being of the entities one is learning about. At the same time the process of learning to be authentic only reaches its full potential of manifesting in the world by way of Dasein's intentional relationships with things, itself, and, most importantly, other Daseins. This then show how conventional learning and learning to be authentic can form part of the same process, and really should unite in authentic learning, for there go be both a true grasp of the being of the entities involved and the manifestation of love and affection in the life of Dasein.

The mixed temporality of authentic learning

The final aspect of a unified account of authentic learning we are looking at in this part of the chapter is that it combines two distinct forms of temporality. As *authentic learning* weaves together two strands of learning, the first, *learning to be authentic*, is momentary, in that it is not cumulative. The second, *conventional learning* is, in contrast, linear in terms of time (in line with the etymology of learning as following along a path), and cumulative as a result. So, there needs to be an integration of, on the one hand, learning to be authentic with its cyclical structure of becoming pre-reflectively self-aware, opening-up, and letting-go, in such a way that it brings the learner to what Heidegger calls the "moment of vision", the moment where there is openness to the being of entities. On the other hand, *conventional learning* has a linear structure, which is cumulative over time, in the sense that there is continuity, that current learning builds on previous learning, and that, as a result, there is a kind of growth that involves increased integration and differentiation.

In this section, we will consider these different temporalities and how they can be combined. Then, in the sections that follow, we will look at three ways in which learning to be authentic and conventional learning interact: we will look at how growth interacts with letting go, how the situation interacts with the circumstances, and how this results in an original sense of the being of entities. Together, these will describe in more formal terms what in the first part of this chapter was given for each of the faculties of Dasein, understanding, attunement, and being-with. In the final part of the chapter, we will then consider the notion of *authentic learning* as a more general way of characterizing this learning. This will tie together the different strands of the investigation into one movement, that of the dissolution of the self. But, as we will see in the final section of the chapter, such moments of authentic learning are themselves a new beginning, because out of them may come a way of being-in-the-world that is truly creative and new.

The first characteristic of authentic learning is that the dimension of learning to be authentic is momentary in nature. Although the description of the process of becoming authentic may at some points appear to imply that it is linear, this is really a function of our language and not of the process itself. First, the movement of learning to be authentic is circular, where becoming pre-reflectively self-aware, letting-go, and opening-up each set into motion the other. Sometimes it is pre-reflective self-awareness that sets the process in motion, as when Dasein understanding becomes transparent to itself. Sometimes letting-go comes first, as when Dasein's articulation of the other falls silent. And sometimes there is first a moment of opening-up, as when the call of conscience breaks through Dasein's habitual way of listening.

But even the very notion of one of the three coming first is, in many ways, misleading, because they all need each other to be happening from the beginning. Thus, pre-reflective self-awareness can only manifest, in so far as absorption into a subject-object relationship is being let-go of, and a degree of openness exists. Likewise, letting-go needs to happen at the level of pre-reflective self-awareness, if it is to happen at the level of the apriori, and is always also an opening-up. And for the same reasons, opening-up contains an element of letting go as well as increased pre-reflective self-awareness.

We find further evidence for the momentary nature of learning to be authentic in the notion of "the instant" or "the moment of vision", which we saw in Chapter 4 is the moment when Dasein takes a resolute stance on the situation it is in. This "moment of vision" is instantaneous, because it is not the result of, say, discursive reasoning or interpreting the situation against an existing background understanding. Rather, it is the moment when Dasein's openness to the situation and the entities in it allow it to see the situation in terms of itself rather than in terms of something else. Conventional learning, it has been argued, always understands a new situation in terms of a previous one, and this implies continuity. But authentic being-in-the-world seizes the moment. And this is true even for the way in which authentic Dasein takes itself as thrown projection – even then the authentic insight in its own temporal nature is instantaneous and not, say, a reasoned conclusion. Thus, Dasein's authentic self-understanding includes understanding the whole of itself as finite, in such a way that the understanding itself is not temporal. You could say that, the only way for Dasein to grasp its own nature as essentially temporal is by way of the moment, the instant: when "one has an understanding of being-towards-death – towards death as one's ownmost possibility – one's potentiality-for-being becomes authentic and wholly transparent" (Heidegger 1962, 354).

This momentary nature of authentic learning then raises the question whether we can still legitimately speak of a process. To reframe the question, can a moment still be processal in nature? The answer to this would be negative, if we saw time as a sequence of "now" within which Dasein manifests. But we saw in Chapter 4 that Heidegger thinks of temporality (the authentic way of experiencing time rather than the, derived, notion of time found in science and common-sense), as constituting the nature of Dasein itself. To repeat an earlier quote, "Heidegger's point of departure is the notion of subject as 'process' (*Vollzug*)" (Schuermann 2008, 57-58). In that sense, Dasein exists *as* turning toward the past, present, or future. And in that sense it is possible for learning to be authentic to be both instantaneous (becoming authentic is not a sequence of events one after another) and processal (in becoming its true self, Dasein becomes finite temporality in a way that is transparent to itself). Or, Dasein as temporality does not exist as an entity within time (although that is true of Dasein's body) but "it unfolds", it emerges, in the sense that "temporality 'is' not an entity at all. It is not, but it *temporalises* itself" (Heidegger 1962, 376-377). In this sense, Dasein understanding itself authentically as temporality means that its becoming transparent to itself, its learning to be authentic, is a process, even if this process is momentary in nature.

If authentic temporality reveals the processal nature of Dasein in the instant, conventional learning has a more familiar form of temporality, that of a linear sequence of "nows". In each of the moments that make up conventional learning, Dasein has its own, authentic form of temporality as "ways in which to be-here is to be 'outside' or even 'beside oneself'" (Dahlstrom 2001, 337). Thus, authentic temporality is very much in line with the notion of Dasein as openness and transcendence, in that its very existence is that of turning toward the past, present, or future, whereas conventional learning consists of a sequence of moments of authentic temporality lined up, in such a way that the sequence traces a change in Dasein's ways of feeling, acting, or thinking.

The question then raises itself as to how such moments of authentic being, each of which has its own temporal structure, can come to form a linear progression that culminates in conventional learning. If the process of learning to be authentic is momentary and needs to be repeated each moment anew, "must be held open and free for the current factical possibility" (Heidegger 1962, 355), how can there ever be the kind of continuity we need for a learning that consists of the modification of existing ways of being, resulting in increased integration and differentiation over time?

Part of the answer lies in the nature of memory as being recorded in terms of that which is salient. For example, when the authentic understanding of a situation reveals this situation as one where a certain skill needs to be learned, this primes memory as to what needs to be remembered. In this way, an initial, authentic grasp of the situation Dasein is in may begin to lay down a trail of memory, for example, when Dasein is shown how to do something by following a number of steps, and it focuses on the steps as shown, these steps will be remembered as steps, as a result of an initial understanding of the situation. But, once the initial understanding is there that the individual steps are to be noted, it can be left to memory to record them, while an overarching sense of openness to the ever-changing situation can remain. The process of noticing those parts of the whole that are relevant to the attitude, skill, and knowledge to be acquired resides, in this way, within a wider, authentic way of being-in-the-world.

Another part of the answer how moments of authentic being-in-the-world can (despite their instantaneous nature) begin to make up a cumulative process of learning as modification and growth lies in the nature of memory as the repetition of ways of feeling, acting, and thinking based in associative principles. That is, an (authentic) way of seizing the moment is able to call up ways of being that are associated with it, and in that way, tie a remembered way of being to one that is given by Dasein's openness to the being of entities. For example, when another Dasein is revealed as *other* and existing *for its own sake* by authentic Dasein, this authentic understanding of the being of the other Dasein can elicit ways of being that are associated with relating to another Dasein as *other* and existing *for its own sake*, which in turn can be recorded in memory, as described in the previous paragraph. In this way, the authentic disclosure of a situation can form part of laying down a sequence of conventional steps of learning.

What is not done here is reveal the being of the entities involved in the situation from out of memory. But once the being of the entities has been revealed from out of an authentic way of being in the moment, associated ways of being in relation to the entities may be recalled. This remembered way of being can then help disclose the situation to authentic Dasein further, though, as authentic, Dasein will always remain open to the being of the situation and ready to take back any particular understanding of being, especially one that has been given through association and not through an originary connection with the situation itself. In this way, the unfolding of Dasein's understanding of the situation through memory and association will occur tentatively and within a wider, authentic sense of the situation as a whole.

If we then take into account the nested nature of memory, where memories of a short timespan make up more general memories, and where the short-time can call up the longer-term ones and vice versa, we can see how a complex skill or knowledge construct can form out of moments that, at one level, are each taken as existing purely on their own terms. For example, the completion of a stage in a complex task may be marked such and remembered as the culmination of a series of smaller steps. This marking of the stage then becomes the higher-level memory that can evoke the, lower-level, individual steps. At the same time, the lower-level steps may themselves call up the memory of the stage to which they contribute, and thus gain guidance from that higher-level memory. In this way, the competence to complete a complex task may be constructed purely out of remembered moments, each of which is experienced within the authentic momentary sense of instantaneousness. And the way these momentary memories are linked can be purely by way of association.

If we now remember that what is recorded as salient in an authentically experienced situation can be guided by what learning Dasein is engaged in, it becomes clear that the kind of longer-term memory I mentioned in the previous paragraph can be shaped by this initial learning demand. That is, the process of exploration, opening up, and letting go of old ways of being is now accompanied by the memory that tells Dasein to record that which is indicated as the steps of task being learned, and to do so in terms of a certain background understanding of the meaning of these steps. In this way the function of memory (continuity) enables Dasein to not only articulate, grasp, or master steps in the process of authentic learning that is unfolding, but also the longer movements that are built up of these smaller steps.

Conventional learning can do this, due to its essential characteristics. Memory is called up by association. More complex ways of being in the world are reconstructed in the engagement with the intentional object rather than, in some unexplained way, stored in the person. There are different levels of memory, where some concern the momentary, the small-scale and some the long-term, large-scale, and where the memory of a large-scale structure can call up, by way of association, its small-scale components and vice versa. In this way, as the longer-term learning projects is recalled repeatedly, there is increased integration of the different elements and the different levels, making for increased integration, differentiation, and stability. Importantly, at any one point in such a complex construction process, it is individual associative mechanisms that record and/or recall the memory, and each occasion of association is itself momentary.

That is, associations have a one-to-one relationship with what they are associated with, and this makes each associative moment momentary in much the same way that the moment of seizing the moment is momentary. This is as true for declarative memories, which come all at once, being, as it were snapshots of previous experience, as it is of the kind of task grammar, where one movement, one thing we do, calls up the next. In more complex learning, some of these memories (declarative or part of a sequence) will be higher-level ones, giving one a more general view, prospect, of the thing being learned. But this should not lead us to posit the existence of anything more than momentary ways of being in memory. And the momentary nature of memory allows it to come and go within a wider context of authentic being-in-the-world, which is itself a continual grasping and letting go of the being of entities.

In this way, the two different temporalities can exist together in the same learning. The instantaneous moment of learning to be authentic can be there in each of the individual moments of conventional learning, when any way in which an intentional object that has been grasped, can become pre-reflectively self-aware and let-go of, so that there is a moment of opening up. At the same time, the very process of conventional learning can exist within a wider movement of authentic letting go and opening-up. In this way, the two can combine to form a single tapestry of authentic learning.

Authentic learning

As we saw earlier in this chapter, it is possible for the grasping of *conventional learning* to be integrated with the letting-go and openness of *learning to be authentic*, when the intentional relationship of conventional learning is embedded within a wider sense of pre-reflective self-awareness, even as from within the intentional relationship this same pre-reflective self-awareness is opening up the relationship. So, with the integration of the momentary temporality of *learning to be authentic* with the linear temporality of *conventional learning* we have now come to a feasible notion of *authentic learning* in both its spatial and temporal dimension.

Such authentic learning, we have seen, resolves the learning paradox we first encountered in Chapter 1, that of the apparent contradiction in our idea of learning as involving both an apriori understanding of the entity one is learning about and an openness to the being of that entity. The resolution of the learning paradox is possible, we saw, because the process of learning that opens up happens at the level of pre-reflective self-awareness, whereas the process of learning that is based in continuity and grasping occurs at the level of the intentional relationship. And these two levels, we saw, can be operative at the same time: the linear path of conventional learning can coexist with the momentary instants of learning to be authentic. Indeed, both processes can, in their own way, grow: as the linear process of conventional learning increases in integration and differentiation, the momentary process of *learning to be authentic* increases in intensity and depth. In this way, we become ever more pre-reflectively self-aware, even as our attitudes, skills, and knowledge become more sophisticated.

This authentic learning, further, brings us closer to who we are, and in this way begins to fulfil the promise of authentic existence, of becoming who we are. It does this by allowing the understanding of being that arises in the openness of authentic being-in-the-world to manifest in actual relationships with ready-to-hand and present-at-hand entities, as well as entities with the nature of Dasein. As was pointed out in Chapter 1, it is especially in relation to the ground of experience, others, and life as a whole that a true understanding of being can only come out of a connection that is based in authentic openness. At the same time, such authentic understanding of being needs to filter through to the concrete things we feel, do, and think, in order for us to be able to say that we have made true our potential for being who we really are. So, again we find that the combination of *conventional learning* and *learning to be authentic* is able to do more than either of the two can on their own: where *conventional learning* on its own lacks openness to the being of entities, *learning to be authentic* on its own still needs to manifest in real-life relationships for its potential to realize.

This merger of *conventional learning* and *learning to be authentic* has been brought about almost purely at the level of process. For the two kinds of learning to manifest together, we do not need to be any particular kind of person, other than a person who can allow both processes to run together. This emphasis on process also means that *authentic learning* can happen at any depth of understanding: regardless of who we are, we can enter the stream of authentic learning, so long as we allow our pre-reflective self-awareness to grow as we engage in an intentional relationship of learning, so long as we follow this pre-reflective sense in its call for us to let go of some or all our ways of being at the pre-reflective level. This process of letting-go even as we grasp, of opening-up even as we focus on the intentional object, has its beginning always in the moment, in the here and now. In this way, authentic learning needs no preparation to merge with conventional learning, because our starting point is the processes and not on any kind of state of being we may or may not have achieved.

There is, in this way, wholeness in *authentic learning*, in the sense that openness is combined with continuity, in the sense that letting go is combined with grasping. This wholeness in learning is also a wholeness in who we are, in the sense that we are openness at the heart of our being, even as this being is pre-reflectively self-aware and transparent to itself. Finally, the wholeness of *authentic learning* is there in our relationships with other Daseins, with other living beings, where we find a sense of oneness with that which is other, a sense of connectedness that is more often than not experienced as affection and love, and which can then become the basis on which others can be called to also open up to the wholeness of *authentic learning*.

Bibliography

Bonnett, M. (2002). Education as a form of the poetic: A Heideggerian approach to learning and the teacher-pupil relationship. Heidegger, Education, and Modernity. M. Peters. Oxford, Rowman & Littlefield Publishers: 229-245.

Bouton, M. E. (2007). Learning and behaviour: A contemporary synthesis. Sunderland, Massachusetts, Sinauer Associates.

Capobianco, R. (2007). "From Angst to Astonishment: Heidegger on the Defining Mood of Dasein's Authentic Existence." Review of Existential Psychology and Psychiatry.

Caputo, J. D. (1986). The mystical element in Heidegger's thought. New York, Fordham University Press.

Cooper, D. E. (2002). Truth, science, thinking, and distress. Heidegger, education, and modernity. M. Peters. Oxford, Rowman & Littlefield Publishers: 47-65.

Crowe, B. D. (2006). Heidegger's religious origins: Destruction and authenticity. Bloomington and Indianapolis, Indiana University Press.

Dahlstrom, D. O. (2001). Heidegger's Concept of Truth. Cambridge, Cambridge University Press.

Davey, G. (2005). Emotional intelligence. Encyclopaedic Dictionary of Psychology. G. Davey, Hodder-Arnold.

de Beistegui, M. (2005). The new Heidegger. London, Continuum International.

Freire, P. (1970/1996). Pedagogy of the Oppressed. London Penguin Books.

Fuster, J., M. (2003). Cortex and mind: unifying cognition. Oxford, Oxford University Press.

Gur-Ze'ev, I. (2002). Martin Heidegger, transcendence, and the possibility of counter education. Heidegger, education, and modernity. M. Peters. Oxford, Rowman & Littlefield Publishers: 65-81.

Hager, P. (2005). "New Approaches in the Philosophy of Learning." Educational Philosophy and Theory 37(5): 633-634.

Hager, P. (2005). "Philosophical Accounts of Learning." Educational Philosophy and Theory 37(5): 649-666.

Hager, P. (2008). "Learning and Metaphors." Medical Teacher 30(7): 679-686.

Heidegger, M. (1954). Was heisst Denken? Tuebingen, Nax Niemeyer Verlag.

Heidegger, M. (1958). What is Philosophy? New Haven, New Haven College and University Press.

Heidegger, M. (1962). Being and Time. Oxford, Blackwell Publishing Ltd.

Heidegger, M. (1976). What is Called Thinking? New York, HarperCollins Publishers.

Heidegger, M. (1980). Hegel's Phenomenology of Spirit. Bloomington, Indiana University Press.

Heidegger, M. (1982). The basic problems of phenomenology. Bloomington and Indianapolis, Indiana University Press.

Heidegger, M. (1995). The fundamental concepts of metaphysics: World, finitude, solitude. Bloomington, Indiana University Press.

Heidegger, M. (1998). What is Metaphysics? Pathmarks. W. McNeill. Cambridge, Cambridge University Press: 82-97.

Heidegger, M. (2000). Elucidations of Hoelderlin's Poetry. New York, Humanity Books.

Heidegger, M. (2004). The phenomenology of religious life. Bloomington & Indianapolis, Indiana University Press.

Ireson, J. (2008). Learners, Learning and educational activity. London, Routledge.

Jarvis, P. (2006). Towards a comprehensive theory of human learning. London, Routledge.

Manukata, Y. and J. Pfaffly (2004). "Hebbian learning and development." Developmental Science 7(2): 141-148.

Marton, F. and S. Booth (1997). Learning and awareness. Mahwah, New Jersey, Laurence Erlbaum Associates

McNeill, W. (2006). The time of life: Heidegger and ethos. Albany, State University of New York Press.

Miner, R. (2004). Truth in the Making: Creative Knowledge in Theology and Philosophy. New York and London, Routledge.

Murray Thomas, R. (2005). Comparing theories of child development. Belmont, Thomson Wadsworth.

Nancy, J.-L. (2008). "The being-with of being-there." Continental Philosophy Review(41): 1-15.

OED (2009). Oxford English Dictionary, Oxford University Press.

Petitmengin, C. (1999). The Intuitive Experience. The View from Within. First-person approaches to the study of consciousness. V. F. J. S. J. London, Imprint Academic.

Piaget, J. (1967/1974). Biology and Knowledge: An Essay on the Relations Between Organic Regulations and Cognitive Processes. Frankfurt, Fischer.

Piaget, J. (2001). The psychology of intelligence. Abbingdon.

Ratcliffe, M. (2008). Feelings of being: phenomenology, psychiatry and the sense of reality. Oxford, Oxford University Press.

Schuermann, R. (2008). Heidegger's Being and Time. On Heidegger's Being and Time. S. Levine. London, Routledge: 56-132.

SOED (2007). Shorter Oxford English Dictionary. L. Brown. Oxford, Oxford University Press.

Sorial, S. (2005). Heidegger and the Problem of Individuation: Mitsein (being-with), Ethics and Responsibility. School of Philosophy Sydney, University of New South Wales **PhD**.

Thomson, I. D. (2004). "Heidegger's perfectionist philosophy of education in Being and Time." Continental Philosophy Review **37**: 439-467.

Van Geert, P. (1998). "A dynamic systems model of basic developmental mechanisms: Piaget, Vygotsky and beyond." Psychological Review **104**(4).

Vandenberg, D. (1971). Being and education: An essay in existential phenomenology. Englewood Cliffs, Prentice Hall.

Volpi, F. (1996). Dasein as praxis: the Heidggerian assimilation and radicalization of the practical philosophy of Aristotle. Critical Heidegger. C. Macann. London and New York, Routledge: 27-67.

Winch, C. (1998). The philosophy of human learning. London, Routledge.

Zahavi, D. (2005). Subjectivity and selfhood: Investigating the first-person perspective. Cambridge, Massachusetts, The MIT Press.

Zimmerman, M. (1993). Heidegger, Buddhism, and deep ecology. The Cambridge Companion to Heidegger. C. Guignon. Cambridge, Cambridge University Press: 240-269.

Zuidervaart, L. (2007). Social philosophy after Adorno. Cambridge, Cambridge University Press.